DREAMS CAN COME TRUE

THE STORY OF JACOB

BARRY ISON

DREAMS CAN COME TRUE

THE STORY OF JACOB
As recounted by Tarku, a ward of Jacobs' and
a brother and close friend to Joseph

Jacob went out from Beersheba and travelled towards Haran. He came to a certain place and stayed the night there because the sun had set. He took a stone from the place, put it under his head and lay down to sleep. He dreamt that there before him was a ladder resting on the ground with its top reaching to heaven, and the angels of Adonai were going up and down on it. Then suddenly Adonai was standing there next to him; and He said:

"I am Adonai, the God of Avraham, your grandfather, and the God of Yitzchak. The land on which you are lying I will give to you and your descendants. Your descendants will be numerous as the grains of dust on the earth. You will expand to the west and to the east, to the north and to the south. By you and your descendants all the families of the earth will be blessed. Look I am with you. I will guard you wherever you go, and I will bring you back into this land, because I won't leave you until I have done what I have promised you".

Jacob awoke from his sleep and said, "Truly, Adonai is in this place – and I didn't know it!"
Genesis chapter 28: 10-16

CONTENTS

DEDICATION

This story is dedicated to Adonai, the Father of an infinite Majesty and His one honourable, true, and only son Yeshua, Messiah, Mashiach, Al-Masih, because He was there, blessing Jacob and Joseph, with His covenant promises, more than three and a half thousand years ago.

ACKNOWLEDGMENTS

Firstly, I would like to acknowledge my wonderful family, a very precious gift from Adonai, my God. Special thanks to Debbie, who with a masters in English and fifty years of teaching the English language has spent many hours editing and proofreading the manuscript.

MESSAGE

As a result of all the research and deliberations that have gone into writing this fascinating and enlightening story, I am convinced that the resounding message has to be of the all-encompassing love of Adonai, Almighty God, for all His creation and, in particular, for those who honour and worship Him.

PREFACE

This is the story of Jacob and Joseph. The Bible, the Tanakh, and the Quran, have a wonderful array of fascinating characters and they are all the very same people. The three great Patriarchs, Abraham, Isaac, and Jacob, who established the children of Israel, are shared in all three religions. Abraham, similarly, has been considered the father of several different nations. Then there are the most amazing leaders, fearless, trusting in their God and vanquishing their foes, like Moses, Joshua, and David. We read of the brave Prophets who challenged authority and proved the supremacy of their God, Elijah, Elisha, Isaiah, Jeremiah; and many more. So many Heroines who risked everything for their people, Deborah, Esther, and Ruth. And then there was the father-son combination of Jacob and Joseph. Jacob who sired the twelve sons of Israel and managed to amass a fortune with his knowledge and skills in selective breeding, starting with a few ill-kempt spotted and striped sheep and goats. And Joseph, who achieved a level of greatness surpassing all of his forebears and becoming, possibly, the most powerful and influential of the sons of the Patriarchs and their descendants. This is a credible history, the events related in this story actually happened, dating from around the late 17th century BC to the early 16th century BC.

In commencing my research about both Jacob and Joseph, the most compelling question for me, was, how did they manage to accomplish all that they achieved? Arriving in Haran as a refugee fleeing his brother's wrath, and with virtually nothing to his name, how was Jacob able to amass flocks and herds numbering many thousands as well as a large family and a sizeable camp following? After slaving for his uncle over fourteen years, for his two brides, Jacob commenced building his own legacy and within six years, he was able to leave Haran a wealthy man. This is Jacob's story. While the message of this narrative is essentially of Jacob's God, Adonai and His many blessings, the following chapters provide some of the details as to how it was accomplished. Where I have indulged in, perhaps, excessive detail, the purpose has been simply to add to the credibility and ingenuity of everything that Jacob accomplished.

Sadly, the bible does not elaborate on the personalities of these two hugely successful ancestors of God's chosen people, Jacob, and Joseph. The reason being, I think, simply because the authors of the ancient texts were primarily focused on God's Covenant, and His nurturing and blessings for His people, rather than proclaiming the glory and achievements of any one individual. True, it speaks of the faithfulness of Abraham, the tolerance and forgiveness of Isaac, and the perseverance of Jacob, but very little about who these great people were as human beings.

Quotations of Biblical texts are from The Complete Jewish Study Bible.

Finally, I recognise that I have made specific choices as these relate to historical events, character traits, and the significance of locations. This has involved considerable research and while I am a historian, this story, its focus, and approach, has been a more recent exciting adventure to my studies, and I would acknowledge that many of the facts and inferences I have selected could be controversial. However, disjointed as specific events in history may appear, the weaving together of these historical fibres can produce some very interesting scenarios. My objective has always been to present Joseph, and his father Jacob, in as realistic and positive a light as my studies have discovered. They were both absolutely amazing people.

Recognising that my story is fiction based on fact, I have called my genre Biblifiction.

CHAPTER ONE

JOSEPH

"Then God took note of Rachel, heeded her prayer and made her fertile".
Genesis 30:22.

My name is Tarku, and I am honoured to share the remarkable story of my dear friend and younger brother, Joseph, who currently holds the esteemed position of Grand Vizier of Egypt. Being intimately involved in his journey since its earliest days, I have been entrusted with the privilege of narrating his extraordinary tale. From the simple origins of a nomadic shepherd's family, to becoming the second most powerful man in Egypt after the Pharaoh and saving the known world from starvation. It's a chronicle of indiscretion, naiveite, courage, intrigue, and triumph; of love, loss and recovery, forgiveness, wholesale destruction, untold wealth and power, and an acknowledgement throughout of the covenant promise and blessings of Adonai, the one and only true God. As the story unfolds, this narrative will delight with all the richness of personalities, extravagant opulence, stunning scenery, brilliant planning and execution, and heartwarming relationships.

In order to adequately cover the story of Joseph's life, I must first devote some time to recounting the tale of his father, Jacob – my adopted father. This is the man, whom I love dearly, who experienced an equally exciting number of adventures throughout his journeys, initially from Beersheba in southern Canaan, then to Haran in the distant north, and subsequently returning to Hebron. Finally, reuniting with his once-lost son, now the Grand Vizier of Egypt, and settling in the land of Goshen gifted to his family by the great Pharaoh Apepi. Jacob's life was particularly remarkable, both in terms of his physical as well as his spiritual journey. During this time, he was bestowed with the new name of Israel, signifying him as the father of a nation that would eventually grow to equal the number of the sands of the sea and the stars of the sky.

Looking back on the kaleidoscope of events experienced by both father and son, it is not difficult to identify a pattern of two major themes which they shared in common. Firstly, of course, were the covenant promises ordained and blessed by their God, Adonai. Secondly was the role of dreams they experienced, both personally and in the lives of others, and the impact these visons had on every aspect of their beings.

1

As a Hittite, my very existence became woven into the life and subsequent journey of Jacob, ben Isaac several decades ago. During his passage from his father's camp in Beersheba to his uncle's home in Haran to the North, he discovered me, abandoned by the roadside as he passed beyond the city of Hebron. At that time, I was just a helpless baby, barely able to walk, and my recollections of my village and family are vague.

Year's later, Jacob, whom I also call 'father', recounted the tragic scene where he had found me. Apparently, our village had fallen victim to a brutal attack by a band of Philistines. The raid resulted in the loss of numerous lives, including many of the villagers. Although we had little to offer as plunder, these raiders sought food, and the brave men of our small hamlet, being Hittites, resisted. Unfortunately, their bravery led to their demise. (It is very unwise to oppose armed Philistines unless one possesses great courage, extreme foolishness, or a substantial armed contingent at their side.)

Now that I have introduced myself, let us begin my story at a point where it always begins, with a tale of childbirth, taking place in the delightfully tranquil setting of rural Haran in Northern Mesopotamia. Jacob, third in line to the prestigious family of Patriarchs, Abraham and Isaac, had arrived from the land of Canaan to his uncle's place in Haran, in search of a bride. He has married two sisters, the eldest, noble Leah, who has given him several children, the younger, his favourite the beautiful Rachel, now after many years, is preparing to offer him her firstborn. Having presented this very brief introduction to the family, let me continue the narrative step by step until it grows into a much fuller understanding of people, places, reasons, motives, and amazing achievements.

It was around noon, and I was sitting under the shade of a baobab tree as the day was very hot. All around me were beautiful rolling hills, surrounded by fields of abundant golden wheat almost ripe for harvest. At the foot of one of the hills a vineyard stretched well into the adjoining valley. Our camp was located in the middle of the sanctuary of palms and a variety of other trees typical of the region. Behind the camp was our olive grove. While we were essentially shepherds which included sheep, goats, camels and some oxen, the availability of a plentiful supply of water together with fertile soils and clement weather easily encouraged our involvement into agriculture. It was altogether an idyllic setting for what was soon to be a tumultuous event within the very camp where we lived.

All was unusually quiet, not a sound except for the occasional call of the hoopoe bird. All the normal hustle and bustle of camp life had come to a complete halt. The pervading atmosphere was a mixture of hope, expectancy, and a small amount of dread. A child was being born.

Not any child: This was to be the first born of the favourite wife of our leader Jacob. There he was seated on carpets beneath a canopy not far from a small but beautifully decorated tent which had been specially set up for the birth. The tent had been made from sections of finely woven linen held together with bold stitches of silken cords. Over the top was a covering of goatskin to protect it from the weather. Both inside the tent and around the entrance were hung beautifully embroidered silk hangings and brocade. Also, discretely placed were special amulets and images that were meant to provide good fortune. No expense had been spared for this very special occasion.

This separate tent had been erected according to the normal customs of the region to ensure the best possible conditions regarding hygiene, comfort, and convenience for the birth, free from any possible infections. That was where Jacob's wife lay on a makeshift bed, surrounded by midwives and healers experienced in childbirth and ready for anything unexpected. This child had to arrive safe and healthy. In preparation for what was going to be a painful ordeal, she had been given herbal remedies to ease the pain and to ensure there was no undue loss of blood or any infection.

I could see my father Jacob wince every time he heard a gasp or moan or cry from the tent. Inside, the air was thick with the scent of blood and sweat, and the only light came from flickering oil lamps that cast shadows on the tent walls. As her labour intensified, her cries grew louder and more desperate. With every gasp, moan, or cry, emanating from the tent, I watched my father clearly suffering his own emotional turmoil as his wife agonised through her birthing pains.

This next brief but graphic description comes from one of the midwives with whom I sat sometime later.

"My mistress was suffering such great pain as her body seemed unwilling to offer her an easy birth, and her stamina seemed very limited. Inside the tent, the air was so heavy, we could almost feel the scent of blood and sweat. According to our customs, the tent flap remained closed, protecting us from evil spirits and possible infections, so the only light came from flickering oil lamps which threw strange shadows on the linen walls.

As the violence of her labour increased, her cries grew louder, causing us all to suffer in witnessing her distress. Her anguish continued to grow, and her face screwed up with the unbearable pain. She held the blankets so tightly that I could see her knuckles glistening white.

Finally, after what felt like forever, she found some last spring of strength and with what appeared to be a final effort, brought forth the long-hoped for little ball of a baby. It was as if time stood still while we all held our breath, we could feel the tension. Two of the older women cradled the baby and were rubbing it with oils, and cooing to the little creature, as if they were calling the baby into life. We were all praying. All we wanted was the sweet sound of a cry. And then it came, loud and strong, it felt like a miracle.

Tears streamed down our mistresses' face, and the joyous emotion spread to all of us inside the tent. Fear and dread were washed away, replaced by beaming wet smiles stretching wide across everyone's faces. Then we all burst out into joyous laughter and crying. It was oh, such a happy and beautiful time. That scene has fixed into my memory for as long as I live. I often think about it and the tears flow once more."

Outside the mood was completely matched with shouts of joy, people running round clapping their hands, laughing, shouting exuberant phrases, crying with joy. Even the children were running around screaming, infected by everyone's happiness.

I must admit, my eyes were also streaming with tears. I could see her husband, Jacob, bent over and shaking with emotion and then he lifted his face and seemed to be saying something. I knew he was praying and the relief and happiness on his face was something to behold.

My father stood at the edge of the tent, waiting anxiously for the women to beckon him to enter. Then he was gone, racing inside, and kneeling down at Rachel's side. His beloved had given birth after so many years of suffering under the taunt and misery of seemingly being barren.

He told me later. "We shall call his name Joseph,' I whispered softly, stroking Rachel's hair. I simply couldn't help myself, smiling from ear to ear. The many years of prayer and hope had brought to fruition this beautiful healthy baby boy."

The relationship I had with my adopted father, Jacob, was extremely close. Even at a young age, he trusted me with his confidence, and totally involved me in the series of life changing events which impacted every member of his family in subsequent years. He also delegated to me the specific responsibility of mentoring, guiding, and befriending his youngest and favourite son, Joseph.

Initially, as a boy, I assisted Jacob in various tasks around the camp, including occasional shepherding duties. As time passed, my role evolved, and I eventually served him as his personal assistant and companion. Despite our age difference of more than thirty years, he found in me someone with whom he could share his thoughts and feelings and feel safe. Throughout my childhood. I addressed him as father. Then once, during my early teen years, I suggested addressing him as 'adoni' or 'my master'. In response, he simply looked at me and said,

"After all these years calling me father, is that what you think of me, your master? You have always been my first son, though not born to me, certainly given to me by Adonai, the Most-High God. Would you rather be my servant or my son?"

Rather humbled, I replied, "your son, of course". And that was the end of that conversation.

Looking at him on this day, father was the most exhilarated I have ever seen him, and so was the whole camp. Some preparations had been made earlier in the hope of a successful birth, though not too many so that the gods would not be annoyed. Now the real preparations began.

But now, all the gods were being praised and blessed and given offerings. Every one of the heavenly deities had to be appeased. I had to sneak away so as to complete my song of welcome which I had been preparing for some time. I have also learnt to play several instruments which I taught myself when I was sitting bored and watching the flocks of sheep and goats. So, I needed to go somewhere to decide which instrument would be most suitable for my song and somewhere no one would hear me.

We were a strange mixture of cultures and religions in our camp population. I'll explain more about this later on, but for now, we had a celebration to deliver and enjoy. My father followed one God, he referred to as El'Elyon, or Most-High God, El Shaddai, or Adonai. For the purposes of my story, I will refer to Him as Adonai. Rachel worshiped Sin, the moon god, Hadad, the storm god and Anu, the sky god. She did this discreetly, as she knew that Jacob worshipped what he called the One True God, and she didn't want to displease him.

But all her life she had known her local gods and this tradition was hard to break because of the strongly felt superstition that angry gods could bring terrible consequences. For me, I was leaning very strongly towards Jacob's God because He seemed the most real and reliable. But traditionally we Hittites worshipped weather gods similar to the Mesopotamians and, in fact, I was named, I have been told, after the god of hunting, and forests, though I have never really lived in a Hittite community so am not sure that is correct. The rest of our camp population followed a mixture of gods in many ways similar, though with different names.

Now came a period of seclusion for Rachel, according to the customs of her people. It hadn't been an easy birth and time was needed to ensure her full recovery. Her isolation was to be for seven days, remaining in the birthing tent, during which time midwives and helpers would bathe her and treat her with various medicinal herbs. Even from the outside, passersby could smell the powerful aromas wafting from within while she was healing. Rachel knew about babies as she had been closely involved in raising the two boys that her maid

Bilhah had produced with Jacob, her husband, and at her request as, for many years, she had not been able to conceive. This time, however, Joseph was her own and she was very jealous about her involvement in his care.

For the following days, the camp was full of busy people. This was to be a major celebration for everyone, including Rachel's family from Haran who would travel out in caravan and spend several days in accommodation specially prepared, simple but comfortable. Everyone had something to do, and they did it with the utmost enthusiasm. While the campsite may not have been a palace, the food and celebrations were to be equal to any royal function.

The seventh day of seclusion finally arrived. Everyone was awake and active as the dawn broke; there was so much still to do and of course there was the feast. A large number of animals had been carefully selected and needed to be prepared for the various pots spread around the cooking area. It seemed like there were dozens: and everywhere I looked, another pot was beginning to simmer away. Even the sounds of the food preparation seemed to be singing in anticipation for this the most momentous celebration the family had ever experienced.

At last, by evening, just as the sun was beginning to set, all was ready, and everyone gathered in a large circle around a fire which had been elaborately arranged on a small altar of stones, so there was plenty of light. In addition, torches on long four-cubit high poles were lit throughout the camp. Almost in concert with this auspicious occasion, the sky was also offering its special blessing, showering the light of its full moon on everyone assembled.

As I walked around the numerous tents and other structures such as storehouses of clay and woven reeds and the occasional awning that offered shade for women toiling over the pots, rolling the spits, grinding flour, kneading dough, and stoking up the range of ovens for bread and roasting meats, I marvelled at the overnight transformation from a rather laid-back family of semi nomadic shepherds to a vibrant community that could conjure up the most luxurious of feasts within such a simple campsite, albeit exuding its own rustic splendour.

For it seemed, as if by magic, the whole encampment had been transformed into a festival scenario with hangings of multiple description and origin, wildflowers and fragrant herbs festooned on every possible raised object and some artistic individual had even painted celebratory designs on the sides of some of the tents using ochre colours of red and yellow, and the white of lime. It felt like walking inside a magic world of sheer happiness, and joy.

I strolled towards the gathering of eager revellers, drawn to the circle formed around the mesmerizing fire. The sparkling, dancing flames painted playful shadows on the faces of the assembled community. The air was rich with the earthy scent of woodsmoke, mingling harmoniously with the aroma of freshly baked bread and the enticing spices of roasting meats. We were a diverse group of men women and children, all belonging to the camp, both freemen, and slave but everyone was honoured with the same respect duly offered to a creation of Jacob's Adonai. There was another group of our people in the pastures minding the flocks. They would be relieved tomorrow and would come and join in the festivities.

Adding to our camp family, were Rachel's parents, Laban, and his wife, along with their extended family and friends who had travelled from Haran to partake in the celebrations. Laban, Jacob's uncle, had amassed considerable wealth through both a healthy inheritance as well as very successful business ventures, principally livestock and mainly thanks to Jacob. Their home in Haran was situated about a two-day journey away from our rural campsite, depending on the mode of travel. Laban had recommended this particular site to Jacob for setting up camp, primarily because it was closer to lush grazing fields for the animals. Additionally, the area boasted a grove of trees, including healthy olive, date, palm, and pomegranates, all nourished by a natural spring. This refreshing environment provided a pleasant and wholesome contrast to the somewhat stifling atmosphere of a city.

There was also the fact that Laban, although he wouldn't admit it, did not want to be embarrassed by the presence of his nephew, who was merely a shepherd coming from the distant land of Canaan, which paled in significance compared to the grand city of Haran. Laban, after all, had established his reputation as an honoured nobleman with a wide variety of investments, a significant proportion of which included the animals being managed by Jacob.

Special tents had been set up to accommodate Laban and his entourage all appropriately decorated in a nomadic rural style, offering the very best available. The caravan had arrived the morning of the celebrations with the women traveling in a cart pulled by oxen, while the men mostly rode donkeys and camels. Although horses were not a common sight among private citizens as they were rather expensive and mainly used by royalty and cavalry, however, a few in this group came on horseback, making a statement about their status. Laban being one of them.

In all, we would have been a company of close to a hundred. I should add, that included a group of minstrels and dancers who had been hired from the city of Haran. I could feel the excitement growing while everyone waited for the arrival of the honoured guests. Meanwhile, the musicians played some soulful melodies, in fact I could even put words to some of the tunes. The rhythmic pulse and mellow sounds resonated with the heartbeat of the gathering, celebrating jubilation, new birth and answered prayer all echoing through the night air.

The master of ceremonies was no other than Leah, the first wife of Jacob and older sister to Rachel. She ruled the day-to-day functioning of the camp and was very good at it. Strong, efficient, determined but also very kind. Everyone liked Leah and obeyed her to the letter, more because of their fondness for her than for her authority. If she was feeling any resentment for the huge fuss being made for Rachel's first born, she didn't show it. Perhaps she was hoping that now Jacob had a child from his favourite, he would pay a little more attention to her as she had already given him so many more healthy and promising boys over the years.

Just then, to calls of welcome and congratulations, Jacob adonenu (our lord) and immeinu Rachel (our mother Rachel), accompanied by several women, midwives, and helpers, arrived. Rachel was beaming shyly under a head covering of fine blue silk. Jacob, adonenu, was strutting proudly as if he had recently achieved something of great significance, and holding a small tightly wrapped bundle behind Rachel came her maid, Bilhah. At the western end of our campsite, a small platform had been erected using rocks covered with beautiful hand-woven rugs and cushions for the honoured guests. It was important for the baby and his parents to be facing east looking towards the rising sun in recognition of the new birth and a very special new beginning. The rest of us were seated on mats woven from reeds and covered with sheep and goatskins. For the more important guests, such as Rachel's family from Haran, rugs and cushions had been added for extra comfort and in recognition of their status.

And so, after days of feverish preparations, finally the actual moment for our festivities had arrived and I had been bestowed the honour of the first performance. All around, necks were craned, smiles and laughter abounded, the sense of anticipation and excitement was almost tangible. I had decided to accompany myself with the melodious notes of a lyre. Many years back, I had crafted my own makeshift lyre using wood for the base, and sheep sinews for strings, with a bridge fashioned from bone. It took several attempts, but eventually, I managed to coax a decent sound from my humble instrument.

However, one very memorable day, my father surprised me with a gift of the most exquisite lyre, its frame made of cedar, and the sides of the sound box of beautiful tortoise shell. The two uprights were meticulously carved bone, intricately painted, while a simple bone bridge at the top held the strings in place. A very impressive carving of a male goat with curved horns, graced the front of the lyre – an image I had previously only seen when the music masters of Haran performed for us. My father explained that this precious gift symbolised the delight and happiness he and his family experienced whenever I sang.

Handing me the instrument, he said, "Whenever you play on whatever musical implement you choose, Tarku, it is as if you had breathed life into that object, and the soul-stirring sound it produces is nothing short of magical".

Apart from its enchanting melody, my choice of the lyre also held religious significance, as it was believed to bring good fortune to its listeners, further adding to the enchantment of the occasion.

So, I sang. The message was a celebration of a new life that had been created after years of trial and sadness. The song commenced with a series of dirges that built up to a crescendo of triumph and creation. My purpose was to highlight the achievements of Jacob, the beauty and patience of Rachel and the final success of their love in the arrival of Joseph. I invoked blessings from above and in respect to Jacob's faith made a specific reference to the one God, Adonai, who rules and blesses according to His good pleasure and being pleased with Jacob, had blessed him with this wonderful new creation.

As there was some sensitivity between the fruitfulness of Rachel's elder sister and herself delivering Joseph as her first child, I did add a veiled reference to the strength and support provided by Leah. I ended with a shout of triumph invoking Adonai's blessing on the life of adonenu Jacob in his role as the provider and protector of his immediate family, and indeed the wider family of all gathered here. Little did I know what epoch-making events were to follow from that joyous evening those many years ago.

So, the celebrations continued. There were dancers whirling around in their shimmering garments. There were musicians playing and singing popular songs from all over the region and especially expounding the foretold glories and beauties of this newborn child. One singer, I can distinctly remember, a woman with the most haunting mellow voice, stood up and began to sing a beautiful and alluring ballad that reached deep into ones being. She was actually one of our camp family whose roots were in Canaan. It was an ancient melody and very well known. When it came to the chorus, others in our midst started to join in with an unexpected perfect harmony pouring love and blessings into each note.

As the joyous occasion unfolded, the air was filled with the enchanting melodies of local minstrels, whose music resonated through the balmy evening atmosphere. With the skill and experience of years of performances, they played on the tambourine, lyre, and flute. Especially beautiful was the haunting sound of the double flute. Especially beautiful was the sound of the double flute. The tunes wove a tapestry of captivating music that transported our gathering to a realm of wonder and celebration. The combined sounds of the rhythmic tambourines, the harmonious chords of the lyre and the mellifluous notes of the flutes stirred our hearts and celebrated our welcome both to the newborn child as well as to our guests from Haran.

Inspired by the exuberant spirit of the occasion, dancers emerged from the crowd, gracefully swaying to the rhythm of the melodies. Their feet gently kissed the earth, and their flowing garments billowed like wings of butterflies in a warm breeze. The dance was one acknowledging the significance of the occasion and honouring the miracle of a new creation; an ancient tradition passed down through generations. The movement mirrored the cycle of life, evoking the essence of natures' rhythms, from the blooming of flowers to the soft rustle of the reeds beside our spring, and gentle swaying of the trees. As the firelight flickered, the dancers' expressions glowed with joy, their bodies telling stories of love, unity, and gratitude. We were all transfixed by the hypnotic effect of both music and movement.

Then there were the story tellers who had such a gift in recounting great events that had occurred among the Akkadian people of the region. One older and very wise looking man told the story of the family's history. I recount a shorter version using his words.

"Gather round, my friends, and hear the ancient tale of Father Abraham – a saga of hot deserts, lonely terrain, and the grand city of Ur to the South, a megapolis of marvels. Alongside his father, Terah and their kin, Abraham set foot upon the soil of Haran, seeking a new horizon.

Following the death of his father, Abraham eventually journeyed down into Canaan, directed by the hand of his God, El Elyon, and blessed by a special divine covenant promising that he would become the father of many nations. Oh, the trials and tribulations they faced, as they traversed scorching deserts, their hearts yearning for the promised land. With this noble destiny, written in the stars and etched upon his heart, Abraham ventured further south into Canaan.

Yet, as life's tapestry unfolds, it bears both blessings and hardships. When a cruel famine swept through the land, Abraham and his beloved family embarked on a daring escape to the great Southern Kingdom of Egypt. Sojourning there for many years, seeking refuge and sustenance in the arms of the Nile.

But fate, like a capricious deity, had more in store for Abraham. The Pharaoh, his heart poisoned by jealousy, coveted Sarah, Abraham's wife, drawn by the forbidden fruits of her beauty. Yet, in divine providence, God warned the Pharaoh against any harm he might inflict upon Abraham. Instead of retribution, the jealous ruler found himself bestowing gifts upon Abraham, beseeching him to depart from Egypt's embrace.

And so, our tale weaves onward, with Abraham's destiny intertwined with the threads of the divine, guided by El Elyon's hand. Such is the journey of a man destined to become a father of many peoples, a wanderer in foreign lands, and a recipient of blessings bestowed by the heavens above. May his legacy echo through the ages and may we forever remember the trials and triumphs of Father Abraham".

But this amazing storyteller didn't stop there. He continued with the adventures of Abraham's defeat of the three Kings of the North. Of Isaac, my father's father whose bride was the beautiful Rebecca from Haran. It was a long but very emotional telling and at times there were many wet faces staring into the fire as their minds identified with all the significant characters and joined in with their exploits, their elation, and their sorrows. When the story came to an abrupt halt, at the most recent birth of Joseph, there was a total silence, no movement, no sound, almost in respect for the venerable ancestors living and passed on who had provided such a legacy to the family's history.

Then at a sign from Leah, the sound of drums, cymbals and double pipes announced an invitation to the feast. Immediately women in flowing garments of earthy browns and vibrant reds gracefully rose and disappeared behind the tents to where, I knew, there were those array of large clay pots simmering with delicious stews of beef, lamb, wild deer, and hare combined with a variety of herbs that saturated the air with delicious aromas. Not far away, I could see several spits where lamb, goat, chickens, and ducks were being roasted. One of my favourites were the beef pies, a real speciality in this part of the world. I also knew to expect a delicious selection of smoked carp, catfish and eels stuffed with a magical concoction of herbs and spices. A wide selection of vegetables, some added to the stews and others steamed and garnished with various herbs would be laid out on long platters. To all of these delicious foods was added the freshly baked flat breads which had their own special flavour and pervading fragrance.

The whole group moved over towards where all the cooking preparations were taking place. There a large square of tables had been arranged, slightly raised with mats and skins to sit on. At the Western end, as in the previous celebrations, a table had been prepared for the honoured guests and their relatives. All the tables had been decorated with flowers and candles at the outside leaving space for the food which was to come. A number of the group who had joined in the previous entertainment, now separated themselves as they were servants, and this was their time to contribute. And it wasn't long before the dishes started appearing and of course, there was the wine. My father's father-in-law, Laban, had gifted a large number of wineskins of old and delicious wines for the occasion. It seemed to have become a never-ending feast, sumptuous dish after dish. Not far away the fire had been stoked up and was sending sparks into the air like a celebratory bonfire. All around us the torches continued to flicker and sparkle. And from the centre of this banquet the music continued to flow and vibrate with beautiful renditions.

The evening was slightly warm with a cool balmy breeze, so typical of this time of the year. I couldn't help looking up into the dark sky, where a full moon shone down but didn't eclipse the brilliance of Sirius, Castor, and Pollux, among several other dazzling heavenly constellations. It was an evening I will never forget. Eventually, it all ended but we were all more than satisfied, physically, mentally, and emotionally. And so, to bed.

I was aware that Rachel would be taking part in several purification ceremonies and wasn't sure whether she would join Jacob in the camp's principal tent where he slept and carried out all the responsibilities of camp management as well as overseeing the expansive and challenging livestock supervision. Both Leah and Rachel had their separate tents where they and their senior maids slept. They would join their husband in his tent upon invitation. For the most part, I would stay in a larger tent occupied by Leah's sons. I had been accepted by all the family as an older brother and sometime mentor. However, on certain special occasions, Jacob would ask me to join him in his tent for company and we would drink some wine together and he would feel free to share some of his thoughts. Although I was still only a teenager, my father and I had bonded years before his marriage and fatherhood, and he looked on me as both an elder child as well as a young friend. Over the years, Leah had been prolific in providing him with sons and each time we had celebrated, though never on this grand a scale, then she would retire to her tent and my father to his.

All of a sudden, I saw Jacob approaching me and I bowed to him to demonstrate both my love and respect as well as the happiness I shared. While at times he could be a very daunting and formidable character, at other times he could completely hide his feelings. In a way, it was a gift as both of these character ploys assisted in his maintaining control in most situations. But tonight, he was different, a happy, content and very gracious new father. He had finally been blessed with a son by his favourite wife.

He put his hand on my shoulder and nodded, so I followed him to his tent. This was father's home, and as he was the Patriarch of his family, in a discreet way, the tent reflected this. While the outer covering was the same as for all tents principally made of goat's skins to ensure it was waterproof, the inside was lined with soft near-white linen hangings that created a more friendly atmosphere and also aided in absorbing and shielding the heat on a hot day. To one side was my father's bed, slightly raised on a wooden frame, the insides of which consisted of a woven reed matting. On top of the matting were several layers of sheep skin with the wool side up to offer a comfortable surface to lie on. Above the bed were several embroidered hangings depicting rural scenes of the hills, valleys, and rivers of our region.

On the other side of the tent was a similar construction but smaller and with cushions for reclining. That is where I normally slept. In front of both of these was a low table, bolstered behind with cushions where Jacob sat when planning, or carrying out business, and in front of the table was a space, lined with an assortment of rugs where visitors could sit. Illuminating the whole was a kind of hanging candelabra containing several oil lamps. On two sides of the tent were small stands where incense was burned on various occasions such as entertaining guests, celebrating special events or hosting one of his wives.

We settled down comfortably, and Jacob kindly poured me some wine, only a half cup, knowing I wasn't particularly fond of alcohol. It was a time for celebration, so I happily joined him. My father then shared that Rachel would be returning to her birthing tent to participate in certain rituals, guided by the midwives, according to those prescribed for women who had experienced a difficult birth. Then she would sleep. They had carefully prepared a crib for the baby, and her maid and two helpers would watch over the child throughout the night to ensure a peaceful and uninterrupted rest. However, Rachel specifically instructed that she be wakened whenever the baby needed to be fed, as she was determined to be present for every precious waking moment with her newborn. Although she had planned to have a surrogate help with feeding later, for the first few days, she wanted to be solely devoted to the child and become an integral part of his life.

Meanwhile, Rachel had also asked for complete privacy for an additional seven days, after which she would rejoin camp life. During this time, she would undergo an ongoing program of cleansing and purification, another traditional obligation. All these ceremonies did not involve Jacob, who, sympathetic and understanding, was willing to patiently wait, knowing that he had many years ahead to spoil and cherish their son, Joseph as well as his mother.

While I more or less anticipated what he would say, I asked father.

'Why did you make this celebration so special?"

"You must know the answer by now Tarku." Was his initial response. "You know my story and even though you were not much more than a baby when you came here, you have followed everything I have done and have watched me plan and, at times maybe conspire, and have seen the results. I only ever wanted to marry Rachel, but I can see now, in the wisdom of Adonai, I was first given Leah, who is a lovely gentle person, though to whom I simply cannot give my love. And now I have many sons and a daughter. But Rachel has always been my only true love".

He continued, "I have tried very hard to love Leah, but then I see Rachel walking past my tent and every affection I have for anyone else simply disappears. My whole world revolves around spending time with Rachel and making her happy. I know it is very selfish of me, but from the very beginning of my sojourn here, she was the single reason for me to stay.

I have tried to make it up to Leah. I have made her the Matriarch of the family, and she is the one to whom I give total management of my household. And, as you know, she is very efficient. The whole camp operates so smoothly mainly because of Leah. I have given her the largest and most attractive tent. I have given her servants and slaves as many as I can afford. She has only to ask, and I give it to her. But when she asks for my love, I can always pretend, but there is simply nothing there to give. I know she realises that, and she suffers for that. But in all my dealings with my family, I have to be honest.

No, don't raise your eyebrows, and don't cough inside. You know my story and when I talk about honesty, you also know of my deceit with my brother. But since then, I have had several encounters with Adonai. My life has changed. I have changed. I am now, slowly beginning to realise that I am part of a divine plan and so I have to be honest with myself and also with all the members of my family. I'm not sure that needs to include my uncle for as you are aware, he has certainly deceived me several times and used me to increase his wealth. Fourteen years of labour for his two daughters, when I only really wanted to marry the younger, is a very high price to pay. Our initial agreement had been seven years for Rachel's hand and then on the morning after the wedding I found Leah in my bed. So, I agreed to another seven years for her sister. Maybe, I will retain some of my ability to connive in order to deal with him. But otherwise, I have to be honest, and one day when I meet my brother again, I hope I can show him due respect and express my deep regret for taking advantage of him, stealing his birthright and also our father's blessing. Don't judge me, pray for me. And I'm going to put the whole responsibility for raising Joseph into your hands".

He still had more to say, "Tarku, you have wisdom far reaching beyond anyone your age would normally exhibit. I am sure you have been brought into my life for a reason. Sometimes the vision of my life and that of my family frightens me. I receive messages from Adonai, astounding messages. I am surrounded by so many different cultures and each with their own gods whom they trust and depend on. So why am I and my family different? My father used to tell me of some of his experiences with Adonai. Who is this one supreme God who is going to create a people more numerous than the sands of the sea? The very same words spoken to my father. How is He different from all the other gods? And He demands complete obedience to Him alone. It is all so new and confusing and I'm really not sure I understand. But He has blessed me with so many wonderful sons, and a daughter, and he has enabled me to establish a family with many flocks and servants and enough to live on. How can I doubt such a God of blessing? And now, finally a child from my beloved. It is all too wonderful to begin to comprehend".

I did have one question to ask him as it had been irritating my brain for days now, so, assuming father to be in a very good mood, I ventured ahead and asked, rather hesitatingly, "So what now adonenu? Will we be returning to the land where your father and family are, in Canaan?" I used the honorific and hoped he would not take offence.

For a while, there was complete silence and then he simply responded, 'I don't know. I have two wives and many children and everything that my father and mother have been sending me from Beersheba, over these fifteen years, but I can't return home empty handed. I'll talk to my uncle tomorrow'.

'Now, I'm tired. Good night'.

And that was the end of our conversation. My mind was still in a turmoil wondering what we would be doing, and I did long to return to the land where I was born. But for now, I had a limited answer, and I was sure I would know more in the coming days. I walked over to my couch and very soon fell asleep.

CHAPTER TWO

BETRAYAL AND ESCAPE

"So, Isaac called Jacob, and after blessing him, charged him" "You are not to choose a wife
from the Hittite women. Go now to the house of B'tuel, your mother's father, and choose a
wife there from the daughters of Laban, your mother's brother. May ElShaddai bless you".
Genesis 28: 1-3

'Jacob, the supplanter, pilferer of his brother's rights, deceiver of his father's trust, driven by greed for what doesn't belong to him'. These were some of the names whispered behind my father Jacob's back. Living with such a legacy must have been extremely distressing. I find it hard to imagine my adopted father enjoying much happiness under such cruel conditions. The truth is that through a combination of necessities, his mother's manipulations, spontaneous opportunism, and unfortunate circumstances all led to Jacob's extremely complicated situation as a young man living in his father's establishment in Beersheba in southern Canaan. This is how it was explained to me, years later in his own words.

"As you know, Tarku, I used to enjoy cooking. One fateful day, I had decided to prepare one of my favourite dishes. It was simple, but cooked the right way, with my own recipe of herbs and spices, this lentil dish was greatly favoured by most members of my family".

He continued, "I was sitting on a bench under an awning where our cooks would work their magic for our daily meals. The dish was bubbling away in its final stages, and I was waiting for the last few stirs after which it would be ready to eat. Just then, my brother Esau, came running up to me, out of breath and seemingly upset about something. He crouched down beside the cooking pot, looked into it, had a strong smell of its vapours and then looking up at me, he said,"

"I must have some of your stew my brother. It is by far the most delicious preparation I have ever tasted; you know it's my favourite. Give me some to eat."

"I don't know what came over me, whether I was serious or jesting, or perhaps I was a little annoyed at his audacity, I'm still not sure, but I replied". "What will you give me in exchange brother?"

"Anything," he retorted, "just name your price, anything, just give me a plate of your amazing creation, I've been out hunting and haven't eaten all day."

"So, I said, alright, if you are so desperate for what's in that pot, give me your birthright."

"What?" he replied, looking up at me startled.

"I repeated my absurd suggestion."

"Give me your birthright."

"He crouched back down, remained quiet for a short time and finally said".

"Oh, alright, what good is it to me anyway? I don't want to spend my life looking after silly sheep and goats, it's yours, now can I have some of your food?"

"And that was it. I gave him the food. He ate it rapidly like a starved animal and left. I didn't think much about it for quite a long time, until one day, in front of our parents, he burst out in anger accusing me of stealing his birthright. Both parents were shocked and then the whole story came out. It seems that by his agreeing to my demand over a plate of lentils, I had actually obtained his birthright. I'm still not sure I really wanted it, but now I had no choice". Explaining the situation, Jacob still seemed rather bemused by what had happened.

He went on, "My father was horrified but my mother was pleased as it meant that I had inherited the right to manage my father's business, something that had been worrying my mother for some time as her eldest, Esau, was never around and there was so much work involved in overseeing everything that my father's business had established".

Then, more seriously, he confessed. "That was my first, I should call it, mistake. My mother took full advantage of the situation and made sure everyone knew the details. She instructed our chief overseer, Baruch, to instruct me in all the complications of the business, and it wasn't long before I was totally immersed in everything related to animal husbandry and management as well as the whole other side of trading and investment".

Jacob continued. "The next major event took place one day when my mother came to me and told me to quickly go and get one of the kid goats for her to prepare some food for my father. I asked why, and she simply said,' just go and get it and I'll tell you while I am preparing the food".

The plot thickened as Jacob explained. "Apparently, she had overheard my father asking my brother to go out and hunt some game and then prepare his favourite food so he could eat it and then give him his special blessing reserved for the first born. My father had been feeling frail and his eyesight was going, and he was sure he was going to die anytime soon. So, my mother had decided I was to steal this blessing".

Now Jacob was revealing a side of him not many people knew. "I protested, but she insisted and her logic at the time seemed very reasonable. She explained that while I may have the birthright, I still did not have full authority and she cited some instances where servants and herdsmen were expressing their dissatisfaction that I, as a younger brother, was over-reaching my authority and they weren't happy. So, for the good of the family business, it was the very best opportunity of which I had to take advantage. I explained that I neither looked like nor smelled like my brother, but she had everything organised".

"This is how it all took place, Jacob described. "Soon after, dressed in my brother's clothes and with young kid goat hair on my arms, I walked into my father's tent and greeted him, saying".

"Father, I have brought the food you asked me to prepare. Now, I knew my father could not see who it was, but he reached over and touched me and replied. "You feel like Esau and smell like Esau, although you have the voice of Jacob. Come closer and give me the food so I can eat."

Jacob continued. "My father fell for the deception, and I breathed a sigh of relief. He ate it and then, telling me to kneel down and place my hands on his thighs, he gave me his blessing. My brother came in soon after and when he learnt of my deceit, he was absolutely furious. I think, if I had been in the room, he would have struck me dead on the spot. Actually, when I think about it, I wouldn't have blamed him. It was a terrible deception on my part, even though the motive was, I thought, reasonable in ensuring adequate management for our family business".

Jacob finished his story; "I know he was wanting me to understand the undesired dilemma he had been placed in, and to gain some sense of absolution for what had happened. "So, Tarku, that's the story behind all of my troubles, and here we are in Haran, fleeing my brother's wrath and looking for a bride."

I was very glad to have heard the full story directly from my father. I found it hard to resolve the issue of integrity and deceit, but I heard my father's tone of regret and as he had commented, he had no need of his father's inheritance now as he was gradually becoming a wealthy man in his own right.

Indeed, the birth of Joseph marked a profound turning point in my father's life and consequently, in the lives of us all. Finally, this birth had the added significance that it was a male heir. This pivotal moment in the family's history is the principle reason why I chose to commence my story with this momentous event because it was Joseph, this innocent baby born out of love and tremendous pain, growing up as the youngest and spoilt son of a father of eleven sons, despised by his brothers, but despite everything, rising to greater heights, power and wealth than all the family past and present combined. His has been a simply amazing story.

For the record, let me explain a little more about the family, its history, and its lineage. My father Jacob was the third in line of the Patriarchs. Adonai had called Jacob's grandfather, Abraham, out of Ur of the Chaldees, situated on the southern coast of Mesopotamia. During his divine encounter, Adonai promised Abraham that he would become the father of several nations. This promise was then reiterated to Jacob's father Isaac.

Later, in a place just outside a city called Luz (which site my father named Bethel, meaning 'House of God'), and occupied by a Canaanite people called the Perizzites, Adonai appeared to him. As with his father and grandfather, Adonai re-affirmed the promise that his heirs would become a great nation, numbering more than the sands of the seas and the stars of the sky. This dramatic experience marked a significant moment in Jacob's mind and in his acceptance of God's promise and consequently in the belief in the ultimate fulfillment of the divine prophecy. What I suspect was that, while Jacob was convinced in Adonai's divine forecasting, he never realised the impact it would have on his entire family and indeed everyone coming within the sphere of Jacob's authority and influence.

Abraham eventually settled in a place in the deep south of Canaan called Beersheba and Isaac, who was Abraham's only child by his wife Sarah, inherited his father's wealth which included his flocks, his servants, and his household. Abraham, determined to ensure that Isaac had no competitors, actually paid off his concubines and their children and sent them somewhere to the east and I understand they became a tribe calling themselves Midianites. However, that is only gossip which I have heard over the years, and they don't appear to be at all significant. Perhaps because they shared the same father, they eventually came under the protection of Ishmael, being their half-brother.

Now, in order to understand this part of the story from the beginning, let me add a little more detail. Isaac was the only true son of Abraham and his wife Sarah, who remained childless for most of their married life. Adonai promised Abraham that he would become the father of several nations, leading him to expect a son. After years of waiting, Sarah, taking matters into her own hands, offered her Egyptian maid Hagar to Abraham in hopes of his fathering a child through her. This desperate plan succeeded, and Abraham did father a son named Ishmael through Hagar.

Then, to his absolute astonishment, Adonai told Abraham that he would have a son through Sarah. Abraham expressed serious doubts, and pointed out to Adonai that he was actually one hundred years old. Sarah simply laughed at the idea. Nonetheless, Adonai's promise came to pass and, amazingly, Isaac was born.

In a truly bewildering turn of events, after many years of joy and contentment shared with his beloved son, Isaac, through his cherished wife Sarah, Abraham received a profound and challenging instruction from Adonai. He was commanded to take his only son to Mount Moriah and offer him as a sacrifice. This devastating demand shook Abraham, but his unwavering commitment to his God led him to obey without question. So, from Beersheba, Abraham assembled a small caravan, and together with Isaac they journeyed the several days journey north to their destination.

Arriving east outside the city of Jebus, they set up camp and early the following morning, leaving the two servants behind, Abraham and Isaac completed the journey up mount Moriah, the place God had directed him to. There they built an altar, and Isaac was bound and about to be sacrificed when an angel of the Lord called out to him".

"Abraham, Abraham …. Don't lay a hand on the boy! Don't do anything to him! For now, I know that you are a man who fears God, because you have not withheld your son; your only son from me".

Miraculously, a ram was discovered caught up in the bushes, provided by Adonai as an alternative sacrifice. This divine provision brought indescribable relief to Abraham, who had just faced the ultimate test of his faith and obedience.

This was a very dramatic story and with great pride and reverence has been passed down from father to son, seemingly word for word.

In recognition of his faithful devotion, Abraham received confirmation by his God, to the covenant that he would become the father of many nations and subsequently he received blessings and prosperity more than he could ever have dreamed of.

Following the passing of Sarah at the venerable age of one hundred and twenty-seven, Abraham was filled with sorrow. Seeking a suitable place to lay her to rest, he approached his Hittite neighbours and requested a burial site. After some negotiations, an agreement was reached and Abraham acquired a cave in a field known as Machpelah, near Mamre, just outside the city of Hebron, which would serve as a family tomb, greatly venerated, for generations to come.

Realizing his own mortality, Abraham felt it was time for his son Isaac to find a suitable wife. He was determined that Isaac's bride would not come from the local Canaanite tribes, as Ishmael, Abraham's firstborn, had done.

To accomplish this, Abraham entrusted the task to his loyal overseer, Eliezer, who was sent to Abraham's brother-in-law, Laban, way up north in Haran. Although gone for many days, once there, Eliezer wasted no time and soon returned with Rebecca, a young and exceptionally beautiful woman. Isaac fell deeply in love with her at first sight.

However. Despite their love for each other, Rebecca like her mother-in-law, struggled with infertility for twenty years. Then, through the prayers and blessings of Adonai, she finally conceived and gave birth to twin boys. The firstborn was Esau, a robust and hairy child, followed very closely by Jacob, who was gentle and smooth.

Year's later, the boys had become grown men. Esau became a seasoned hunter and brought his father wild game to be prepared into his favourite meal. Jacob mostly stayed in the camp spending his time absorbing knowledge and skills related to looking after livestock and even delved into agriculture, as Isaac had very prosperous fields of grain. Jacob loved animals and wanted to know all about them. He also enjoyed listening to stories of days gone by from some of the older members of the camp population. One particular elder taught him the basics of reading and writing, which was highly unusual for people following his way of life. Although expressing his distaste for violence and weapons, his father insisted he learn some basics in self-defence, but beyond the simplest of elements, he refused to go any further.

Rebecca found that as Esau was spending most of his time with his Hittite wives, and feasting and hunting with their people, it was up to her to manage her husband's affairs which were extensive. Abraham had been a very wealthy man and his inheritance left for Isaac was substantial. On top of that Isaac also proved himself extremely successful in raising animals as well as crops.

Fortunately, Rebecca had inherited a very capable overseer, named Baruch, the son of Eliezer, Abraham's valued chief servant and manager of all he had. When Abraham died, Eliezer retired to his hometown of Damascus, but left his son to help in managing the affairs of the camp. Rebecca relied very heavily on Baruch and had him train Jacob in all the knowledge and skills required to supervise and grow Isaac's wealth. Although Baruch was a freeman, he decided to remain in the employ of Rebecca and Jacob, which in fact was a very comfortable living as he was the most senior in the family after mother and son.

A key figure in the lives of both Abraham and Isaac was Abimelech, King of Gerar, peopled by the Philistines, a seafaring people who had settled on the coast of Canaan. Initially, Abraham lived close to Gerar but there was a falling out between them over his wife Sarah, who being beautiful had attracted the attention of the King. Earlier, Abraham, fearing he would be killed by the Philistines so that they could take his wife had told her to say they were brother and sister. Adonai came to the rescue and warned the King not to meddle with Sarah as she was Abraham's wife and as a consequence, the King gave Abraham what seemed like a bride-price and asked him to move away from the city. So, Abraham settled in Beersheba. Many years later, Isaac, having inherited his father's wealth was faced by a famine. Adonai told him to stay in the land and so he moved back to Gerar where he prospered, even taking up cropping of barley and wheat.

There ensued some quarrelling between his herdsman and those of the king over wells and water, so he moved back to Beersheba. Again, it seemed like everything he put his hand to reaped enormous bounty. His prosperity was so remarkable that King Abimelech himself, accompanied by his army chief, visited Isaac in Beersheba to establish a peace treaty. The meeting demonstrated the high regard and recognition Isaac held in the eyes of regional rulers.

The king explained his reason for the treaty to be that he felt Isaac had become more powerful than himself. While such a claim might have been met with scepticism by many, as Isaac did not have a standing army, nevertheless, King Abimelech had to be vigilant due to the numerous enemies among the Canaanite tribes who sought to challenge his authority. Although Isaac employed no professional soldiers, on the other hand, he possessed substantial wealth that could potentially support the recruitment of a formidable army. Thus, the mutual interest in forming a settlement that established a mutual peace accord and support between both parties, seemed like a reasonable way forward being beneficial to both Abimelech and his Kingdom as well as Isaac and his family.

As a gesture of his on-going desire of accord and friendship, Isaac confirmed that he had no aspirations to seize anyone's land or authority as witnessed by his refusal to contest King Abimelech's herders, who reclaimed wells that Isaac's father had dug. The King vowed loyalty and a willingness to come to Isaac's aid in times of any aggression he might face by rival families contesting grazing rights.

One highly favourable outcome, from Isaac's perspective, although he might not have fully appreciated it at the time, was King Abimelech's gift of one of his foremost warriors. Ithai, a skilled Philistine soldier, belonging to the esteemed Pelethite group, who was specifically trained to guard the King and was renowned for his prowess in all forms of combat. Accompanied by four of his fellow men at arms, Ithai took a solemn oath of commitment to protect Isaac and his family and to train the young men of the household in the skills necessary for an active participation in their defence.

Then, on the insistence of the king, a ceremonial feast was prepared with much fanfare, during which sacrifices were made, Isaac to his God, Adonai, and Abimelech to Dagon, confirming pledges from both parties for a pact of peace and mutual assistance. One of the highlights of this ceremony was the sacred swearing-in, held in high regard by the Philistines, for the induction of five noble and accomplished combatants into the service of their new overlord. And so was solidified a bond initially established between King Abimelech of Abraham's time and subsequently confirmed, more officially, through his son Abimelech during the life and times of Isaac.

Now, recalling my conversation with father, earlier on where he explained his duplicity with both his father and his brother, I had also concluded that, according to the laws of the land, he had been wrong. Although we were all a great mixture of tribes in the land of Canaan, with differing origins and beliefs, many of our customs and values were shared.

All right, to be fair, let me qualify that. I suppose it depends on which side of the family one prefers to sit in judgment. From his brother, Esau's perspective, he stole his birthright for a bowel of lentils, followed by a deception with his father, many years later, stealing his father's blessing normally belonging to the first born. However, from Rebecca's and Jacob's point of view, it was simply fate and divinely appointed to be. Adonai ordained it and Jacob was by far the better option to carry on the family line. Esau was a great hunter but that is all he could ever offer his family – hunting for wild game. What did he care about raising animals? How would he know the intricacies of negotiation or formulating any plans which could benefit the family in a land of warring tribes; always requiring political savvy, patience, and tact?

Besides, Esau had married Hittite women which immediately disqualified him from being the source of future heirs. Yes, from this perspective, all the generally accepted moral and ethical considerations could perhaps be rationalised as having less importance than the priority of lineage. The family of Fathers Abraham and Isaac needed someone competent to ensure a positive future, besides which, Adonai had predicted this would happen and, very clearly, gave it His blessing. But all that considered, was it still, right?

The fact was, Esau considered it a major betrayal and his father Isaac could not help expressing his disappointment. Sensing potential danger from an angry Esau, Rebecca, whispered into Isaac's ear.

"We need to consider an heir for you, my husband. Esau has married Hittite women, and I am sure that is not pleasing to Adonai. We need to send Jacob back to Haran to find a wife and to keep your inheritance untainted for future generations".

I must say, I really feel sorry for Rebecca. History will brand her as a conniving wife, manipulating her husband and favouring, even spoiling, her special son Jacob. Here she was, Matriarch of an establishment that was very significant and of incredible value involving hundreds of servants and slaves and thousands of animals. She was married to a man who was almost blind and determined that he was dying. Her eldest son had married Hittite women who sought every opportunity to harass her and even confront and dishonour her husband. Her son Esau had absolutely no interest in managing the family business. There was unrest amongst the shepherds and herdsmen over Jacob's management of affairs as they considered him the second son and lacking authority. What was she to do?

Well, to her credit, she acknowledged the problems, secured the support of Baruch, and focused on how she could manipulate her younger son into the required position of a manager possessing both the right and the authority. This she accomplished, but it all seemed to fall apart when Esau started to threaten death and destruction. What was she to do? Any confrontation between her two sons could have led to the death of one of them. She loved them both, although she had favoured her younger son. But the last thing she could have wished was anything hurtful to either of them.

So, dear beautiful, Rebecca, decided that Jacob had to leave. She instructed him to follow her line of appeal and go and explain to Isaac his desire to return to their family roots in Haran to find a bride and so ensure a pure bloodline, rather than seeking a wife from anyone of local origins.

Isaac was aware of the trouble his wife had been enduring from Esau's Hittite wives and, in fact, he had also suffered occasional humiliation, so, without a great deal of discussion, it was agreed.

Within a short time, everything was readied. It was decided that Jacob was to leave Beersheba, accompanied by several servants, a line of camels, and a couple of donkeys, carrying everything that he would need to maintain the level of comfort that his father had always provided, as well as gifts for his intended bride. Isaac also insisted that Ithai and one of his soldiers (actually a young Egyptian mercenary who had enlisted under the banner of King Abimelech) accompany him to provide protection on a potentially perilous journey. Isaac now had protection both from the Philistine King in Gerar, as well as through a growing number of his own retainers who had been taught various skills in handling weapons.

As much as I love and respect my adopted father, I must admit that he had a weakness; he was not accustomed to physical hardships, well, certainly not in those early years. While his brother was out hunting and embracing the rugged lifestyle of a strong and hardened man of the land, Jacob mostly remained close to the tents of his father's camp and was indulged by his doting and ambitious - or perhaps I should say protective - mother.

What my father Jacob did possess, in abundance, was perseverance. Although he may not have been a man of the land, living and roaming with his father's flocks, he was determined to learn as much as he could about animals, as much as he could about cropping, and, in fact, as much as he could about every aspect of the family business. His priorities lay in developing the use of his mind over his muscles.

Time and time again, I have explored many perspectives in an attempt to explain or excuse all that occurred during the somewhat tumultuous family intrigue of that period. Undoubtedly, Rebecca was looking out for the overall benefit of her husband's business and welfare, and I'm certain that Isaac, an aging but intelligent man, was fully aware of the significant differences between his two sons and understood that Rebecca had a genuine interest in preserving all that he and his father had built. He knew his wife favoured the younger son, and though he tolerated this reality, he sought to compensate this by focusing more attention on his eldest, Esau. Nevertheless, it is clear that everything Jacob did went against the traditions, norms, and obligations of the times.

"Yes Tarku, I know that many people have felt that I abused my responsibility as a younger son by stealing both Esau's birthright as well as the blessing my father wanted to give him", Jacob once explained. "However, remember this, my father also gave me a second blessing which involved his request to Adonai to grant me the same benediction and divine covenant that He had given to both my father as well as my grandfather, Abraham. This was a blessing that foretold of becoming a great people and inheriting the land of Canaan. While trying not to compromise on the principles relating to honesty, I truly see all of this as simply the will of Adonai, however much it may have broken traditions, laws, and expectations".

He continued with, "Yes, I did have my doubts and had expressed these to my mother on several occasions, but in the end, the need for managing my father's affairs, as Esau was not interested, as well as providing him with an heir other than that from a Canaanite woman, convinced me to go along with my mother's schemes as the best course for the family and its future. Without my father's blessing, I would never have had the authority or credibility to conduct business in his name. And now I am a long way from home, so maybe it has all fallen apart anyway."

While Esau would have loved the opportunity to ambush and punish his brother during the course of his journey, in fact he had threatened to kill him, and he certainly had the means and the network to make that happen, he knew it would break his father's heart and he dearly loved Isaac. So, he compromised with the fact that Jacob would be out of his life and anyway, anything could happen between Beersheba and Haran. Perhaps he would never return.

Perhaps the most surprising element in this new chapter in Jacob's life was Isaac's second blessing. In fact, it evolved into a double blessing. Firstly, for his journey and its successful accomplishment. But secondly, and more importantly, a request to his God, Adonai, to bless Jacob with the same promises that He had given to both Isaac and Abraham; a blessing of the land and of becoming a great nation.

Actually, Jacob had originally asked his father if he could travel simply and alone, perhaps accompanied by one servant. However, Ithai had advised him otherwise supporting his reasons with very graphic descriptions, based on his own experiences, of what could happen to him on the way if he was to travel by himself. He explained that most people planning a journey of this nature and distance would normally attach themselves to a caravan heading north. My father was definitely no warrior and had very little experience with a sword or anything else to defend himself, so it wasn't too difficult to convince him that a journey alone would have been tantamount to suicide.

Listening to my father as he reflected on those early days and talked about his preparations for a journey of considerable distance with many unforeseen challenges, it was clear to me that, in leaving Beersheba, Jacob was a deeply anxious and troubled young man. His thoughts consumed him, spiralling off into every possible direction. He feared the immediate future, from a very angry older brother. He sensed the disappointment from his ailing father. Additionally, he couldn't help but wonder what awaited him at the end of this journey. Would he be welcomed, or would he face rejection? Was there a suitable bride waiting for him, or would be find himself alone?

Then there were the physical challenges. During the day, everyone in the caravan was expected to walk as that was the customary mode for travellers like Jacob's group. Horses were rare, and only when absolutely necessary would those unable to walk ride a donkey, or a camel. The latter being the preferred mode for desert travel.

So, as Jacob was poised to commence this long trek north to Haran, a journey that would most likely take more than sixty days, engulfed with the challenges of past present and future, he was having to deal with both physical as well as mental torment: principally a combination of painful blisters as well as a guilty conscience.

However, before we venture into that narrative, I would like to provide a little more about my father's background and experiences up to that point in time, and hopefully this will illuminate more about the man I have grown to love and respect and help us commence this new chapter on a note of optimism.

Indeed, Jacob's life had been rather pampered up to this point. He would tell me of one of his favourite pastimes being in the evening, sitting around a campfire with the elders of their people, sipping wine and listening to the riveting tales shared by the wise old men who had spent their whole life working for Abraham and then for his son Isaac. They were the experts growing up under the tutelage of the first Patriarch, learning all there was to know about rearing and expanding the flocks. This was a side of Jacob that so impressed me, his insatiable curiosity, wanting to explore every aspect of caring for livestock, including the many intricacies of successful breeding.

Let me add, so as to adequately share the Jacob I have known for many decades, he has always been a very strong personality, highly intelligent and extremely knowledgeable, particularly when it comes to animal husbandry. To his credit, during those troubled times, my father had the strength of character to realise he was needed, and he stepped up to fulfill that role with significant commitment and a generous amount of ability. It took time, but with the guidance of Baruch and occasional inputs from his father, he learnt fast and by the time he was in his late twenties, he had become the master-in-waiting.

Then there was the great trek south. Once a year, Jacob would follow his father's custom of travelling south to a camp site which the family had called Beer-Lahai-roi located in a wadi, or dry riverbed, also blessed with several wells, not far from the city of Rekem. In fact, it was on Isaac's return journey from this annual trade pilgrimage, that he first saw Rebecca who had come from her father's house in Haran. Brought back by Abraham's faithful Eliezer, both Rebecca and Isaac immediately on seeing each other, fell madly in love. This is how Jacob shared the story told to him by his father Isaac.

"After several weeks away enjoying the delights of our camp just outside of Rekem and the genuine friendship of the royal family and their people of that amazing city, I was riding my camel and looking forward to relieving my weary body from hours in the saddle. Just ahead I could see our tent city. It was a welcoming sight, and I knew our caravan would generate a whole new level of excitement with all the treasures we had brought from the south. I had just ordered my beast to lower itself, when, in the distance, I saw a number of animals approaching from the north. I waited and watched as the lead camels lowered themselves and I noticed several people alight and commence walking into the camp, one a woman, seemed to have covered her face. As they drew closer, I recognised our Eliezer and so I asked him who were those accompanying him. He replied, "This fair woman beside me is to be your wife".

I was stunned but turning towards her, I asked respectfully whether she would permit me to see her face since she was to be my bride. She gently removed her veil, and my heart almost stopped, for there before me was the most beautiful women I have ever seen. Young, vivacious, fresh, and amazingly attractive. We all proceeded into my mother's tent, where she also expressed her delight and approval. That was the happiest moment of my life. All thoughts of my recent adventures in Rekem simply vanished. And I am still madly in love with Rebekah. That is why I allow her to do whatever she pleases in my establishment and among my people".

Now, Rekem was a major city that attracted trade from all over the region. Abraham had first journeyed through Rekem when he took his family to Egypt to escape a major famine in the land of Canaan. Being a large and wealthy family, Abraham had met the ruler of Rekem who suggested he set up camp at the wadi not very far from the city, because of its location, the shade provided by its trees, as well as its many wells. On his return to Canaan, Abraham once again met with the ruler of Rekem and from that time on he would carry out an annual visit for trade and the renewal of friendships.

Isaac continued this tradition and eventually it became the duty of his son Jacob to also carry out this long expedition which would take anywhere upwards of five days, traveling through the Negev east where eventually the route joined up with the King's Highway that connected Mesopotamia in the north to Egypt in the south. The route was over dry and arid land and each day's travel was determined by the location of a series of springs along the way. Because of the nature of the environment and weather, the camel train usually commenced during late Winter or early Spring.

Jacob would be accompanied by a retinue of servants to look after the pack animals and set up camp once in Beer-lahai-roi. Ithai and several of his Pelethite warriors escorted them for protection, although there was an understanding throughout the region that caravans of trade were to be left alone. Otherwise, combined efforts would be made from various city- states with vested interests in safe and reliable trade to totally eliminate any potential threats.

The caravan from Beersheba would be laden with a variety of agricultural products, including wool, grains, fruits, oil, and wine; various metal and metal objects such as bronze weapons forged by skilled Philistine artisans; Canaanite and Philistine pottery was well reputed and in demand both in Rekem as well as among traders from other parts of the region; woven garments, dyed fabrics and ornamental textiles also fetched good prices. On the return journey, the caravan would bring back luxury goods such as precious stones, perfumes, spices, and exotic goods from the east. While in Rekem, Jacob would be feted as an old and trusted friend and so the camp site at Beer-Lahai-roi would be set up to support the whole company as well as to be able to reciprocate food and feasting to Jacob's friends in the royal household.

Now let us return to Jacob's intended journey north. A feature of the land of Canaan was its historical function as a land bridge between Egypt to the south and Assyria and Mesopotamia to the north. Caravans had two principal routes to choose from. The easiest route followed the flat lands along the coast, referred to as the 'Way of the Philistines,' as it traversed their territory once they arrived in Canaan. The other, perhaps shorter but somewhat more challenging journey, possibly due to the arid terrain, was known as the 'Kings Highway', as it was the preferred passage for conquering armies as well as regular trade convoys travelling south and north.

Upon their arrival in Canaan, two additional roads became available. Perhaps the most direct was to traverse the central range of mountains, locally known as the 'Central Hill Country'. For Jacob's journey north, Ithai chose this third and most direct route, leading over the mountains to Shechem. From there, they would cross to the north of the Sea of Kinneret (also known as the Sea of Galilee) and proceed to Damascus, where they planned to rest for a few days, allowing both the animals and the group a well-deserved break. Afterward, they would embark on the longest stretch of their journey to Haran, situated far to the north, beside the Balikh tributary, and nestled between the two great rivers, the Euphrates, and the Tigris.

The route selected was possibly the most physically challenging, especially for someone unaccustomed to walking. Hence, a couple of donkeys were included for Jacob, who had to trust in Ithai's judgment. There was, in fact, a fourth route, along the Jordan valley, but their plan was to cross the river further north, just beyond the Sea of Kinneret, and then join up with the King's Highway. For the initial leg of their journey, they aimed to reach Hebron, Luz and Shechem which would take close to seven days or even more, accounting for rest periods and anticipating potential days of rain.

The first leg of Jacob's journey took them past Hebron, which they deliberately skirted, aiming to avoid major urban centres at this early stage, although it also held several chapters of their family's history and was, in fact, the site of Jacob's grandfather's tomb. Hebron is a picturesque city nestled amidst rolling hills. As they traversed the countryside, Jacob was greeted by the breathtaking sight of blooming wildflowers and lush green fields, so much in contrast to the views around the much drier Beersheba. It was during this part of their journey that fate intervened, leading them to discover me – a stranded and orphaned baby. Beyond this incident, there isn't much else to recount, except for the fact that they promptly strapped me to a donkey, and

Djoser, our Egyptian mercenary who came to us from Gerar along with Ithai, assumed the responsibility of caring for me throughout the rest of our travels.

There was not much for Jacob to do on this journey as he had all the help he needed. Each evening, they would set up camp. There was no need to unpack the tents, but they always had a campfire. Whether walking or riding, Jacob always had time to think. Why couldn't Esau show greater responsibility towards his father's business? Why did it have to be himself? Why didn't Isaac insist that Esau become more involved in the family business? If Isaac loved Esau so much, surely, he could demand greater loyalty and involvement? Now he had to be seen as running away. What would people think of him? Was he a coward? Was he really afraid of Esau, and would his brother genuinely have threatened his life? If the people who served his father were to accept his authority, it would be logical for Isaac to give his fatherly blessing. Didn't Isaac and Esau see this?

Then, in the evenings, after eating, Jacob preferred to move a little away from the firelight and his companions, so he could look up into the bejewelled night sky, filled with the most beautiful array of stars, many of them familiar because of the stories he had heard growing up; tales of heavenly beings and their mighty deeds, represented by the various constellations and star signs. His favourite was the Pleiades, which, like all of the constellations, received its names from our neighbours the Greeks in the west. As told in many of their mythical stories, the Pleiades are seven sisters born of the titan Atlas (the big strong man of muscle who holds up the world on his shoulders) and Pleione, an Oceanid nymph or divine spirit.

Now we come to a part in my father Jacob's story that was not only life-changing, but initiated and transformed his relationship to his God and impacted everything he thought, said, and did for the remainder of his life.

Luz is an old Canaanite city occupied by a small tribe called the Perizzites. The city itself is a very busy centre for trade, receiving and distributing goods from all over the region. Jacob and his companions made camp just outside the city, distant enough not to be disturbed by the noise and smells and close enough to be able to send in for food. As usual, they lit a fire and gathered around it for warmth as the nights did tend to get cool and this particular evening there was a fresh wind blowing from the southwest. It almost felt like rain.

Having eaten, Jacob moved several cubits away, under a large tree, found a rock for a pillow and draping his cloak over him lay back looking up into the night sky, which was especially dark illuminating even more stars than usual.

My father frequently shared this encounter at Luz with me, it was such a special memory, and, as he revisited that experience, I would see his eyes grow wide and bright in wonder. I could never tire of hearing the story, which, each time, had some new detail added or some additional memory of his thoughts and feelings. For him to have a personal meeting with his God, was beyond anything he could have imagined. Whenever he recalled that incredible experience, it was as if it were yesterday, and he simply could not believe it was happening. In fact, on occasions he would become quite poetic.

"I had been walking from mid-morning until almost sunset and was hungry and very tired, my blisters were almost healed, and, with stubborn determination, I refused the offer of the donkey, although still in pain. Sensing this, the servants quickly lit a fire and prepared a stew of lentils and smoked meat, which they presented together with some fresh and hot flatbreads. Despite my exhaustion, the food tasted good and being washed down with some of the family's best wines, it was a wonderful way to settle me down for the night.

I wandered off as I knew the others would sit up all night talking about the journey and recalling stories of similar journeys and I simply needed peace and a time to think a bit before falling asleep. As I started to lie down, I couldn't but help noticing the beautiful soft golden hues of the afterglow of the sun already below the horizon, casting its warm radiance across the rolling hills and the silhouette of the city in the distance. This time of the year, the twilights were short and then, all of a sudden, it was dark. I had selected the cover of a large oak tree and looking up, I wondered at the history that those ancient branches, spread out and offering some protection from possible winds and rain, could tell of the passing of nations and the kaleidoscope of people living in this area.

The coolness of the rock pillow against my cheek served as a reminder of the earth's grounding presence beneath me. And as the night became cooler and darker, a profound stillness settled around me. The sound of nature such as the gentle rustling of leaves and the distant hooting of an owl, created a peaceful atmosphere. Stars began to twinkle around the silhouette of the tree, painting a canopy of light across the distant night sky.

Suddenly in the midst of this serenity, I felt a presence. It was as if the very air around me had become charged with a divine energy. A deep sense of awe and reverence filled my mind and took control of my whole body as I began to sense an encounter with someone or something other-worldly, even supernatural. Could it possibly be anything to do with Adonai, my God? Then a radiant light appeared, seeming to surround the ground where I was sleeping. It was both comforting and terrifying covering everything with a unique heavenly glow. My words really fail to adequately express what was happening all around me. A deep sense of inadequacy overcame me as I realised I was in the presence of a Being far greater than myself, one that held both blessings and challenges for my future. I have had several meetings with my God whom I now know to be the one true and only El-Elyon, but this was my very first experience. It was awe-inspiring and so very special as it was the beginning of an incomparable, blessed, and holy covenant with Him.

One minute I was looking up at the sky and the next I was seeing a stone stairway stretching ever upwards into the infinite distance beyond. I wasn't sure if it was a dream or a vision or a trick of the firelight against the dark night, but I distinctly heard a voice reminding me of my heritage and of promises made. I was puzzled and not just a little afraid. This stairway was teeming with celestial beings, angels ascending and descending upon it. It seemed as if this heavenly highway was offering a direct connection between our terrestrial realm and some sort of divine location. As I witnessed the mystical light, I perceived a vague Being, perhaps Adonai, my God standing above the ladder, addressing me.

"Who are you, Lord? I asked, trembling."

The answer came back. "I am El Elyon, the one true God. I am the God of your grandfather Abraham and your father Isaac and the one you have been worshipping all your life."

"What do you want Lord? What do you want me to do?" My voice was shaking.

"I promised your grandfather and your father this land of Canaan – when your ancestor came to this city so many years ago, and I said to him,

To your seed I will give this land'. Then when a famine had come upon the land, I appeared to your father Isaac and said, *'Do not go down to Egypt. Live in the place where I tell you to live. Stay in this land for a while, and I will be*

with you and will bless you. For to you and your descendants, I will give all these lands and will confirm the oath I swore to your father Abraham. I will make your descendants as numerous as the stars in the sky and will give them all these lands, and through your offspring, all nations on earth will be blessed."

"I am Adonai, the God of Abraham your grandfather and the God of Isaac. The land on which you are lying I will give to you and your descendants who will be as numerous as the grains of dust on the earth. You will expand to the West and to the East, to the North and to the South. By you and your descendants all the families of the earth will be blessed. Look I am with you. I will guard you wherever you go, and I will bring you back into this land, because I won't leave you until I have done what I have promised you."

'Then the voice vanished, gone, and all was quiet, strangely quiet; except for the sound of a soft wind rustling through the tree and an occasional hoot from a night owl. In total contrast, my mind was racing, my limbs in shock, frozen, and my skin shivering. What was all that about? I have just met Adonai, my God. How could that be possible? How should I respond? What does someone like me do or think or feel after a divine visitation?

There I was, fleeing from the wrath of my brother, now a refugee and a nobody with possibly very little to look forward to in the future. Suddenly, from nowhere and without any introduction, I have a visitation from my God, Adonai, with promises of blessings for my journey and a repeat of the covenants He gave to my father and my grandfather. As you know, we all worship the God of our fathers, and consequently, I continued to bow down before Adonai because my father and grandfather did. Now, the God of my fathers, Adonai, had appeared to me in a place seemingly of little consequence which, to me, had now become very sacred and of incredible importance.

My mind was a total mix of astonishment, awe, surprise, excitement and quite a bit of fear. Can Adonai really care enough about a person that He would deign to visit him, me, someone of no account? It took more than a little time to totally digest all that I had experienced but finally I came to the irrefutable conviction that it really was Adonai whom I had met. My mind was so adamant that it could have been no one else, and then my fears began to grow. What if I had misunderstood the message? What if there was something I missed? What should I do now? I waited until the sun started creeping over the horizon. Everyone in the camp was still sleeping. Total silence".

Every time my father spoke of this his first encounter with Adonai, he would pause, and I knew it was my cue to ask him.

"So, what did you do when you woke up?'

"My mind was a total mix of astonishment," he replied. "And my feelings were equally a tangle of emotions".

He then went on to explain, "One thing I was determined to do was to mark the very spot where the encounter had taken place. So, I took the stone which I had used as my pillow and made it the foundation stone of a pillar to the Most-High God, Adonai. After all these years, and several meetings with El Elyon, I still cannot believe how, as a young man, reasonably ambitious though with absolutely no reputation, that Adonai would have deigned to visit me in such a genuinely personal encounter.

I further made the commitment to Adonai that if all this was to take place as promised, I would ensure that this very site would be remembered in honour of the one true and only God, Adonai. That was the least I could do to ensure the memory of that amazing experience."

Once, and only once when I was quite a bit older, did I venture to ask:

"Father, how did you know it was Adonai who was speaking to you?'

Jacob's response was so adamant and so assured, that I never raised that question again.

"You really had to have been there to fully understand, Tarku. It was a presence and an atmosphere combined with a deep conviction of a divinity communicating with me – I had absolutely no doubt it was the God of my fathers, and I was truly petrified. Can you imagine a stairway – all the way up to heaven filled with Beings moving up and down? Although, I can also remember a special peace, and feeling of tremendous joy, as well as a realisation of something there, supremely powerful, all happening at once. Yes, I have had several encounters since then, but that was the first and it has always remained the one with the greatest impact and the most re-affirming of all".

Jacob continued, "Having completed building the stone pillar, I knelt down, and looking up to heaven, I dedicated this place to the Almighty, Bethel, because I knew as surely as I could feel my heart beating, that God had been in that place, so it was fitting that it should be called 'the House of God'. I can't remember how long I was there on my knees, when a voice interrupted the silence".

"Master Jacob, what are you doing? What is this you have built? What has happened?' It was Ithai.

I was not in a mood for a detailed explanation, so I simply said,

"I had a dream and wanted to mark this location in honour of that dream."

Then I walked towards the fire, newly refreshed by the servants and with hot flat bread baking on a clay griddle. My mind was still in considerable turmoil, but at the same time an incredible peace descended upon me, as if I had received a special blessing and a confirmation from above. It was in this mode that I lived throughout the rest of the day, not speaking, just recalling the voice, the message, and my feelings, and offering an occasional prayer of thanksgiving. That was it, I did not speak of that event again throughout our whole journey, although the memory has remained amazingly vivid, even to this day."

JOURNEY TO HARAN

"Jacob woke from his sleep and said, 'Truly Adonai is in this place – and I didn't know it".
Genesis 28: 16.

The land of Canaan, to which I belong, has many different tribes, each with their own designated territory, although the borders do tend to remain fairly flexible and from time to time, they change according to the power and influence of each city state. Every tribe has their favourite gods and so there are many to choose from in the celestial abode. However, these gods are all residential and do not move around. So, the gods of Canaan remain in Canaan, the gods of Mesopotamia remain in Mesopotamia and the gods of Egypt belong only to Egypt.

Although Isaac had taught his two sons to worship and revere the one and only true God, my father Jacob was fully aware of the pantheon of gods supposedly ruling the land of Canaan. Now here, just outside Luz, he had been given the privilege of coming face to face with the God of his ancestors who reminded him of the divine covenant promise granted to them, and subsequently to be realized by his descendants. That everything around him, the mountains, the valleys, the fields, the crops, the rivers, and the walled cities; these were all to belong to his family. It certainly was a lot to take in.

Several years later, I was still a boy, but circumstances seemed to have afforded me a maturity way beyond my years because both father and Ithai included me in many very personal conversations. We were seated around a fire; it was winter, and overhead was a sky full of the most wonderful illuminations. My father was in a particularly good mood, having returned from overseeing his flocks. These were the speckled and striped flocks that his uncle had agreed to give him. His plan for building his own establishment of animals was paying off in leaps and bounds. As the two of them, my father and Ithai were bantering about his strategy, Ithai made a comment:

"That night at Luz, Master, so many years ago, I couldn't help but notice the change; how it brought you out of your youth and into such a new and increased maturity".

My father looked at him for a long moment, and then, shrugging his shoulders, moved the conversation onto plans for returning to the land of Canaan and his father's domain, something he had longed for these many years.

"It won't be long now my friend. We will leave this beautiful site with all the mixed emotions it conjures up. I love it for the family it has given me. I hate it because it represents so many years of exploitation. I honour it because it has brought me incredible wealth. But overall, I will be happy to leave."

So, several days later, when the opportunity seemed appropriate, I asked Ithai.

"What did you mean, Nasi, (my leader), when you told my father that his experience at Luz, whatever it was, had transformed him from youth into maturity?"

"Perhaps you are too young to understand, as you, Tarku, are very much in your youth, but for Master Jacob it was almost an overnight transition. For the first two weeks of our journey until that experience, he would start out determined to complete a day's walking, but by the middle of the day, had to resort to the back of a donkey. The Master has always been a very determined and capable leader, but he lacked stamina. The morning after the Luz encounter, it was as if he had been re-born. There was a spring in his step and a confidence and purpose that had appeared overnight. This was not the same person I had been traveling with for the past many days. He didn't have to say anything, it was written all over his face and stature. He never climbed onto that donkey again all the way to Haran".

Several years later, I was in my mid-teens, very curious, and hoping for an opportunity to venture a question with my father that had been burning a hole in my mind. We were seated under the awning in front of his tent at our campsite in the region of Haran. It was late afternoon, a time to relax and ponder over the day's work. All around was a wonderful feeling of peace and calm. So, risking a lecture, telling me to mind my own business, I ventured with the question.

"My lord, father, how did your experience with El-Elyon, the one and only true God, in Luz affect you?" I was hoping that the use of the word 'lord' would simply reflect my respect.

His answer was very short but completed a story I had been constructing over the years.

"Well, Tarku, it was like this. Immediately after that first encounter, I determined, if Adonai would be with me and would guard me on the journey I have embarked upon, giving me bread to eat and clothes to wear, so that I could return to my father's house in peace, then Adonai would be my God; and that stone which I had set up as a standing-stone, would one day be God's house; and of everything that He gave me, I would faithfully return one tenth".

He was speaking, not simply about his journey to Haran but more completely of his life's journey.

Resuming, their passage to Haran, my father, it seems, now led the caravan as if he was running out of time; compelled with a new energy. The proposed route was to be first Shechem, east into Bashan, crossing over the Jordan north of the Sea of Kinneret, then Damascus, that great and renowned city, and finally on to Haran.

However, one particularly significant incident seriously interrupted this, so far, trouble free quest for a bride. He has never really shared the details of that episode, so now I will let Ithai tell this part of the story.

However, before my friend embarks on his memories of those events almost twenty years previously, let me tell you about Ithai. As I have shared, he is a Philistine and one of King Abimelech's best warriors. He was gifted to Isaac in exchange for a treaty before the birth of Esau and Jacob. He was, and still is, in his prime a well built and healthy forty-something-year-old, from a good family who had dedicated him to their King in gratitude for his protection and the restoration of their lands from marauding Canaanites of the north. Ithai had been well trained having been under the protection of his king, and he had benefitted from the tutelage of Phicol, himself a distinguished warrior and leader of King Abimelech's army. As a soldier of repute, in Gerar, he had been housed in simple but comfortable accommodation and given the best food considered appropriate for someone of privilege above the rank of an average warrior.

Ithai was a little under 4 cubits which was unusual and considered very tall for us in those days. He had smooth skin burnished by years under a hot sun, a short beard and had acquired a reputation in several skirmishes against warring Canaanite tribes who considered the Philistines as newcomers and trespassers in a land in which they had no heritage. Ithai was physically strong but more importantly, emotionally, and intellectually calm and reliable. He had never married but seemed to have dedicated himself to his masters. His major weakness lay in his intolerance for injustice. I have many stories exemplifying this, where I saw his face light up in anger transforming him into a fury of rage against perceived oppressors. So much character and so much to tell, but now is the time for him to progress this story.

"Alright my friend, here is how the rest of the journey transpired. For a start, I can tell you, it was a very special journey, filled with the most amazing scenery, the mountains, the vast plains, the colours of the flowers, shrubs, and other vegetation; all so new and different from where we had come from. Although I am simply a soldier, and not much of a storyteller, I will do my very best to try and transport you into our experiences, of what we saw and felt and, of course, there were the adventures.

As I have previously mentioned to you Tarku, Master Jacob was a changed person after that evening in Luz. Somehow, he had gained a whole new life full of confidence. Gone were his worries about the blisters. He had energy and enthusiasm bubbling out of his body. So now it was he who had become our leader. It was something I had hoped for, but never anticipated so early on in our travels.

After another two days, we arrived at Shechem. Actually, the outskirts of the city. And this is where our adventures really started. We were just descending from the hills, when suddenly we found ourselves surrounded by more than twenty warriors. There was nothing much we could do as we were vastly outnumbered. Then up speaks Jacob, demanding to know what they were thinking of. We were a group of innocent travellers, harming no one and simply going about our own business.

'My name is Jacob, son of Isaac of Beersheba. Who are you and by what right do you accost us like this?' Very brave words for someone who has hardly wielded a sword in his life.

"We are the King's watchmen. We guard the city. Do you remember the grove of trees you walked through earlier this afternoon? Well, that is the most sacred site of our people where we honour our gods, and no one is permitted to enter there on pain of death". The speaker, we later found out, was Hamor, the son of the King of Shechem.

"So how were we to know?' was Jacob's reply. 'If the grove is so sacred to you, why are you not guarding it? Obviously, you don't seem to place much value on the safety of your gods".

These were fighting words, and we were not in a position to offer any resistance. We were five grown men and a baby. Although everyone had some experience in the use of weapons as I had insisted on at least a basic training for all of Master Isaac's company, we would have been no match for bows drawn and swords at the ready of four times our number".

"At a sign from the leader of the troop, the warriors surrounded us. 'Follow me and we shall see what your brave words can do for you, Jacob of Beersheba", was the leader's final command.

"Master Jacob looked like he was going to do some resisting. I moved up beside him and whispered". "Master let us go, if we were anyone else, we would have been cut down without a second thought. Obviously, they can see you are from a good family. So, we followed as commanded.

By late afternoon, we found ourselves standing in front of the awe-inspiring walls of Shechem city. These bastions were not only impressive but reliably solid and guarded by sturdy wooden gates clearly built to confidently protect the city's inhabitants. At least fifteen cubits in height and six cubits thick, the walls presented a daunting challenge to any force attempting entry. Much like Luz, Shechem thrived as a bustling trading centre, attracting caravans from both the north and south. To facilitate the influx of these merchants and their animals, expansive areas outside the walls were designated with enclosures and corrals to enable the conducting of their respective businesses.

As we were marched through the city's narrow streets, I estimated a possible population of about three thousand permanent dwellers, simply based on my experience with other cities in southern Canaan, similar in size and activity. After another short walk, we arrived at a rather imposing dwelling, with its own gates, guarded by a half-sized wall surrounding it. We were jostled unceremoniously inside, and I could see Master Jacob was starting to build up quite a rage as people were staring at what they assumed were a group of captives heading for a very dark future. It was a taste of humiliation that my master had never experienced.

We walked through some imposing doors centred in a pillared portico, with marble floors and frescoes on the outer walls. This was clearly the dwelling of a wealthy noble family. Inside it was much cooler and soon we entered a large hall and were told to wait. It wasn't long before a group of men in expensive robes seemed to float in from a side doorway. It was their manner that struck me. There was a strong aroma of perfume and an attitude of absolute disdain. These were privileged people who clearly considered themselves of a far more exalted bloodline than anyone else in the room, except perhaps for the leader of the soldiers who had brought us here. Though feeling considerable anxiety at my master's rage, I could understand his anger which had increased even more since we had entered this building".

"Bow before the King and do not look at his face. Bow you worthless peasants – now".

"Was the barked command from someone who seemed to be the vizier or senior royal steward. I immediately hated him as an obnoxious and obsequious sycophant of a human being. I could happily have run my sword through him if it was the last thing I did, but our weapons had been taken away and although I did have a knife tucked away in my leather jerkin, any move towards accessing it would have resulted in an immediate sword through my back.

We were all stunned. Our slow response resulted in several of the soldiers hitting us on the shoulder and kicking the backs of our knees, forcing us onto the floor; simply reinforcing our humiliation. The most imposingly dressed individual and wearing something that looked like a crown, sat down on what must have been his throne and asked the head of the warrior group".

"Who are these people and why am I even looking at them?" He asked with an air of arrogance that was insulting to the extreme.

"Father," this was from the rather arrogant leader of the troupe that had accosted us, "I found this group of people after they had crossed through our sacred grove. They have no excuse and I really think they should be dealt the harshest penalty of the law, so as to set an example."

"Who are you and where are you from and why have you come here?" came from his majesty, addressing all of us in general.

"I looked at Master Jacob, appealingly hoping that he would show some restraint".

"My name is Jacob, son of Isaac and grandson of Abraham, hailing from Beersheba." Jacob said surprisingly with a calmness I knew he was not necessarily feeling.

"So why should we show you any clemency and spare your lives despite your committing a trespass warranting death?" This was from one of the members of the King's entourage, a rather bulbous apparition who seemed very fond of himself. From my perspective it all seemed rather comical with all these weird characters obviously enamoured by their importance.

"My father is a well-established man of the land, living in Beersheba and having very close relations with his neighbours, in fact he has a treaty with his majesty King Abimelech of Gerar" was the response from Master Jacob. I did admire his composure given the degree of rage I had seen earlier and the abominable treatment we had so far received.

"Never heard of him and as for Gerar, it is no more than half the size of our city and really of no account," was the King's cynical reply.

"My grandfather is the Abraham that routed King Chedorlaomer of Elam, and which was recorded as a great victory for the people of Canaan." Jacob added.

Let me further explain briefly what Master Jacob was referring to. Many years ago, the Kings in the south of Canaan, namely of Sodom, Gomorrah (these two cities have since been destroyed by fire, a volcanic eruption, I believe), as well as Admah, Zeboiim, and Zoar, who paid tribute to the Kings of the north in Mesopotamia, being of Elam, Shinar, Elazar and Goyim, decided that twelve years of punishing levies was enough, so they revolted. The Kings of the north came down and defeated the Canaanite Kings and ransacked their cities. In the process, they abducted Abraham's nephew, Lot, and his family. Abraham gathered his forces, pursued the northern army, and defeated it, rescuing his kidnapped family, restoring the stolen booty, and giving it back to the defeated Kings. It was a very impressive victory.

"Yes, I have heard of that, my father spoke well of him but with some reservations," replied the King, "Your grandfather did also have the remnants of the army of the south and Chedorlaomer and his troops were all drunk celebrating their success. So maybe the victory was not that significant after all. But now to you and your situation. What are we to do with you? We have no reason to stir up trouble with our southern neighbours, but you have crossed a serious threshold and there will be a price. My son, Hamor, what have you to say?"

"Father, these people are of no account and even if their death results in come reaction from the south, our walls are massive, we can withstand a siege, and we have many kings from city states in our region who pay us tribute and would come to our aid." Shechem, the king's son insisted.

"I agree my son", The king responded, "but the trespass was not deliberate, and a great deal of our trade comes from the south, in fact, I do recall a caravan not so long ago from a wealthy source around Beersheba. Perhaps that was your father? Whatever we do, we will be judged by our peers, and we must appear to be just. In any event, let's be generous and see what these ill-kempt people are willing to give for their lives, supposing they possess anything of value at all".

"Father", the son persisted, "while I was escorting these people into the city, I noticed a baby boy strapped onto the back of a donkey. You know that one of the ways to appease the gods of our grove is the offering of a baby boy. Maybe that should be the price for their freedom."

"I was horrified as was the Master and it was clearly written all over our faces".

"That is a good idea my son. What is the boy to you?" addressing Master Jacob.

"I am his guardian. To me he is like a son. That is not an option and in no way would I be willing to agree to that demand," Jacob's reply was polite, but very firm.

"Enough of this bargaining. What will you offer in exchange for your lives and especially that of this little boy, of no apparent consequence?" The king was clearly becoming impatient.

"Now, I was totally at an end of options and wondered what the Master would come up with. I looked over towards him expecting to see the total disgust and fury bursting out of his face. But whatever depths from which he obtained it, his face was calm, and his voice was both authoritative and respectful".

"Noble King, on behalf of my company and of my family and of my heritage, I would offer you our absolute apology for our indiscretion. You know it was totally inadvert. We would never deliberately transgress your laws or your beliefs or anything you held sacred. I have in my company several camels all loaded with gifts for my intended bride whom I am hoping to find in Haran. My uncle is a very wealthy and well-connected member of the council of Haran. May I offer you two of my camels with all that is on them together with a lump sum of fifteen hundred shekels of silver in coinage as well as three hundred shekels of ornate gold jewellery. That would buy you many slaves and the contents of my camel packs will delight your ladies as they include the finest textiles and precious stones brought from Rekem."

"That certainly is a fine offer but what would prevent me from killing you and taking all of your camels?" Was the king's response.

"Your, majesty, you have suggested that you would rather not stir up any animosity with the people of the south. That animosity could also very likely reverberate from the north as well. Both my father and my uncle are significant businessmen and control trade throughout the region. I trust that you would see this as a very fair offer, and we will be happy to be on our way the minute you release us." Jacob continued, focusing on the king's sensitivities towards regional opinion, trade and relationships.

"A very loud silence ensued. I know we were all holding our breath and I, particularly, couldn't believe what I was witnessing from my Master as his presence and his response was so calm and measured and persuasive."

"But father?" Protested Hamor.

"Enough, we have spent too much time over this paltry affair, its done, see to it and make sure these people leave us immediately. The sooner they are out of our kingdom and our minds the better." The king made a final decision.

"So, we survived, thanks completely to Master Jacob. I have often thought about this experience. Was this the real Jacob that we never fully understood? Was this a Jacob that had been transformed after his experience at Luz? I still don't know, but we were all greatly relieved and very impressed.

Leaving Shechem, we set off on our northward journey aiming first for Dothan and then on to Damascus. The weather belied our feelings of defeat and shame. I was less affected than the Master, so I could appreciate the beauty around us. The sun-bathed landscape in every direction was painted in hues of warm yellows and oranges as the bright orb of the sun slowly and majestically set in the West. The air was filled with the scent of olive groves basking within an exquisite sea of wildflowers, and the song of birds that were sheltering in the trees lining our path. Somewhere nearby, we could hear the sound of rushing water as a stream ran down rocks offering life-giving water to the fields below.

As we ascended further north, the terrain became more rugged. The path meandered through rocky outcrops and winding valleys, offering glimpses of the plains beneath. At its height, we stopped to rest, and I watched Master looking back. His lips were moving, and his face was hard and unforgiving. Later he told me that he had vowed to return and seek his God, Adonai's sense of justice in exacting a serious vengeance for what we had all endured. I thought I had always had a fierce sense of right and wrong, but this far exceeded anything I could have mustered. It was a deep and enduring anger that consumed him, and I felt a pang of dread if my master was to ever be in a position to exact his revenge.

Within the next day and night, we were well clear of Shechem, lighter by two camels and a lot of silver coin and gold jewellery, but we were alive. For three days Master Jacob said nothing, simply keeping to himself and we honoured that. Then finally, one evening, as we were sitting around the campfire, he expressed something that stayed with me for years until I personally witnessed an event that demonstrated the depth of his need for retribution - his curse".

"May, Adonai, the God of my father and my grandfather inflict upon the royal family of Shechem as much and even more than they have done to me and my people. May their progeny cease. May their businesses fail. May the sky dry up its rain so that the fields and crops perish. And may all that remains of that kingdom remember the wrath of Adonai who has promised to bless his chosen ones and their descendants forever."

"Expressing his deep anger in a curse that seemed to focus his mind on a future vengeance, seemed to somewhat assuage my master's fury and he appeared to relax somewhat for the remainder of our journey, although we avoided all towns. Only when our food was almost exhausted, did he permit our servants to go into a village and obtain bread, vegetables, and meats, mainly fowl and smoked lamb".

One evening, when I thought he was displaying a more affable mood, I asked him, "Master, what are we going to do about gifts for your intended bride? Everything of value is gone. After a short silence he looked up at me, almost with a twinkle in his eye, and replied.

"Not everything Ithai my friend. I placed the most valuable of the jewellery in saddle bags on the donkey that our young Hittite is riding. That will be enough to start with and meanwhile I intend to send back to my father's house for more to replenish that which was stolen."

"That was a side of my master I had not seen before, clever, and discerning. Obviously, a large beast would be carrying the best, so offering two camels would distract from anything that might be stored in a humbler beast, like a donkey.

I should make mention of the boy. All along, he had been strapped into a makeshift saddle on one of the donkeys. He never spoke, although he was probably too young to have much of a vocabulary. But he never expressed anything like boys his age should have, neither fear, nor anguish, nor amusement. Nothing. Tarku, looking into your large dark eyes, I would wonder what horrors you had witnessed and what kind of thoughts you must have been thinking in your tiny baby head. You simply accepted, and followed, and sat, looking ahead. And there you were, all the way through Shechem, where your life was very nearly sacrificed, to Damascus and finally to Haran. You simply sat. My heart went out to you and, adding a comment after many years of knowing you, I do confess that you have become someone very special to all of us. Bless you young Tarku, but you've never really shared some of your earliest memories.

There was a lot I could say, but I merely added, "Thank you noble Ithai, I have very dim memories of those days in the saddle other than that I felt looked after and safe. I find that I have been blessed with a short memory of things evil and a happy recall of everything pleasant to remember".

"So, moving on, we passed through quaint villages and fields, until we finally arrived in front of ancient Dothan. Nestled amidst the undulating landscape, Dothan's golden fields of grain swaying gently presented a friendly invitation to enter and taste of some comfort and good food. However, my master deliberately vied away from the town and passed onto higher ground overlooking the urban settlement surrounded by high stone walls, like most Canaanite towns of any size. There we spent the night, enjoying the softly shimmering lights below and the free and open sky above together with the warmth of our campfire and the excellent companionship of those who had survived that perilous ordeal a few days earlier.

We broke camp before dawn the next morning. The sun starting its slow climb, guided by the northern star with our determination to reach Damascus as soon as possible. The landscape transitioned into a mosaic of rolling hills and expansive plains, adorned with vibrant wildflowers that splashed colour in the midst of the surrounding greenery. The road stretched ahead, flanked by groves of olive and fig trees and the aroma of all this vegetation filled our nostrils blending the intoxicating smells of herbs and flora with the warm earthy scent of the countryside.

I think it was during this stretch of the journey that I experienced the most beautiful vista anyone could ever imagine blessing their eyes. It was early morning on the fourth day after leaving Dothan. Once again, we had broken camp before sunrise, so walking in the pre-dawn light we crested a hill and there below us, shimmering silver, and bronze like a massed army of burnished shields, reflecting the new rays of the sun slowly rising in the east was the stunning Sea of Kinneret. Growing up in Gerar, I had been told of the fabled sea, a fisherman's delight, and source of the freshest and sweetest waters. Now here it was in front of me – dazzling and inviting, an amazing image indelibly etched onto my memory. As we descended towards its shores, we could see fishermen in their boats returning after a night's netting through the deepest waters."

"Time for breakfast," came from Master Jacob".

"So, we approached one of the boats and asked if they would sell us a fish. Very willing to oblige, we were offered several and finally chose five of the largest, catfish and mullet I believe they were called, two for the morning's repast and the others, salted and packed, for the evening meal. We feasted on grilled fish and fresh flat bread from a nearby village, the simplest of meals, but absolutely delicious. While our own bread was very palatable, our servants couldn't match the age-old traditions of a village bakery.

Reluctantly, we left that exquisite panorama of the northern shores of the sea and simply took our visual, auditory and tastebud memories with us. Now for the long haul, but we were visibly more relaxed as we had left the land of petty Kings and were now on a route traversed by regular caravans, traveling towards the King's Highway. I estimated the remainder of our journey would take another thirty sunrises, giving us and our animals time to rest in places we found particularly appealing. I had suggested that this might be a good opportunity, if master Jacob wanted, to send back to his father for another caravan to replace what we had lost at Shechem, but he considered it wiser for all of our company to experience the total journey to Haran, identifying towns and villages of risk and those that were friendly to ensure safe passage for the future. Excellent thinking.

After resting and feasting, we travelled north and crossed the Jordan river not far before the Waters of Merom. For me it was like crossing a major hurdle, turbulent and unpredictable, as we had to try and locate a suitable crossing for man and beast with little knowledge of the rushing torrents. My experience of rivers had been limited to those in southern Canaan which were, in comparison, no more than brooks. However, later, after experiencing the mighty Euphrates and the Tigris in and around Haran, the Jordan, in contrast, resembled little more than a stream. I should add, though, over time we discovered so many more historical and physical reasons to consider this humble body of water as being incredibly significant in the lives of everyone living in the land of Canaan. And it had a very distinct personality of its own.

As we proceeded northeast, we encountered the hill country of upper Gilead, with even more steep slopes and rocky mountain gradients that challenged every bit of our stamina. What I simply could not get over was watching master Jacob, up ahead, striding forward with such determination. I continually wondered at the kind of encounter he must have had at Luz, which he had named Bethel, that had resulted in this amazing transformation. But we never spoke of it, and then again, there had been the trauma of Shechem.

At one point we passed the impressive heights of majestic Hermon, the highest peak in the region. Looking up into the clouded peak, I couldn't help wondering what particular god dwelt there and which of the Canaanite tribes claimed his or her allegiance? The towering height was sovereign and overpowering, and somewhat fearsome beyond anything I had ever seen. Now we found ourselves passing through dense forests, and I had to remind everyone that our enemy was far more likely to be walking on four legs, so to keep a look out and if we had the misfortune of finding any beast in our path, we would simply remain stock still and let it pass. Fortunately, nothing other than an occasional herd of deer and even a pack of wolves appeared within our vision, but nothing threatening. Then, finally we arrived at the King's Highway which linked Mesopotamia in the north to Egypt in the south and which was very popular with marauding armies, as well as caravans trading every conceivable product from around our world and sharing them between these two great civilizations.

The mountains that had so far sheltered us from the elements during our most recent travels now served as a new challenge, weaving through steep passes, then descending into deep valleys. We persevered until finally, we arrived, almost breathless, into the plains and the road leading towards the bustling streets of the famed and ancient city of Damascus. We all stopped, let out a deep sigh and looking at each other, I sensed a shared feeling of both weariness and excitement. We had braved treacherous terrains, life-threatening moments, endured a range of weather extremes, finally arriving at this pivotal moment, Damascus.

So, mobilised by a fresh vigour, we started our final descent and within a very short time we were back on easier walking ground. As we continued, we could see the faint outline of the city in the distance. In what must have been no time at all, the reality of a considerable metropolis grew before our eyes, depicting an amazing and varied tapestry of life. The city walls, ancient and weathered, seemed to enclose a labyrinth of narrow alleys and grand boulevards. Buildings of various shapes and sizes stretched towards the heavens, their architectural wonders a testament to the rich history and culture of this ancient and amazing civilization.

We stopped. Almost having to look up, I could imagine the vibrant marketplaces bustling with merchants, the aroma of spices wafting through the air, and the melodious echoes of prayers from sacred places of worship. The Master looked around and seeing an open field backed by a crop of trees not too far off the main road, he led us into that direction. We were going to set up camp outside the city. Not only was it close enough to access the conveniences within the walls, but it was also a far healthier place to rest.

We remained there for several days, giving our animals time to recuperate, and allowing us to relax before the next long stretch up to Haran. Not to be denied the luxuries of the city, we sent in some of the men to purchase the very best the markets had to offer. And we were not disappointed, Fruits, nuts, meats, wine from the very best of orchards. We had both donkeys loaded up with the excellence of Damascus' produce. I suppressed any mention of my longing to walk the famed streets and taking in sights that I had only ever heard of in stories; the palaces, the mighty walls that would discourage any but the bravest of armies, the temples, the bustling marketplaces offering every imaginable delight from around our known world, and of course the enormous storehouses, perpetual reminders of the possibility of famine or siege. This city, more than most, emanated tales of intrigue, passion and adventure going back centuries. However, perhaps the Master read my mind, as one evening, he beckoned to me and said."

"Ithai, we are going into Damascus tonight. Place Djoser in charge and tell him we will most likely stay the night and return early the next morning."

"So, we set off, walking. Leaving our camp just as the sun was setting, it was almost dark by the time we had arrived a short distance before the imposing walls. Approaching the gates, we stopped and looked up at the towering edifice before us. It was more than impressive, it was awesome. We continued past a group of guards who paid us no attention as we would have blended with most of the people entering and leaving. Just inside, the Master went up to what looked like an official and asked him for directions. His mother Rebecca had maintained contact with Abraham's servant who had endured the long journey to Haran to claim her as a bride for Isaac so many years earlier. Eliezer had successfully reached a very healthy old age. Every year, she would send a small caravan with gifts and food and a range of both necessities and luxuries to him, so she knew where he lived and had passed this information on to her son.

Master Jacob came back and nodding his head in the direction slightly to the left of the gates, he headed down some narrow streets until he came to a square which, during the day would have been filled with market stalls. At night it transformed into a vast array of eating sites offering roasted meats and every kind of delicacy available in the region and further afield. Master Jacob stopped at one food stall selling sweetmeats and asked for further directions and then took off straight ahead until he stopped in front of a walled doorway behind which a building of significant quality rose to at least three stories.

He knocked, and after waiting a very short time, it was opened by what would have been a servant doorkeeper. Master mentioned to him his name and that he was here to see Master Eliezer and immediately the door was flung open and the servant, bowing bid us both enter. He asked us to be seated under a balcony covered with a flowering creeper and went inside. We heard a lot of loud voices rattling off a string of commands and out came the Master, Eliezer, Abraham's faithful servant. Master Jacob immediately bowed low touching his feet and expressing his joy at being able to finally meet him again. Master Eliezer picked my Master up and ushered him into the house, straight into what would have been a large square surrounded by the storied edifice.

For the remainder of the night, both of the master's sat together and talked and laughed and cried, it was something to behold my Master enjoying this so very special reunion. I was shown to a room and after eating my evening meal, which was particularly welcome, as the food on our journey, apart from one or two exceptions, had always been rather basic, and then I slept. The next morning, we breakfasted on bread and fruit and cheeses, and then Master Eliezer walked us to the door and after a protracted series of hugs and goodbyes, we left to return to our camp.

The following few nights were almost like a celebration, so much so that I had come close to forgetting the horrors of Shechem. But not so my master. While he joined in our banter over the campfire, his face still resonated with a mixture of anger and vengeance. His meeting with an old friend and mentor had softened his features, but he was still hurting from that horrendous ordeal now many days away. So, we avoided any talk of the past, simply anticipating excitedly our arrival in Haran.

After an additional fourteen days of walking and enjoying pleasant scenery, having occasional meetings with other travellers, watching shepherds with their flocks, and passing by picturesque villages, one mid-afternoon, we topped a slight rise and there in the distance was our destination, Haran. The landscape transitioned from fertile fields to orchards and groves, with blossoming trees providing a fragrant and visually enticing vista into which, it seemed, we were being invited to enter. We stopped to take in some deep breaths, relief, and a feeling of achievement. We had been many weeks on the road, so we simply stood there to drink in the panorama of the land, the city, and the rivers, such as we had never before seen. Everything was like a new world, and so impressive.

My master came over to me and pointing towards some movement in the foreground, he said we should move forward to where it seemed as if some shepherds had congregated their flocks near a watering place. We advanced until we were in speaking distance and my Master asked whether anyone was familiar with the house of Laban?"

"Friends, we have come from a long distance and are seeking the house of Laban? Do you know him?"

"The answer came in a friendly reply from one of the shepherds, saying".

"We are gathered here to water our flocks and once everyone has arrived, the stone against the side of the well will be removed to allow the water to flow into the troughs below. Yes, we do know the house of Laban and as it happens, here comes his daughter to water their flocks".

"My master looked up and was about to say something when, seeing a young woman come towards him, walking with a confidence and manner that told him she knew what she was doing, and for the first time in his life, he said he actually felt his heart stop. The rest is history. Master Jacob had fallen in love. He insisted, despite objections from the other shepherds, on releasing the passage of water so that her sheep could be watered and while he was doing this, she raced away back to her house to tell her father the amazing news that his nephew had arrived from Beersheba.

We eventually set up camp about two days walk from the city among groves of olives and figs and date palms and beside a spring fed pond. Much of the surrounding land was owned by my master's uncle, Laban, and beyond that were lush fields for grazing, even up into the distant hills and valleys. It was an amazing sanctuary and one where, as you know, we have lived for many years.

With love in his heart and looking forward to his union with the beautiful Rachel, my master made a contract to work for his uncle for seven years and I watched as his enthusiasm paid huge dividends for his uncle, expanding his flocks more than he could ever have expected. Master Jacob had a special gift for animal management, breeding, healthcare, protection, and everything to do with sales and marketing, more than anyone I have ever met.

The rest of my story, Tarku, is part of your growth from a boy to a teenager. As you have been a part of the family and all that has related to its growth. You know how our life has revolved around our campsite here outside Haran, and I must admit it has been an environment I could only have dreamed of, in its beauty, its convenience, and its productivity. Little did I envision the duplicity and intrigue that Master Jacob has had to put up with, robbing him of so many years, along with cherished hopes and aspirations. But you have totally exhausted my memory and creativity in recounting those early adventures. The remainder is for you to tell".

CHAPTER FOUR

THE HOUSE OF JACOB

"Jacob had fallen in love with Rachel and said, 'I will work for you seven
years in exchange for Rachel your younger daughter".
Genesis 29: 18

My father Jacob arrived in Haran with two camels, two donkeys, a baby boy and three herders plus two men at arms. The camels carried everything required to set up a reasonably comfortable camp comprising the main tent for Jacob, a smaller tent for Ithai and Djoser and another small tent for the three attendants. I was given a cot in Jacob's tent although my immediate care was delegated to Djoser. Finally, there was a tent for stores and a half tent-like awning for the cooking.

Our camp site was located some way from Haran and nearer where the flocks and herds were kept. Although the latter did move around a lot, a base facility was established offering sanctuary for animals when the weather was bad and storage facilities for animal fodder. The site also offered a place for herders to return to after they had brought in animals in need of special attention. Finally, a special tent was set up for when Laban came to vist his flocks.

It didn't take long for Laban to realise that in Jacob, he had an experienced manager for everything related to his livestock and agricultural interests. So, he asked Jacob what it would take to employ him to look after his flocks, herds and other farming activities which included fruit trees and vineyards. Jacob repeated that his principal reason for coming to Haran was to look for a bride and he declared that he had found the woman of his dreams, Rachel. Although Jacob had brought gifts in the saddle bags of a donkey, hidden from the greedy eyes of the King of Shechem, easily sufficient for the bride price of a princess, Laban needed Jacob's skills and management. So, while accepting some of the more valuable items, he offered his daughter in marriage in exchange for seven years of Jacob's labour, a very high price to ask. However, after all, Jacob knew there was some serious animosity towards him back in Beersheba and having been totally smitten by Rachel from his first sighting of her, he agreed.

Over the succeeding years, our simple site in the countryside outside Haran, had gradually grown in size. Soon after setting up camp, Jacob had sent one of the herders accompanied by Djoser back to Beersheba to ask for additional supplies and a few months later a caravan of many camels arrived together with a dozen additional servants, all with particular skills meant to add comfort to Jacob's situation. One of these was a nurse maid for me. Each subsequent year another caravan arrived and, after leaving a wide range of supplies and comforts behind, would then return to Beersheba with trade goods from Haran; a business also managed by Jacob. Isaac, meanwhile, seemed to have recovered from his temporary blindness and fear of an imminent death, and was back into managing his affairs, and Rebecca, it would be safe to say, was greatly relieved, and focused her energies on encouraging the caravans to Haran. Then, of course, they still had Baruch, to make sure everything in Isaac's affairs continued to function smoothly.

So, now we come to the end of the seven-year period and the highly anticipated marriage between my father and Rachel. The only problem was Uncle Laban. In addition to accepting a very generous bride price, which Jacob was not really obligated to give as he had worked every bit of his seven-year commitment, Uncle Laban switched brides and the morning after the wedding Jacob woke up to find Leah, the eldest daughter, in his bed. Extreme disappointment and a fierce rage would hardly describe Jacob on discovering the deception. I remember seeing him storm out of the camp on one of the newly acquired horses, he had become a natural on horseback, straight to Haran. We all held our breath for the next few days wondering what would eventuate. I also remember feeling especially sorry for Leah. It was her father's intrigue that had created this situation, she was hardly to blame. I have always liked Leah. Physically, while she had the most disarming smile and infectious laughter, she was not very attractive, but her real beauty was genuine and locked up inside a hardworking, capable, and loyal personality. Leah's total internal make-up was the valued pearl of our family, through and through. She was both admired and really loved by all who passed through her life.

Jacob's return was much more leisurely and accompanied by an entourage. The whole camp stopped work and gathered to see what was happening. A central feature of the caravan was a covered wagon. Jacob got off his horse, gave the reins to a waiting attendant, and walked back to the wagon. Lifting the cover, he offered his hand and out stepped a woman, smiling from ear to ear. It was Rachel. Impromptu and resounding applause erupted from everywhere together with a few calls of '*mazel tov*' or congratulations. We were all very happy and so, in fact, was Leah, because now she had her younger sister with her, they had been very close growing up. It was certainly a time for celebration and that we did.

Prior to the wedding, a separate tent had been erected and furnished for Rachel, and it had been adorned with some of the most exquisite tapestries and beautiful carpets that Jacob could find. Now it was Leah's tent. Another tent was hastily erected for Rachel with strict instructions that it was to be fitted with only the best of whatever remained. However, we knew where Rachel would be sleeping for the following several nights after this evening's auspicious celebrations. Meanwhile, the whole camp was bustling with preparations. As for me, while I had been sharing my adopted father's tent for the past few months, I had been moved to share a tent with Ithai and Djoser. I was not yet ten years of age, so moving was of no consequence, and both of these warriors had plenty of stories to share in the evenings before it was time to sleep. All very exciting.

Immediately it was realised that now was a time for celebrating Jacob's wedding with two sisters, the preparations began. Both Leah and Rachel had brought along their special maid attendants. Leah had Zilpah and Rachel had brought her maid, Bilhah. Both the sisters had grown up in a household of plenty and although they had been required to contribute their share of labour within the family, Leah in the kitchen and organising the household, and Rachel helping with the animals, there had been other attendants who assisted them. In fact, Zilpah and Bilhah were daughters of two of the families who worked for Laban, so they had grown up with Leah and Rachel, almost as surrogate sisters.

For the most part, that evening was pretty much normal except that Rachel and Jacob disappeared into Jacob's tent fairly early after the sun had set and we didn't see them again until mid-morning the next day. But preparations continued at a feverish pace. Everyone wanted to make this a celebration to rival every other, with the intent of welcoming both sisters. This was going to be historic. While there had been festive occasions such as the annual remembrance of Jacob's arrival, an array of religious feasts, and the welcoming of Laban and his household at various times, this was going to be a star-lit ceremony of the best food, wines, and music that the camp could offer, an event that we would all remember for many years to come. This was just for us, the members of Master Jacob's camp, so everyone contributed their very best to make it as perfect as possible for their master Jacob – whom I recall, even at my relatively young age, had earned the respect and loyalty of each and every member of our camp family - and his two brides.

There must have been about thirty of us, all seated around a massive campfire. On the west side, facing the east as was the expected auspicious seating arrangement, were Jacob and his two brides one on the right and one on the left. I must admit to feeling a little sad on noting that Rachel had been given the preferred right side, which for many reasons should have been given to Leah. This unfortunate detail in their relationship continued to sadden our camp for many years to come. I suspect it was a combination of Rachel and the impact her beauty had on my father the moment he saw her, as well as the fact that he was a second son, as was Rachel a second daughter. So, both his affections and his affinity made her his favourite. But for tonight, it was pure celebration time.

We had a few musicians, one older storyteller, some dancing, mainly contributed by Zilpah and Bilhah, and then there was the food. Our chief cook was someone sent up from Beersheba by Rebecca two years previously, as a special gift from mother to son. She was brilliant. A variety of animals had been slaughtered the previous day and hung overnight, our vegetable gardens had been vigorously raided for the very best, breads and cakes had been baking for hours and that ever so tantalising smell permeated every corner of the camp.

We all sat on the ground around a huge campfire and ate. We were seated on a variety of rugs and animal skins and our plates were simple wooden platters, but the food was fit for any royal banquet. After eating and drinking for a longer time than I had ever spent over a meal, we relaxed with delicious fruits; grapes figs, dates, pomegranates, and a range of special sweetmeats that we had never previously experienced, the offering of our very esteemed chief and master cook. I watched her standing there besides the cooking pots, looking at us all filling our bellies with a very satisfied grin on her face. Her name was Nefertari, of Egyptian heritage, and we were blessed in having her with us for the remainder of her life. Even once she had grown too old to be involved in preparation, she would hobble around with a staff, supervising, and if excellence was not achieved, she could be very cranky. Her status within our camp was always a combination of significant fear and reverence.

The moon had risen and then had almost disappeared by the time we were ready to retire. A small number of attendants were designated to clean up, ensuring that no food was left lying around to attract wild animals into the camp. Their rising hour would also be delayed. Most of our company were quite intoxicated with the finest wines Jacob had to offer. I was allowed a small quantity of the newer wines, but I really preferred the exquisite sherbet our wonderful cook created using goats milk and a variety of herbs and spices. She only ever produced it on special occasions and in my memory, there had only ever been two or three such before this evening. So, we all settled into our beds and slept very soundly.

And so it was, for the next several years, each of the wives lived in their tents with their maids in attendance. Leah was the productive one, giving Jacob two sons, Reuben and Simeon. But she didn't stop there; two more boys were added, Levi and Judah. The tragedy of Rachel's barrenness hung over the camp as she was unable to give Jacob the favoured son that he so desperately wanted. She was his favourite without question, and he longed for a son borne of his love for her. It seemed not to be, so she offered her maid Bilhah, and from her came two strong baby boys, Dan followed soon after by Naphtali. Rachel took the two boys into her own tent and nursed them as if they were her own. But she knew and so did everyone else, it wasn't the same as having her own special child.

Leah had also stopped producing so she offered her maid Zilpah and from her came two boys, Gad, and Asher. Then, as if by a miracle, Leah started producing again and gave Jacob two more boys, Issachar, and Zebulun. Now Jacob had ten healthy boys, but he still wandered around the camp as if his life was unfulfilled. Where was the offspring of his dearly beloved? One evening, I was walking past Jacob's tent when I heard raised voices. It was Rachel accusing Jacob of her barrenness.

"Why can't I give you a son of my own womb? Why can't you talk to your God and ask Him to put an end to my barrenness? What have I done to deserve this? Pray to your God, the one and only true God. Why does he not bless me with a child?"

"What are you saying my love?" Jacob, sounding defensive, responded, "Am I a god that I can give you a child? Will my God hear me after He has given me ten healthy boys? Please don't give up. I will pray, but don't blame me. I am simply a mortal with no powers other than what God has already given me".

And so, I noticed for the next many days, Jacob walked around with bowed head and lips moving. I could guess, pleading with his God to open Rachel's womb and give him a child by this his most beloved.

And then one day, there were shrieks of delight; screams of happiness. Rachel was expecting a baby. Jacob was out inspecting the flocks and herds. As I was a teenager now, I would normally go out with him, both as a ward learning the ropes and as an assistant to look after his needs. But today, I had stayed behind because Ithai was giving a special demonstration on self-defence as part of a regular program for the young boys and myself. So Djoser had gone instead. Now, I wondered, who was going to break the news?

It was Ithai. As Jacob climbed down from his horse, Ithai approached him, smiling but head bowed,

"Master Jacob, I have good news,' he stopped waiting for his master to encourage him to continue".

"Well, Ithai, speak up, let me know the good news, don't keep me waiting".

Ithai went up closer to him and whispered in his ear, "You need to go and see Mistress Rachel, she has something to tell you. She is in the bath house Master". Ithai, beaming, added, "Maybe you could wait in her tent".

Father was adamant, "No – never I have to see her now," and he raced off towards the bath house. We were all watching. Without hesitation Jacob went straight inside. Everywhere was absolute silence. Everyone was holding their breath, waiting. Then it came – a shriek of sheer joy. A baby! Rachel's having a baby!" The rest of us simply broke into hilarious laughter and tears in total accord with how our Master and Mistress must have been feeling.

Then occurred something we would never have expected. Jacob chased everyone out of the bath house, and it is reported that he got into the bath with Rachel. We will never know, but they were in there together for a long time. As soon as he had emerged, he beckoned the attendants to enter the bath house and complete their tasks. Then he called Ithai and myself.

"Saddle the horses, we are going for a ride, and bring four men to help, and bring along one of the lambs. Make sure it is unblemished".

We left soon after, followed by the men riding on camels. One of them had the lamb draped across the saddle. We headed north to where the hills began and after climbing what would seem to have been the highest, Jacob stopped, and getting down stood and looked around.

"Here, this is where we must build an altar to my God". He began. "He has heard my supplications and has blessed my beloved with a child. I will sacrifice to him today".

Ithai quickly explained to the men what was required of them, he had seen an altar near the camp beside the spring that Jacob had built on the occasion of his marriage to the two sisters, so he knew what was expected. All natural stones were to be used, nothing to be cut or shaped.

Jacob walked away to a quiet spot beneath a tree, the crown of the hill was covered by a mixture of local trees, some of them ancient and weathered. Sitting down between one of its jutting roots, he bowed his head. We knew he was praying; his face was lifted up, and I could see it shone with a glow of both joy and reverence I had rarely seen. All I could surmise was that somehow, he was in the presence of a very great Divinity.

Satisfied that all had been prepared according to instructions, with the altar facing east, we all sat around in a semi-circle observing the simple structure and the ceremony that followed. One of the men assisted Jacob with preparing the animal, and another lit the fire. As the flames grew, the sacrifice was placed on top of the altar, and Jacob raised his hands, his face reflecting complete happiness and gratitude. We could not hear what he was saying, but we certainly understood the auspicious occasion that was represented here, and in our own way, we joined in the thanksgiving. Not only was it a time for expressing thanks, but for many of us, it was also an immense relief; Rachel was finally going to have a child, Jacob's love child. To the west, the sun was setting, the sky displaying vivid reds and oranges fading into purples and blues, with the stars beginning to appear, and all around was silence except for the sound of the fire blazing; a reverent scene, long to be remembered.

As we descended the hill, in the far distance we could see the beginning of flickering lights coming from the city of Haran, the temple towers and silhouettes of some of the taller buildings stood out against the darkening sky. We were fortunate this time of the year to have long and delicate twilights, so for most of our descent we could see all the country around us bathed in the most beautiful, diffused glow of the disappearing sun. The silver streaks of both the Balikh river closer to us and running beside the city shone the brightest, while further in the distance, the grander and mighty Euphrates wound its way until fading over the horizon. In the foreground and stretching as far as the eye could see were the vast plains chequered by fields of various crops, a patchwork of colour. Behind us were the hills and valleys, the perfect environment to graze livestock, protected and fertile. By the time we had arrived back at the camp, everyone was busy preparing for the evening meal. Jacob went straight into Rachel's tent and remained there the whole night. Anticipating this, Bilhah had made herself scarce, but we had many tents and lots of room.

A few words about the city of Haran: Viewed from the top of the hill we had been on, it looked vast, which in fact it was. It was by far the largest city most of us had ever seen, and some said the population was anywhere between twenty to thirty thousand people. The surrounding region was mostly an agricultural haven, producing every imaginable food source that the earth could produce. Barley, millet, and various types of wheats were the grains. There were vegetables of every kind, including lentils, onions, garlic, leeks, cabbage, turnips, lettuce, and cucumbers and some whose names I still cannot recall. Orchards were filled with figs, olives, pomegranates, apples, mulberries, and date palms. Then there were the livestock: sheep, goats, cattle, camels, donkeys and, for the rich, horses. Fresh fish, mainly catfish and carp, were raised in ponds fed with water from some of the tributaries of the two mighty rivers, the Euphrates, and the Tigris. I should also mention some of the more exotic items that were available, such as honey, nuts, oils and wines, herbs, spices, balms and bouquets; all in abundance.

One day, as Jacob was riding through the streets of Haran on the way to his uncle's, he passed a line of shackled men and women being taken to the local slave market. One particular individual caught his attention. She appeared to be middle-aged, around forty to fifty, dirty and unkempt, with long straggly hair and a wild look in her eyes. Clearly, she did not belong to any nearby ethnic group and seemed to be in poor condition; her wild demeanour and behaviour had seemingly resulted in regular beatings as some of the bruising was clearly visible.

Jacob approached one of the men escorting the slaves and inquired about the women and the reason for her violent treatment, as a damaged slave would fetch very little in any market. He was informed that she was from the north, did not speak any of the local languages, and was completely unmanageable. Jacob inquired about the asking price for this poor soul, and after some bargaining with her keepers, who were obviously eager to be rid of her, he purchased her. He then instructed two of his attendants to place her on a donkey and transport her back to the camp, a journey of at least two days. Jacob emphasised that no harm should come to her during the journey and issued a stern warning that if he ever discovered she had been mistreated, the culprits would face severe consequences.

Warnings of this nature were generally unnecessary among Jacob's people due to their love and respect for him. However, in this case, the woman's wild nature could have led to unforeseen circumstances, prompting Jacob's caution. Upon returning to the camp, Nefertari assumed responsibility for the woman. She needed to be kept loosely bound to prevent her running away. By the time Jacob returned, she had calmed considerably, and Nefertari had even begun to communicate with her using a combination of sign language and a few words they had learnt from each other. Nefertari learned from the woman and the woman from Nefertari.

Her name was Mzia meaning sunlight, which seemed far removed from her appearance when she first arrived at the camp. However, with the patient and loving care that only Nefertari could offer, we soon understood why Mzia had been given this name. She became such a ray of sunshine in all of our lives, especially because of her healer's knowledge and touch. Nefertari had some experience in the healing arts mainly due to her familiarity with herbs and spices. While helping Mzia develop her cooking skills so she could contribute to camp life, Nefertari noticed her deep knowledge, recognition, and application of local herbs, some of which even Nefertari had never known about. After months of coaching, it became apparent that we had gained our own apothecary, and what a delight she was, particularly popular with the shepherds and herders who were now able to carry poultices for snake bite and wounds from wild animals.

Once Mzia had become totally absorbed into camp life, I took the opportunity to have a conversation with her, asking about the poultices. She shared the story of a renowned healer who resided in the village next to hers. He had conducted experiments to obtain snake poison by having them bite into bread. He would then allow the bread to mould for a period before blending it with various herbs and his unique combination of ingredients to create a poultice. When applied to the wound from a snake bite, it significantly reduced the effects of the poison, and in most cases, the victim survived. Mzia had visited the healer numerous times in her youth and observed him creating a wide range of poultices, including the specific one for snakebites. Over time, she had conducted her own trial-and-error experiments and eventually developed a range of remedies that appeared to save lives.

The call of nature – had a huge impact on our lives. Not simply because it was a basic necessity, but because of all the additional ramifications that this simple but essential act would uncover. For example, most of the injuries to shepherds occurred when they had to find a quiet location to relieve themselves. They could inadvertently encounter a snake, perhaps a cobra or an adder, or unintentionally disturb a lioness or a mother bear with her cubs. In either case, chaos would ensue, and the shepherd would receive the brunt of the consequences. Thus, each shepherd would receive training on how to treat both snake bites as well as animal wounds and at least one of them would carry around a bag with poultices and various remedies to apply when needed. Although they weren't specialists, at least an immediate application would stem the bleeding or dilute the poison or bind up a fracture.

Horses are highly valued animals in this region and have been primarily used for transportation, agriculture, or military purposes. They are well suited for pulling heavy loads and provide a faster means of travel compared to other available options. Horses in this region are frequently used for pulling carts and chariots, something that is not all that common in other parts of the region further south.

The most significant source for horses was Anatolia to the west. This region was known for its fertile lands and suitable climate for horse breeding. Among the inhabitants of this area included the Hittites known for their cavalry, chariots, and prowess in battle. Hittite warriors were skilled horsemen and their demands for the finest animals spurred an effective breeding program. Trade routes connected Anatolia with the known world and the demand for their renowned horses extended as far south as Egypt, throughout Mesopotamia, and even far east to the famed Harappa civilisation surrounding the mighty Indus River. Haran situated in the middle, had the opportunity to select from the very best of these animals.

While my father Jacob was not a great walker, he became an excellent rider. His knowledge about and love for animals seemed to have bestowed upon him the gift of earning great loyalty from all creatures with which he came into contact. I belong to the people that are known for their skill in battle; I am a Hittite. However, we, the Hittites of Canaan, trace our origins to a period when, as we were told, two brothers vied for the throne, and the loser was banished. He and his followers subsequently migrated to Canaan, where we find ourselves today.

This might be an opportune time to paint a broader picture of what was happening in the world around us. To the east, Anatolia is home to various civilizations, including the Hittites, a powerful empire that gained prominence around the time our Father Abraham arrived in the land of Canaan. They superseded and absorbed the former civilisation of the Hatti people, and are renowned for their advanced military tactics, their use of chariots, and their expertise in modern weaponry, including a very new and strong metal called iron. They pursue an active policy of influencing their neighbours, whether through peaceful means such as trade and diplomacy or, if necessary, through force.

One of the features of the Hittite people is that they built underground cities into which they retreated whenever faced with threat or aggression. These are elaborate systems of chambers carved into rock formations resulting in quite complex establishments. They include living quarters, storage areas, ventilation shafts and even stables for their horses. Of course, I have never been there so I'm not sure exactly what they look like, but that does sound impressive. The name of one of the cities is apparently called Derinkuyu.

Mesopotamia, also known as Akkadia, is the region situated between the Tigris and the Euphrates, where we currently reside and extending to the southern waters of the gulf. This region is home to several city states and kingdoms. Babylon stands out as one of the major cities of the region and its most famous king Hammurabi, known for his code of two hundred and eighty laws, covering matters of justice, trade, property, and family law. I have particularly mentioned this famous ruler because many civilizations surrounding the Mediterranean have adopted his code into their own systems of administration. Included within Mesopotamia is our city of Haran and the very ancient and famed city of Ur far to the south.

Moving north from our location, are the Mittani people. Their primary city is called Washukanni, and they are celebrated for their chariots and their skills in working with various metals, and some say also with iron. While they may not wield significant influence at the moment, it is believed that their time is yet to come. Nonetheless, they are steadily establishing a notable presence in the region.

To the east of Anatolia, the Mycenaeans inhabit powerful city states, and I'm told are frequently engaged in conflicts among themselves, showing limited interest in our part of the world. However, based on conversations with various traders who visit our camp, it appears that this civilization has much to offer in terms of warfare and peace once they consolidate and become more unified.

Then, of course there is Egypt, which is possibly the most advanced and powerful of all the civilisations of our time. At the moment the people ruling Egypt, according to Djoser, are called Hyksos, whom some people refer to as the 'keka-khasut', or foreigners. They entered the northern part of Egypt over a long period of time mostly from areas within and nearby Cannan, principally the Amorite people, drawn by the fertile soils and the sparse population there. Finally, led by a more aggressive people, the Hatti, who had migrated from Anatolia in the north together with their armies, they took over control of the country. These newcomer's superiority in ways of war, especially in the use of chariots, together with advanced weaponry, gave them dominance and eventual victory over the previous Egyptian rulers, the Pharaohs of the Old Kingdom, who have now moved to the southern city of Thebes, in what is referred to as Upper Egypt. The Hyksos, who are now ruling what is called Lower Egypt, principally around the Delta Region, seem to be calling themselves the new Pharaohs. It's a bit confusing really, but they have adapted their lifestyles to that of the Egyptians, mostly anyway, and have continued the earlier traditions of trade and regional influence. I believe that my information is sound, but I could have missed out some details.

Three other peoples I should mention, are the Minoans who are a very old civilization found on the island of Caphtor. They have been around forever, and their ancient cities are called Knossos, Phaistos, and Malia. I had earlier mentioned the Harrapan people in the far east and the Shang dynasty north of them. But I know very little about them so I will leave it as simply a brief mention. And finally, a very aggressive people seem to have commenced their rise to power called the Assyrians, located to the east within Mesopotamia, and concentrated around their main city Ninevah, but once again, I have little information about them as well.

Now, that I have sketched a somewhat limited picture of all of our neighbours, let's return to my story. One day one of the shepherds brought in a basket full of wolf cubs. My father Jacob initiated a program of crossbreeding between these domesticated wolves and local dog breeds to create an animal adapted to both guarding sheep and serving as camp sentinels during the nights. In the fields, the herding dogs were trained to bond with the animals and sleep with them, living alongside them constantly, ensuring their safety and discouraging them from straying.

Jacob gained two brides after seven years working for Laban. However, this commitment also required an additional seven years of work to pay off his second wife, Rachel. Meanwhile, the camp site expanded, along with the number of workers, primarily driven by an ongoing trade between Haran and Beersheba. As a result, my father's expenses were covered, and he was building an experienced team to care for the animals.

At the conclusion of his second seven-year contract, my father began contemplating a return to Canaan in the south and began planning to make it happen. Then, one day, Laban appeared at the camp and initiated a conversation with Jacob about his intentions. When it became apparent that my father, his family, and his retainers were considering departure, Laban realized that this would negatively impact his current accumulation of wealth. My father and his team had substantially elevated Laban's status, transforming him from a moderately wealthy businessman to someone who was now extremely affluent, and he certainly did not want to witness any decline in either his earnings or his social standing.

More recently, Laban had even received an invitation to a banquet celebrating the marriage of the King of Haran's third daughter. As we all came to understand, Laban was, put simply, a covetous man. Having discovered that his wealth also afforded him power and influence in Haran, he recognised the need to sustain the lifeblood of this influence which meant retaining Jacob and all those working with him.

All this resulted in a new contract with my father for another six years with the difference being that he could now start acquiring flocks of his own. Finally offered an opportunity to build his own wealth, Jacob, determined to succeed, negotiated what to Laban seemed very reasonable terms. He would keep all the spotted, striped, and speckled animals and Laban would receive the unblemished flocks. Little did he realise the pit into which his avarice-fed destiny was to lead him. His focus on money had blinded him to the reality of Jacob's depth of knowledge about breeding animals.

CHAPTER FIVE

FAMILY, FORTUNE, AND CANAAN.

"In this way, the man, (Jacob), became very rich and had large flocks,
along with male and female slaves, camels and donkeys".
Genesis 30: 43.

Jacob's first decision, following his new contract, was to move the camp further away by another day and a half's ride to the south, close to a regular supply of water and pleasantly protected by an existing grove of trees as well as not far from some of the best pastures in the region. With fourteen years of experience, he could now plan his new establishment for efficiency and comfort starting with the first pitched tent.

His next task was to separate Laban's flocks from his, which to begin with was easy as Jacob started with only a meagre number of rather unhealthy-looking marked and marred sheep and goats. I could imagine Laban, watching this separation and chuckling to himself about how clever he was and how much richer he was going to become. However, my father had other ideas.

Now Jacob focused on planning and setting up a camp that catered for the needs of a considerably increased and diversified population of men, women, and children.

The main tent, situated in the centre of the camp, belonged to Jacob. It was a large structure with an awning in the front spacious enough to accommodate a U-shaped arrangement of a slightly elevated wooden platform covered with rugs and cushions. Here, he conducted meetings with various senior members of his establishment. Inside, there was a similar arrangement for more personal or friendly gatherings, such as with family or when Laban came to visit. Behind this area, was a curtain of embroidered linen that screened off the sleeping quarters. This area featured a bed made of skins and soft coverings, slightly raised to allow for air circulation, which was particularly important during the hottest months of the year. On either side of the bed, rugs and cushions were positioned, tastefully for relaxation. The interior of the tent was adorned with hangings of light-coloured linen, creating a comfortable and friendly atmosphere, and helping to reflect the limited light from the front entrance. A large hanging lamp in the centre of the tent provided illumination during the evenings.

Either side of this main tent were two smaller tents one for each of Jacob's wives, Leah, and Rachel. They also had awnings, although more compact, where the ladies could sit together with their senior maids in the cool of the evening, and perhaps even be joined by their sons. Inside the arrangement was quite different. While the walls were draped similarly to Jacob's tent, they were adorned with numerous tapestries and silks that reflected luxury and comfort. The entire space was filled with rugs and cushions, featuring a large bed in the middle. Small tables were scattered about, holding oil lamps and censors, either bowl-shaped vessels of clay or the more elaborate four-horned censers for burning incense. From the four corners of the tents various herbs were hung to add a pleasing aroma which was especially important during the hot and humid months of the year. Both Leah and Rachel also had stone carved censor stands with depictions of gods on each side for burning incense during their prayer rituals. While respecting father's very devoted worship of Adonai, they continued to serve their own gods, much to Jacob distress, but it was not something he wanted to insist on, not just yet.

Jacob, the innovator, had added windows at the top of each tent, covered with a flap to aid in protection from the elements and a light silk curtain to avoid any foreign intrusion such as insects. This inclusion provided a very welcome addition of cool air during the summer months.

Beside Leah's tent, was the largest, accommodating the sons of Jacob. By the time we had moved to our present location, Jacob had acquired eleven sons: Reuben – the eldest from Leah; Simeon – the second from Leah; Levi – third from Leah; Judah – fourth from Leah; Dan – from Bilhah, Rachel's handmaid; Naftali – the second son from Bilhah; Gad – from Zilpah, Leah's handmaid; Asher – the second son from Zilpah; Issachar – the fifth son from Leah; Zebulun, Leah's sixth, and finally the son he had always wanted, Joseph – Rachel's first son. Reuben, the eldest was seven, and Joseph the youngest was not quite one. Apart from him, all the boys lived in the one tent supervised by Djoser who was in charge of the dormitory. Joseph continued to stay with his mother Rachel for another year, when, at the age of two, he joined his brothers. Finally, I should mention Dinah, born from Leah and my father's only daughter, and slightly older than Joseph. Also, like Joseph, she was spoilt from birth being the only girl in the family, in fact everyone spoilt her, and her brothers were particularly protective, vying to look after her each day. Surprisingly, Dinah didn't turn out to be at all a precocious little girl, instead she exuded confidence and radiated a very special beauty.

While they were still very young, and over the following few years, I began to assess some of their personality traits; their positives and those areas where it seemed they were not so strong. Events later in their lives, for the most part, confirmed my early assessments. Here I will list them:

Reuben had leadership qualities, was sensitive and compassionate, but would back down when under pressure.

Simeon had a strong sense of justice but was hot tempered and tended towards violence to satisfy his anger.

Levi showed a particular tendency to aggression, which when defending someone was good, but could also be a failing. He was frequently involved in trouble in the camp.

Judah was courageous, responsible and for the most part honest with a strong sense of integrity.

Dan valued fairness and justice and frequently voiced complaints about unfair play among his brothers.

Naftali was athletic, loved running and was exceptionally fast.

Asher was a food enthusiast, loved eating and often could be found looking for snacks in the kitchen tents.

Issachar would enjoy putting on displays of strength at a very young age and tended to test out his ability on items unusual for a boy of his age.

Zebulun loved water, and always had a strong attraction towards the springs near the campsite, despite not knowing how to swim. He was a worry.

Joseph was far too young so I could only hope he would turn out much like his father.

Dinah was spoilt by everyone, however instead of becoming affected by the attention, she grew up to be a beautiful and confident young woman displaying a very attractive personality.

I was the big brother who sorted out disagreements, took them off on excursions, accompanied them as their tutors taught them basic literacy, comforted them when they were distressed and sat with them most nights telling them stories.

In front of Jacob's tent was a large fireplace built on a base of stone. It was lit most nights, a beacon of warmth in winter and otherwise for light around the camp. In addition, torches were set in specific locations such as the cooking area, around the food tent, near most other tents and out towards the main toilets which were pits surrounded by goatskins for privacy; there were six of them: two for the women and four for the men, reflecting the gender balance within our camp population. Nighttime could be dangerous as wild animals were attracted by food smells. Our guard dogs were mostly an effective deterrent, but it was considered best to take every precaution and a well-lit camp became an added benefit to our security.

On the other side of the campfire was the food tent which also doubled as a tent of meeting. The cooking areas were not far away. Some preparations took place in the open air and others such as the baking, and for when it rained, awnings provided shelter. Breakfast was a stretched-out affair with people coming and going, and usually Jacob, Leah and Rachel had theirs in their tents. Lunch too, was rather haphazard in terms of scheduling, as most people had a range of times when they were expected to be on duty, either within the camp or with the animals. Whenever the flocks were grazing at some distance from the camp, food was usually packed up in the morning, sufficient for two meals, breakfast, and lunch, and sent out to the shepherds and herders. Depending on the location and conditions of the fields, Jacob insisted, as far as possible, that the animals were brought close to the camp site in the evening.

Everywhere around us was open country which meant more than adequate grazing options for the flocks. However, Jacob had organised a system of rotation to prevent over-grazing in any one area. Open country also meant wild animals, so a number of folds had been erected around our residential areas, using stones and thorn bushes into which the animals were herded. Each pen, which could hold as many as three hundred animals, was guarded by a shepherd and two dogs. We actually rarely lost an animal. As the size of the flocks grew, so did the number of folds, and eventually it proved essential that we establish additional folds away from the camp because of the need to access fresh fields.

Jacob insisted that the evening meals be spent together. All of us other than those still on duty with the animals, would gather in the evening as the sun was setting. The food tent was constructed with a wooden table in the shape of a big U. Benches were placed beside the table. At the head of the tent, was a low platform on which Jacob, Leah and Rachel would sit. This arrangement was not meant to signify status but rather allowed Jacob to remain seated while addressing everyone, ensuring all could see and hear him. Overhead, a goatskin covering stretched out a few cubits beyond each side of the tables in case of rain. During heavy rain, we even had flaps that could be lowered. Ithai was given a seat of honour close to the head, but for the rest of us we all sat wherever there was room. As our number grew, so did the need for additional food tents, but placed close enough for everyone to see and hear Jacob. Beyond the food tent was a series of smaller tents that accommodated married couples. Initially, there were about a dozen of these but as our establishment expanded, more were added.

Thus, the camp centred around and faced the three tents of Jacob, Leah, and Rachel. Behind these three tents were three separate toilets and three bath houses. A toilet was a simple pit with a seat structure on top of it. The bath houses were small tents made of goatskins and inside were wooden tubs if a bath was required, and a large round earthenware container always filled with water was available for washing.

The insides of each tent were lined with heavy cotton to keep out the drafts and the cold. The tent floors were made of slabs of stone with cotton mats on top, providing added warmth. The space between the tents and the bathroom facilities was illuminated by torches at night. Behind these structures was a palisade made of upright timber poles, each one and a half the height of an average man. The palisade came around the three main tents and at the end of each side began a large semi-circle of tents extended towards and around the married quarters, spanning from one side to the other. On the left-hand side were the women's tents and on the right-hand side were the men's tents, although there were almost twice the number of men's tents as the women's quarters.

At one point a delegation from the women came to Jacob asking that they be provided more protection, so the palisade was extended to continue to circle behind where the women lived ultimately ending against the tent of Ithai. For the general camp population, several bathing structures had been erected beside the spring, so that once inside the occupant had access to fresh water there was no need for any containers inside. As with the other bath houses, the floors were of fitted rocks with the roof sloping down to walls made of goatskins.

Proof of the effectiveness of our security came one evening, rather late, when one of the maids was walking towards the cooking area to heat some milk for one of the smaller children, she heard a growl and looking up, she saw three large animals, with yellow eyes flashing and teeth bared. She screamed, and immediately a loud shouted command came from nearby, and almost instantly six large dogs had appeared, standing in front of her and growling in reply. The scene was dramatic. A lioness with two grown cubs had wandered into the camp, drawn by smells of cooked meat. At the rear was the maid, squatting, holding herself and trembling, in front of her were the dogs with barred teeth and possibly twenty cubits further away were the three large cats. It was a standoff threatening an imminent clash, only at that moment, two armed guards appeared, shouting and hurling rocks at the invasive animals. Finding themselves outnumbered the lions retreated into the dark.

Everyone and the dogs were safe, although it could have been disastrous. The lions were easily capable of taking on the dogs and perhaps even the guards, but with all the noise and being in an unfamiliar environment, they decided to look elsewhere for their food. After that Jacob and Ithai revised the nightshift and guard routine, incorporating four armed guards in each shift. While one guard kept a watchful eye beside the fire, the other three would carry out regular patrols around the camp, ensuring that all torches were lit and there were no unwanted intruders. The night time duty lasted from just before sunset and was divided into three periods, ending once the sun had risen well over the horizon.

Having established a new contract with Laban which offered Jacob an opportunity to build his own flocks and herds, an innovative plan was rapidly put into implementation by Jacob based on selective breeding, one of his specialities. His objective was to successfully increase his own flocks, while left to the less experienced shepherds working for Laban, the quality of their animals deteriorated, principally from neglect. Here is how Jacob, spurred on by a confidence built up over years of acquired knowledge, succeeded. We are still in awe of his amazing achievement.

Jacob understood domestic animals. He had explored the minds of seasoned shepherds and shared ideas with the best of experts wherever he went, from Isaac's camp in Beersheba, to his friends around Rekem, and more recently among his own people in this region near Haran. In the animal business, Jacob had become a master, and possibly the first of his kind to apply selective breeding, in this part of the world. This was his strategy.

Jacob took fresh cut branches from poplar, almond and plane trees and made white streaks on them by peeling off the bark. Then he set the rods he had peeled upright in the watering troughs, so that the animals would see them when they came to drink. And since they bred when they came to drink, the animals mated in sight of the rods and gave birth to streaked, speckled, and spotted young. Jacob divided the lambs and had the animal's mate with the streaked and brown in the flock of Laban. He also kept his own livestock separate and did not let them mix with Laban's flock. Whenever the hardier animals came on heat, Jacob set up the rods in the watering troughs, so that the animals would see them and conceive in front of them; but he did not set up the rods in front of the weaker animals. Thus, the more feeble were Laban's and the stronger Jacob's. By this way, Jacob became very rich and had large flocks, along with male and female slaves and donkeys. Genesis 30: 37-43.

Let me, now, interrupt my description of camp life and share something relating to the other principle focus of my story, Joseph. Starting life as a beautiful and healthy little baby, Joseph continued to grow into a handsome and accomplished young boy. Until he reached the age of two, he remained in Rachel's tent. Then with Jacob's encouragement, she agreed to let him spend more time with the other boys. For the next twelve months or so, his lodging would alternate between Rachel's tent, the boy's tent with Djoser, and Jacob's tent, when I stayed there.

Joseph was a very bright youngster with the three particular gifts that our teacher Nabu-Ahh told me were the essential elements in the learning process: Curiosity, Creativity, and Confidence. He had all three in abundance. In fact, it wasn't long before he gained the nickname 'Ragil' which comes from the family's language meaning enquirer. He was always asking questions.

Every morning, after breakfast, all the boys would attend a program of exercise and receive basic weapons training. Then they would freshen up, have a snack, and enter the food tent which also served as a tent of meeting as well as their schoolhouse. Their academic curriculum included reading, writing, mathematics, some basic tenets of law suitable for children of that age, a limited amount of literature, primarily consisting of myths and legends, a simple version of the geography of the region, and religious education. A scribe named Nabu-Ahh, happy to also be called Apkallu, or 'wise one', originally from Babylon became a willing member of our camp family. He was brought from the house of Laban, as there no were no longer any children there requiring an education.

Jacob has always been a bit of a trend setter and there were a few issues about which he would not compromise. He insisted on all his children being fluent in literacy and numeracy. And, looking back to those early times, I have been interested to notice how this tradition has continued down through the generations.

I would frequently attend these teaching sessions and, although I was considered an adult, I chose to call him ach Nabu or big brother Nabu, out of respect for his learning, wisdom, and age. He was married but his children had all grown up and lived in Babylon, so he was assigned one of the family tents. The boys had all grown up in this Mesopotamian environment and so were fluent in the Akkadian language, which, in fact, was the most commonly used around our establishment. However, they were also learning their father's language, with its roots in Canaan. Religious education became the responsibility of Jacob as he, at this point, was the only one who worshipped Adonai, that is apart from the boys, with whom he held regular prayer and praise sessions.

Joseph was undoubtedly the most active participant during these teaching sessions. Not that the other boys minded as it relieved them of some pressure to perform. His greatest fondness was for using the word, 'why', almost excessively. It wasn't as if he was a boy genius, but his curiosity was insatiable. He delighted in exploring the world around him and delving into everyone else's world as well. Whenever he wasn't in the teaching sessions, he would be following me around repeatedly asking 'why?' If I couldn't locate him among the boys, my first stop was to Mzia's tent, now designated as the 'Healer's Tent'. There he would be asking Mzia all about her potions and herbs and the human body and how it all functioned.

Whenever Joseph and I shared his father's tent, Joseph overflowed with questions about anything related to his father – his past, his grandparents, and his grandmother Rebecca. On one occasion when his father inadvertently mentioned his dream in Luz, Joseph couldn't contain his curiosity and persistently sought to uncover every detail, asking 'why? Then he would accompany the herders when they entered the camp, eager to learn everything about the animals.

Jacob had also been experimenting with crop cultivation, primarily for fodder, but, in addition, he had planted various types of wheat and millet. He had gained some experience in Beersheba, as his father also had a significant history of success with crops. So, Joseph would pester those responsible for agriculture, especially when it came to irrigation methods, or, as he like to phrase it, 'feeding them water'.

I know, it does sound a little bizarre, but it wasn't as if Joseph was asking complex or scientific questions, it was simply curiosity from a boy of four. However, I must admit that, at times, it was quite exhausting.

Joseph was very curious about nature. On one occasion, a maid came running up to me asking for my immediate help because she found Joseph playing with a snake and she was too frightened to go near either of them. It was by the spring and the serpent had slithered over for a drink. In fact, it was a cobra, not the spitting kind, but nevertheless very dangerous. Joseph was not playing with it, just watching it, but the cobra's reaction was a raised body and an extended hood as if ready to strike. I walked over, moving very slowly towards Joseph, gently picked him up and backed away cautiously. We stood stock still for a short while and eventually the snake, feeling less threatened, crawled away into the bushes. I promptly took Joseph to Mzia and asked her to educate him about the serpent world.

I turn to the subject of languages. Our camp's population included Canaanites, people from Mesopotamia, Egyptians, Hittites, Philistines, and even one from way up north in the Caucase area. Jacob insisted that we all learn his language. For most of us we had a foundation in Canaanite languages and simply needed to adapt to the way my father's language had evolved. Father Abraham had come from Ur of the Chaldees and spoke a Sumerian language. He would have called himself a dubsar, or writer of the cuneiform of the language he was brought up with in the great city if Ur.

He travelled up to Haran where they spoke an Akkadian language and later moved to Canaan, residing next to the Philistines who spoke their own Semitic language. Father Abraham also spent some time in Egypt where they had an entirely different language. Thus, over the years and generations, the language he had brought with him from Ur underwent changes out of necessity and common use. It had become similar to many of the Semitic languages but retained its own peculiarities, constantly evolving by adding and discarding words based on their utility.

One particularly remarkable aspect was that this language developed by Father Abraham began to merge into its own written form, initially based on his knowledge of the Sumerian cuneiform. While in Haran, he adapted this to the local cuneiform. Finally, on moving south into Canaan, perhaps for reasons of convenience, he commenced incorporating some of the local scripts which included pictorial representations within the various letters.

By the time of Jacob, the family language had passed through several stages incorporating various script forms and finally adopting elements of a Semitic script which was quite different but easier to use and thus more practical. It remained much more rudimentary compared to the Mesopotamians and Egyptians but was far more convenient. I even witnessed Joseph, on one occasion, writing some letters in the moist silt near the spring. Father Abraham had acquired the skill of making papyrus scrolls while he was in Egypt, and introduced his simplified cuneiform writing onto this material which was much more convenient than clay tablets. Thus, our camp culture embraced an early form of writing for communication, such as when Jacob would send messages back to his father and mother in Beersheba.

Writing our language was as important as reading it, so our camp teacher Nabu-Ahh ensured a complete package of literacy for Jacob's children. This was unusual for most families in the region and one particular challenge was obtaining suitable materials for writing. The most commonly used media in Mesopotamia was on clay tablets, so Nabu Ahh would have the children make their own tablets and practice writing on the wet surface, erasing it each time, and re-using it, until finally preserving and drying the finished version of each lesson in order to show their father their progress. Jacob, himself, used an assortment of materials for writing. Most preferred was the papyrus brought up from Egypt in the annual caravan from his parents in Beersheba. He also used parchment, made from sheep or goat leather, and more commonly used in Canaan. Although this was not as readably available and was more expensive to produce, it was the most preferred when the supply of papyrus was exhausted. While it was easier and cheaper to use the clay tablets of the local region, he found this media rather cumbersome when it came to storage and the longer term keeping of important records.

By the fifth year of his six-year contract, Jacob had accumulated significant flocks, numbering around three thousand sheep and two thousand goats, apart from the camels, donkeys, and horses. His flocks were kept quite separate from those of his uncles, and it soon became obvious that the unblemished animals of Laban's possession, started to look decidedly inferior to the speckled, spotted, and striped ones of Jacob. As Ithai once commented,

"Master's flocks didn't only look healthier; you could also taste the difference!"

On one occasion, Laban visited our campsite and in discussing the state of his flocks, made the comment about the differences as it related to the health and vigour of the animals. Jacob's reply was simply that animals thrived on what they ate and if Laban's animals looked poorly, he should take it up with his chief herders. There was nothing much else his uncle could say, but Jacob realised that discontent was growing and that he should make plans to leave before relationships became violent. He would definitely honour his contract, but immediately after, he decided he should be gone. His people in total numbered even more than those of Labans, but his uncle had many commercial interests in Haran and was on good terms with the King, so he could muster an armed force that far exceeded anything Jacob had.

In planning for a reasonably imminent departure, he gave the responsibility to Ithai, who, after considerable thought, suggested the following. To start with, a gradual reduction of the camp population would be the initial step towards implementation, commencing with a forward party which would move down into, preferably, the hill country of Gilead, somewhat south and slightly east of the mountains around Mount Sion (Hermon). They would identify a suitable location and establish a temporary campsite. Meanwhile, the physical structures, of the present camp should remain intact. Over the subsequent months, similarly sized groups would be despatched, except for the flocks and herds as their reduction would be noticed by Laban's people.

Having travelled through this region on his journey to Haran, Jacob was somewhat familiar with the territory and as his father's caravans had covered the long trek each year from Beersheba to our campsite, he had several people who knew the best potential locations. He selected a group of forty-five or so persons including some shepherds, who would explore the best grazing lands, several herders to look after the larger animals, a camp supervisor, one of the older and capable members of our family together with his wife, a dozen servants to erect the campsite and prepare everything in readiness for the hundreds that would follow, and a dozen armed guards led by Djoser. All the people involved in this secret enterprise were sworn to secrecy, which really wasn't necessary as they were totally loyal to their master Jacob.

A caravan of camels left us one night shrouded by total darkness and, once more, led by our inspiring leader, Ithai, who would confirm the location and then return. This first contingent included Mzia and a few maids, as well as our scribe Nabu-Ahh. Djoser and the small contingent of warriors would serve as protection although no one was particularly worried about security. After all, there wouldn't be anything of particular value in this small start-up establishment.

According to my conversations with Ithai upon his return, everything succeeded as planned and during the following months, we were all encouraged by the knowledge that our main departure was in good hands, and group by group, gradually our population decreased, without any specific evidence of a reduction, while our camp family was slowly being bult up in Canaan.

The key element of our plan for the main decampment from our much-loved current location was to move quickly and efficiently. We needed to put as much distance between ourselves and Laban as possible before he found out that we had left. True it was that his people would frequently visit us either for food, fodder or just friendship, but the departure of the first contingent would have been seen as another caravan heading back to Beersheba with trade goods. Subsequent departures were carefully selected as involving members of our family with duties that were never in the limelight; less noticed. Nevertheless, as a fail-safe measure, people were sent out to remain at key locations from which Laban's people could approach our camp and to tell them the very sad story about a contagious disease currently sweeping through our population. Every contingency had been considered, discussed, and planned for.

Now was also the time for some clever deception. Laban's flocks were several days walk away from the campsite, and more than four or five days from Haran, thus there was a need for some distraction that would avoid the shepherds noticing that Jacob's flocks were no longer where they should have been, and the timing was crucial. So, prior to the determined day for Jacob's flocks to commence their long trek, several of Jacob's shepherds went into the hills behind where Laban's flocks were grazing. At an appointed time, they came running down from the hills, shouting about a raid of Mittani marauders from the north. All very plausible as although the Mittani were yet to become a power in the region, their people were traditional rustlers raiding for plunder which of course included animals. That started a panic among Laban's shepherds, some of them simply ran into the hills and hid, others tried to move their flocks into a safer location such as a valley that was less visible, but generally everywhere dissolved into confusion. Jacob's people promptly left knowing that it would take several days for Laban's men to find and reassemble all the animals, meaning no one would be visiting Jacob's flocks for quite a while.

Now was the perfect time for their departure. Everybody was ready. On the very day that the six-year contract had been concluded, the final caravan was primed and prepared. Most of the major tents were still standing, although they were simply shells with their interiors totally empty. A casual observer would not have noticed anything unusual except for the absence of any human presence. So, it was no wonder that it took quite a few days before Laban's people became aware that the campsite was deserted, and everyone had left. Several days prior to the departure, Leah and Rachel had travelled to Haran with two of their youngest children to spend a day shopping and allow their grandmother some time to be with her beautiful grandsons and Dinah. Apparently, Laban was away at the time, however grandmother thoroughly enjoyed her time with the boys and their very special sister. Then they all returned to the camp the following day.

It was early spring, carefully selected as the most comfortable time of the year to travel overland into Northern Canaan, arriving at their pre-selected and established campsite in the hills of Gilead. The animals and their herders had departed several days earlier, as their progress would have been much slower. Thus, the final caravan consisted of Jacob leading out front and setting the pace, riding his favourite horse. Following him were Leah and Rachel, along with the youngest boys, Leah's Issachar, and Zebulun and her daughter Dinah, as well as Jacob's pride and joy, Joseph, all riding behind in a horse drawn cart. The remainder of the boys together with myself had our own horse drawn cart.

We broke camp at first light. Everyone knew where they were to be seated, they had responded to the call of nature and were fully aware that there would be no stopping except for a midday break for food and to rest the animals. The sun was just lifting its head over the horizon as we rode out, the air was crisp and I could feel the excitement exuding from everyone, looking forward to this daunting but blood stirring adventure. This momentous event stood as a testament to the resourcefulness and determination of our leader Jacob. It was very clear that we all felt immensely proud of all he had done over the past twenty years and were confident that our future was in safe hands.

Ithai was riding up front alongside Jacob with his contingent of ten warriors following behind and either side of the column with two bringing up the rear. They were on either horses or camels depending on which animal they were used to. One cart carrying the senior women, including Zilpah, Bilhah, Nefertari, and two older and senior members of the family followed pulled by two bullocks. Six larger carts with the rest of the women sitting on benches on either side of the cart, ten per cart was followed by another ten carts similar in size holding ten men per cart who were servants responsible for a wide range of general duties.

Twelve camels were ridden by men with a variety of roles within the family and each of them led another three camels laden with everything required to support their intended campsite. Another ten of the more proven servants who had a reasonable degree of skill with weapons, rode the remaining camels. These last rode alongside the warriors. Fifty of the herders had accompanied the animals several days previously, supported by fifteen warriors and all the donkeys which accompanied them as pack animals.

A lot of discussion had gone into the planning of this enterprise as it was quite an assembly. It spoke of the significant success that Jacob had achieved with his breeding program and, not to be overlooked, his very strong conviction that Adonai had blessed him. It had been estimated that the animals and herders would take sixty days plus five days rest along the way, and the caravan would take fifty days plus five days rest along the way, so the two groups should have been arriving in the new campsite in Gilead, roughly about the same time.

While this would possibly be considered a retreat or an escape, my father was fully aware that it was totally justifiable within the conditions of his agreement. Right was on his side, but in this part of the world, right was not always fair. His decision to return to his land of birth was nurtured by his longing to return to his family as well as to escape from the very obvious exploitation of his uncle. Jacob was fully aware that his uncle had discovered his manipulation of the selective breeding program, but, at the same time he had come to terms with the fact that his uncle would never acknowledge the exploitation of his nephew, of his abilities, or of his contribution to his newfound wealth. Laban's rationalisation would have been that Jacob's involvement in his animal husbandry business had provided him in becoming wealthy but that was simply his due, as a return for allowing him entry into his family, marrying his daughters, and living off the land for the many years he had been privileged to serve. Consequently, Laban would have considered it totally justifiable to do anything in his power to prevent the loss of both prestige and wealth.

It was quite a few days after Jacob had abandoned his campsite, and only after they had recovered all of their animals from the false alarm over Mittani raiders, that Laban's herders observed that they no longer saw any sign of Jacob's flocks. Of course, they may have moved further into the hills, but they weren't sure. All the more reason for them to carry out a thorough investigation before relaying any dire message to their master Laban. That gave Jacob's convoy several additional days in favour of their escape. This I found out from Ithai sometime later when he had the opportunity to talk with one of Laban's people on that eventful day when they entered Jacob's newly settled camp at Mahanaim with thoughts of violence. While Jacob and Laban were talking terms of mutual accord, Ithai managed to find out what had happened once Jacob and his family had left Haran.

The daily routine, which we adhered to in the strictest sense, meant leaving early and stopping for the night as it grew dark. A fire was lit, and the women would prepare the evening meal. The cooks would get up early and prepare a simple meal for everyone to break their fast. They would also prepare packs of food, stored on the camels, to be distributed during the midday break. Everyone was expected to sleep early, ready for another gruelling day of travel. The journey was going to be demanding, with little time for rest, but that had been made clear from the start and Jacob had asked his people to give him their support and cooperation, promising that by the time they had reached Gilead, a very pleasant land and comfortable lodgings would be waiting for them.

All was quiet, except for the creaking of the carts laden with people and a wide range of equipment that was too large to be placed on the backs of camels. The carriages swayed gently as they trundled forward, their timbers echoing with whispers of countless stories of events past. The carts were open allowing plenty of fresh air and a view of the surrounding countryside. However, in anticipation of a sudden spring shower, covers had been folded alongside and could easily be drawn up and over the framework on top. There were people among us who had rarely ventured outside the camp, so this was an exhilarating opportunity for them to enjoy totally unfamiliar scenery, and of course once everyone had settled down, there was plenty to talk about.

Mounted warriors, their steeds galloping gracefully, flanked the caravan. They were few in number but nevertheless formidable and sufficient to deter any curious brigands looking for easy pickings. Clad in sturdy armour, their swords glinting in the sunlight, these guardians formed a shield around the vulnerable procession, their horses kicking up small clouds of dust carried them with an air of both power and grace.

Intermingled with the warriors were the camel riders, some armed and others leading baggage laden animals behind them, all swaying in a semi synchronised rhythm with the gentle wind. The camels were an essential element for this convoy famed for their ability to withstand any arduous journey. With their languid yet determined pace, they added a touch of traditional grandeur, and a degree of confidence that they could be totally relied upon.

The road stretched before us, winding its way through vast stretches of wilderness and varied terrain, day after day, after day. The sights transformed as we travelled from the fertile plains of Haran, through endless open and dry lands, mostly uninhabited and sometimes particularly inhospitable, stretching endlessly over the horizon. Then there was the respite offered by glimpses of nature's splendour, a kaleidoscope of spring colours from vibrant wildflowers, wadis of palms and baobabs and in the distance the outline of majestic oak and cedar trees.

As we advanced, the rhythm of the journey became the background soundtrack of each day, punctuated by songs and laughter, the clattering hooves, and the creaking of wheels. The scent of spring blossoms mingling with the dust kicked up created a now familiar aroma that bathed our minds and bodies auguring in hope for a new life to come.

Everything progressed exceptionally smoothly except for one brief but almost adventurous encounter. We found ourselves in the midst of nowhere, surrounded by flat plains and dry dust. Suddenly, seemingly as if out of thin air, a troupe of twenty to thirty riders on camels appeared. My father halted our caravan and instructed the drivers of the carts to form a circle. Then he called out an instruction to those in our midst who had experience with the bow, and there were quite a few, many of them women who had relished the opportunity to compete with their menfolk in providing a defence for our camp family.

Lining up the archers, almost twenty persons, he then told all those on horses and camels to circle around and draw their swords so they would flash in the sunlight. As the camel riders approached, my father told the archers to let loose a volley of arrows and immediately prepare for another shot. The riders stopped, another volley. The camel riders came to a complete halt, perhaps conferring among themselves. Shortly, thereafter, they pivoted and proceeded off in the opposite direction. The clear warning had been heeded, and wisely realised that attacking our caravan could have been an ill-advised choice. We all breathed a collective sigh of relief.

Despite the distance covered and the occasional longing for respite, no one walked. The importance of speed was paramount, and every effort was made to maintain a relentless pace. It was a test of everyone's mutual resolve to accept everything this undertaking and their leader Jacob would throw at them, leaving the uncertainty of Haran behind. Ithai had carefully plotted each day so that when it came to stop for the evening, wood for the fire and water for everyone and the animals was ensured. We were traveling along a tried and tested route called the King's Highway, north from Haran to south and Egypt. So, all the basic needs of our caravan were always available and reliable.

After many days along open plains, the caravan finally commenced its climb into the hills, and I could almost hear a universal sigh as everyone realized we were close to our destination. Within a few days we had topped a particularly steep climb and there below us, nestled in a valley and next to a stream was what we had been longing to see, our new home, at least for however long Jacob was willing to remain here. We were all extremely weary, the animals too, but this was definitely a sight worth enduring all that the journey had sucked out of us. We had arrived in the land of Canaan, covenanted by Adonai to the third Patriarch, Jacob and to his descendants; the 'Promised Land', offering new hope and an endless array of opportunities.

I climbed down from the cart along with all the boys who immediately took off screaming and yelling with sheer delight. Over to one side I saw the cart carrying Leah, Rachel, the youngest boys, and Dinah. Joseph was there trying to tear himself away from his very protective mother, so I went over and lifted him down as his face was alive with the longing to join the other boys, and he took off. Everyone else simply sat down on the grass or a rock, looking around and soaking in the magnificence that was now our new home, which, later on, we learnt to be a place known as Mahanaim.

For the immediate future, they could relax, everything had been prepared for their arrival, giving them some time to adjust to solid ground, fresh air unpolluted by dust, a vista to die for, and a secure future to look forward to. The newcomers were soon invited to move over to a dining tent, similar but smaller than the food tent of Haran, and there for the first time in weeks, they feasted on roast lamb, fresh vegetables, and newly baked bread, washed down with delicious wines. Although the camp was decidedly smaller, everyone's accommodation was catered for - a bit squashed, but comfortable. Having eaten, they were free to unpack their bags and move into their sleeping quarters, and some of them even took advantage of their free time and curled up, wherever they were, and went to sleep. Tomorrow was another day and that meant back to work.

CHAPTER SIX

ESAU

*"Then the man said, 'From now on, you will no longer be called Jacob, but Israel;
because you have shown your strength to both God and men and have prevailed".*
Genesis 32: 28.

Our newest home, Mahanaim, was a picturesque expanse, a tapestry of natural beauty. Towering mountains adorned with lush greenery encircled the campsite, serving as majestic sentinels that seemed to protect and embrace our company with a welcoming caress. The camp had been set up several hundred cubits away from the north-south route we were on to afford us some privacy. The Jabbok River, known for its gentle flow and crystal-clear waters, descended in a series of small waterfalls and rapids until finally reaching the Jordan river several thousand cubits below us. The stream beside which our camp had been erected, offered a soothing murmur in the background punctuated by the occasional calls of the shrike and sunbird, while overhead gliding through the wind currents were the magnificent kestrel and sparrow hawk.

We were generously surrounded by natures portraits of iris, poppy, tulip, daisy, and sunflowers splashing colours over the mountain sides, and the distinctive aromas of lavender, jasmine and sage wafting across the valleys mingling with the fresh and pungent scent of the pine forests. On both sides of the campsite, a tall lining of majestic trees, offered everything we could have required to enjoy this refuge which we were to call our new home for, as it turned out, the next two hundred days.

The shepherds and herders with the animals arrived the following day. They had found short cuts suggested to them by fellow herders on route and so had made very good progress. With that number of animals, it was essential that they be immediately moved into nearby valleys which had already been sourced by the earlier scouting team, so while the newly arrived herders were rested, others took over, helped by the dogs, and moved the animals away and into sheltered valleys where they could be properly managed and offered a plentiful supply of pasture. There was still a lot to be done, with folds and corrals to be built, but for now they were in safe hands, and we could all relax, as the strenuous energy required for moving over such a vast space had been totally exhausting and everyone, especially the keepers, needed rest.

While the sun commenced its slow descent below the horizon on that first day, casting a warm glow across the valley, we new arrivals settled into the camp with a huge sigh of gratitude. Vaguely listening to the sounds of laughter and conversation mingled with a gentle symphony of crickets and nocturnal creatures, I lay back and looking up into the canopy of stars, I experienced an overwhelming sense of peace and satisfaction. My mind wandered over the many stages of our recent journey, and I couldn't help but muse over how incredibly well planned and executed it had been. With a new certainty, it became clear that Jacob had at last commenced his claim on the covenant promised him by his God, and startling myself, I realised that He was beginning to become my God as well.

I was busy with my own thoughts, resting beside the stream away from the others who had newly arrived and so I was rather surprised when I heard my father calling me from his tent. The forward party had erected tents for everyone, but it also meant sharing. Leah and Rachel shared with their youngest, the boys in one tent where I was expecting to sleep, several tents for the men and a smaller number for the women. Until we were sure of how long we would be staying, there was no point in setting up something more permanent. I went over anticipating being given some instruction on my immediate responsibilities', but instead I was told.

"Tarku, could you please find Joseph and bring him along so we can have our evening meal together?"

As the shadows deepened and night approached, I located Joseph, and the two of us went over to our father's tent. We heard voices, so I called out softly, "Father we are here".

"Come in," he replied.

I was quite surprised to find Rachel already inside and seated opposite her husband. This tent was quite a bit smaller than the tent Jacob used in our campsite outside Haran, but it was still comfortably arranged. As there was no awning outside, it seemed that we would be eating inside, but the presence of Joseph's mother had me guessing. Clearly there was a very close bond of affection between the two as young Joseph went over and hugged his mother and then sat next to her, closely, holding her hand.

Jacob began, "We will be eating soon, but first I wanted to explain the purpose of this meeting, with my wife, my son and myself together with you Tarku. Yes, I know that our family is much bigger and includes all the boys, Dinah, and their mother Leah, but tonight our discussion is about this part of the family, and I want everyone involved to listen to what I have to say and to be given an opportunity for questions and discussions."

"You are the father my husband, so whatever you decide, we are in agreement", Rachel responded."

"I am more than happy to do whatever you require of me, father," was my response.

Joseph said nothing, simply staring at his father. Then began a rather long discourse from Jacob, recalling historical events, his relationship to Adonai, his love for Rachel, his great joy at the birth of Joseph, his dreams, and at the end, my future role in the lives of this small family unit.

"I wanted to share many things with you all," Jacob began. "Much of what I am about to say, you already know. Some of the things I'm going to share are deeply personal, but everything I talk about, and that we later discuss, is extremely important to me. Young Joseph, if I say anything that you do not understand, stop me, and ask me to explain," Jacob added to ensure Joseph's inclusion.

"Yes, father, but I'm not really that young anymore. I can even ride a horse and I know a lot of things about animals and our family history, gossip about our camp family, and everything that happens in our camp life," was Joseph's reply.

Smiling at this small outburst, my father continued, "very well, my son, I hear you, but just ask if you need to".

So followed a long narrative from Jacob, much of which I knew, but was possibly new to Joseph and even, maybe Rachel. "Now, first of all, maybe I don't need to say this, but I want to assure all of you here, that you are very important to me and are the main reason for everything I do. All my decisions are very influenced by the persons in this tent. That is not something that you should be talking about outside, you understand that? Joseph, that is not something you should be going around telling your brothers. I love them too, of course, but you are your mother's first-born son, and you know how much I love your mother'".

Nodding, Joseph responded, "Yes father."

"Let me now commence my narrative, starting with my grandfather, Abraham, may Adonai rest his soul. Adonai spoke to him and so he and his father Terah left Ur, way down in southern Mesopotamia, many years ago now, and travelled to Haran, where they stayed for several years. After Terah died, Abraham left part of his family in Haran and, together with his nephew, travelled south into Canaan. Adonai had made a covenant with him, promising that all the land of Canaan would be given to his family which, somewhere in the future, would number as the sand of the sea and the stars of the sky. This promise has been repeated to my father Isaac and more recently to me. I am still very unsure how all this is going to happen, but I am convinced that the God of Abraham and Isaac is my God, Adonai, and having so convincingly proven himself in protecting and blessing me and my family, I am absolutely assured that He is the one true and only God of Heaven and Earth.

Having said all of that, I need to add a little more to this history lesson. This is our ancient heritage, stretching back many generations. My great grandfather Terah's father was Nachor, his father was Peleg, his father was Shelah, his father was Arpachshad, his father was Shem, and his father was the great Noah of the flood. After Noah, our ancestors reach way back to Adam the first man, but we need not go into that detail. Enough to say, we have a very old and honoured lineage.

Now, let's come to the present and to our little family group here. Maybe you don't know about this side of my life, but over the past twenty years, I have had dreams, many dreams, and each time I hear Adonai directing me. Crazy you say? I thought I was going crazy the first time this happened. It was near the city of Luz. We will pass by there one day. I saw a staircase going all the way up to heaven and angelic figures moving up and down between heaven and earth.

Tarku knows about that dream as I have frequently shared that experience with him from long ago. However, since then, I have had more dreams and the most recent one was just before leaving our campsite near Haran. Adonai told me to leave and return to Canaan. That is the main reason why we left, quietly and in a hurry.

For me it was, unashamedly, an escape an exodus. I came to Haran possessing very little other than what my mother and father sent with me. I left with thousands of animals, hundreds of servants, and slaves, two wives and twelve children, and of course you Tarku. I must also add the faithful Ithai and his warriors. For twenty years I felt like a bond servant, and at times, in the early days, even like a slave, owned by your father Rachel and with very little appreciation. Laban was a heavy taskmaster and he demanded so much from me. But you know that. You have shared your feelings with me, as has your sister. Both of you have told me how you felt like property rather than daughters when your father bargained you away to me for fourteen year's labour. So, when Adonai told me to leave, it was with a great feeling of release, a sense of freedom and completely with His blessing, so I left.

Now here we are. We are in the land of Canaan. I know no one in this part of the land. The people are Ammonites, not too dissimilar to what we have become. In fact, I am related to them through my great uncle Lot but that was a long time ago. The two famous cities further north, which we avoided on our way down here are Ashtaroth-Karnaim and Edrei. The first one was captured by my grandfather Abraham during his fight with the 'Kings of the North' from Mesopotamia, but now exists independently and ruled by its own kings. They are Amorites and thus a different tribe, however, we shouldn't have any trouble with the people here as we have been traveling on the King's Highway which is generally protected by the rulers of the lands through which it passes because of the value of the trade it brings.

Nevertheless, avoiding any mention of my grandfather would probably be a good idea as we don't want anyone spreading rumours that could filter up to Ashtaroth and Edrei. They also have in their service the Rephaim, who are giants. The story I have heard is that some of the angels in heaven looked down on earth and seeing the beautiful women living here, came down and had children by them. They have become the giants, and kings all over Canaan are looking to hire them as their secret weapon of war. I'm just adding this because no one really knows the truth as it happened so long ago. There are the Rephaim and the Nephilim, and the Moabites call them Emim, while the Ammonites call them Zamzummim. What I do know is that they are real and that they are very big men and mighty warriors.

Now, however, my most formidable challenge is my brother Esau. For years I have agonised over my deceptions. When he came to me where I was cooking my special lentil recipe, simple, yet just a stew, he was hungry. My response was really a spur of the moment thing; give me your birth right! What was I thinking? He is the eldest and the birthright is his. What was I going to do with his birthright? Everyone knew that he was the first born, so my being given it clearly would have involved some form of trickery. Then there was the blessing. My mother, bless her, was so concerned about her husband's affairs, and here was her eldest son running around after Hittite women, feasting and hunting with people other than our own. Esau had no interest or even understanding of how to manage a livelihood based on several thousand animals. What was she to do? So, she plotted for me to steal my father's blessing. At the time, I thought it a good idea as I was virtually running most of the family's affairs anyway. But afterwards, the disappointment written all over my father's face when he challenged me, the betrayal, it was almost too much to bear. And over the years, my guilt has become even worse, even though I now have the assurance of Adonai's covenant. I need to make my peace with my brother."

"Father," Joseph interrupted, "how did you know your dreams came from Adonai? How did you know?"

"Because He told me". Was my father's simple reply.

"But how did you know it was Adonai and not just a voice or your imagination, or just a strange dream?" Joseph needed more assurance.

"Yes, I know what you are asking my son. It was a voice. A voice that was soft and gentle but with total authority, penetrating my whole being so that I knew it could be nothing else but from Adonai my God. It was a feeling of total assurance. I was raised to believe in Him and encouraged to pray to Him and so I knew of His existence, and I had heard of the many stories of how He had blessed both my father and grandfather. So, when I heard the voice, it was as if everything I had been told about the one true and only Most High God, Adonai, came together and I knew this was from Him. Why do you ask?" Now Jacob was curious.

Joseph further explained. "Father, I am embarrassed to tell anyone, but I know you will understand, I have strange dreams too. Most of them I forget, but I am left with a feeling that someone is trying to tell me something." This was a new revelation to all of us.

Jacob replied kindly, "Don't worry, Joseph, when you get a message that is important, you will remember it. But if you have doubts come and talk to me about it."

"My husband, I wanted to ask you, what if my father comes after you?" Rachel changed the subject but voiced her concern.

This caught father by surprise, "Why would he do that? We are a long way from Haran. He knows that everything I have, I have earned and is mine. Why would he travel so far south?"

"I just have a feeling, that's all," was Rachel's reply. But now I was curious.

Jacob continued, "So now, I have to deal with my brother, and I am not sure how he will react. I am sending some people, led by Ithai down to Seir where he has established his camp, and have asked him to come north and meet with me here. I am hoping he has forgotten and forgiven my past misdeeds, but I have to prepare for every possible outcome. I wanted you to understand the importance of this meeting so you will fully support my decisions, even if you think them strange.

Alright, I have been speaking for a long time, if there are any questions, please share them". As no one said anything, Jacob continued. "Otherwise, the last thing I want to say to you all is the role I have decided Tarku will play in all of this. Earlier, when you were born Joseph, I had asked Tarku to watch over you as a special big brother. Now, I am making it official in front of you and your mother. I am appointing Tarku to be your guardian in your day to day growing up as it relates to your education, your relationships with your brothers, all your training and with almost everything you do. I would like to get your opinions about that. Rachel, you first?'" My father really wanted an honest response from this his small but favourite family.

Rachel, bless her, provided her opinion, "I have always had a soft spot for Tarku and am completely in agreement with your decision, my husband."

My father turned to his son and said, "Good, now Joseph, how about you?"

"Of course, Father, you know I like Tarku, but does he have to follow me around all the time? Can I do stuff by myself?" A typical young boy's response.

Jacob explained, "No, I am sure he won't follow you all day every day, but just as long as you know that anytime you have a question or are troubled or need advice, I am here. However, because I am also frequently not around, you have Tarku, and in any really serious situations, like leaving the camp, or climbing a mountain, or even riding a horse, you must listen to what he tells you."

Joseph seemed a little relieved, "Yes Father."

Then abruptly, Jacob brought everything to a close with "Now let's eat."

While we were waiting for the food to arrive and the three of them were talking about family matters, I couldn't help but notice something new and fascinating about Rachel. Every time she looked at both Jacob as well as Joseph, her eyes would light up and her face would respond with a special lustre that I could only put down to a very deep love and adoration.

She was very beautiful, Rachel, with dark eyes over arched and outlined by fine eyebrows, a smooth and silky pale skin and long dark hair that cascaded over her shoulders. Her nature was gentle and the only time I ever heard her upset, was when she chastised her husband for not providing her with children. I know that, because I had overheard the conversation and later, Jacob had shared the hurt with me. Despite rumours of her jealousy towards her older sister, that was sheer gossip, because Rachel loved and respected her sister and admired the way she managed all the business of the camp. I must admit that at times I considered her physical condition as somewhat fragile. She was very unassuming and would often be there helping someone without their asking, simply because she saw a need. Apart from the great love Jacob had for Rachel, for me she has always been a very special person. The one word that most aptly embodies all that Rachel represents is the word 'love'. Her world evolved around the love for, and the love from the two most important men in her lives, Jacob, and Joseph. At the same time, it was her love for everyone around her, that so captured the hearts of our camp family. Every day, her presence and her nature and her acts of kindness spoke of loving, and caring, and helping.

Then there was Joseph. What a fine young lad he was turning out to be. He would be seven years old in a few days. Like his mother he had beautiful eyes and soft and fair skin, although tanned a gentle brown by his constant love of being out in the open. He was tall for his age, comparing him to other children, particularly those of Leah, in the camp. Physically, he was slender, perhaps wiry, but clearly strong. Already he had learnt to ride a horse and his skill with a sling, sword, and bow, given that he was only just seven, was impressive. Like his father, he was extremely curious and his search for knowledge was endless. In our lessons with Nabu-Ahh, he was almost always the first to ask a question or respond to the teacher's query. That was when his nickname was mostly used, by his brothers, during class and expressing something of a taunt, 'Ragil, the inquirer'.

During his younger years, Joseph was clearly a favourite among his brothers, but as he grew older and his search for trying to understand 'everything about everything' developed into almost an obsession, his popularity was transferred to their sister, Dinah, and his presence was more tolerated than actually sought. They considered him a bit of a know-all, which, unfortunately was true. He knew a lot about almost any subject one could think of. While this was something I and most adults could admire, it was not something that teenagers found amusing. The boys felt rather intimidated.

I should, however, qualify this as there were ten brothers and each one had some distinct character trait, so not everyone reacted with the same degree of animosity to their youngest brother's knowledge and intelligence. No, it wasn't exactly animosity, not at this stage. It was more akin to mocking him whenever he displayed his curiosity and knowledge. And whereas all the brothers were in some way or other actively involved in looking after their father's flocks and herds, Joseph tended to stay within the camp boundary or perhaps wander into the surrounding hills, strictly to observe nature, or admire the wonderful vistas from the top of a rise, always accompanied of course. Simeon and Levi were the most antagonistic, while Reuben attempted some protection and Judah would occasionally stand up for his little brother. The others simply went along with whoever seemed to be in charge of the situation. My role became more and more complex as the years went by, but for the present, I simply played the role of peacemaker and usually it worked.

Several days had passed, in fact seven, and I was sitting under a tree playing my lyre, when I saw some riders approaching. That was strange as most of them seemed to be riding camels and some on horseback, and they were clearly armed, so they weren't any of our own people, and they appeared in a hurry.

One rider, at the head of the group, which must have numbered around fifty, and riding a fine white Arabian stallion, drew closer and to my surprise, it was Laban, Jacob's uncle. What was he doing here, so far from home? I walked across to my father's tent and told him of this unexpected arrival. Jacob immediately walked out and straight across to his uncle who had, by this time dismounted.

"Welcome Uncle," he commenced, "what brings you so far south and without any notice of your coming? We would have prepared accommodation and food for you had we known".

With no attempt at responding to the friendly welcome, Laban burst out, "Where are my daughters, my grandchildren, and my gods? What have you done sneaking away like a thief and taking everything, I have ever given you? What have you to say for your utterly disgraceful behaviour?"

These were fighting words, and I could see a movement behind the tents where Ithai was gathering a few of our warriors and others skilled in defence, readying for a possible fight. I'm not sure where my father found his restraint, but he bowed towards Laban and invited him into his tent, calling for Ithai and myself to accompany him.

Calmly, Jacob, showing considerable restraint, added, "Please uncle, let's not be hasty in our accusations. Kindly enter my home and be seated and rest yourself. Let me offer you some refreshment after your long and tiring journey and let's discuss what you have to say in a manner befitting the close relationship I have with you as your son-in-law through both your daughters."

He beckoned to his uncle while also making it clear that we should now behave as respectful hosts to his men, still seated on their animals. Djoser and some of the other senior members of the camp moved forward to invite the mounted arrivals to leave their animals in the hands of the servants ready and waiting to be of assistance, and to accompany them to several awnings where they could rest and be served a variety of fare, which given the short notice, would have been water, wine, and fruits.

I, along with Ithai walked behind my father and his uncle into the tent and sat down wondering what would be the next explosive accusation? Laban had obviously worked himself into a rage during the many days it had taken him to travel down to Gilead. His face was puffed up, and at normal times it was not the most pleasant of features resulting from his affluent lifestyle, but today it was decidedly red and ugly.

We all sat, Jacob on one side of the central table and Laban the other. Ithai and I sat closer to the tent opening. My father offered his uncle a cup of wine, possible hoping it would tone down the level of aggression. It was accepted and emptied almost in one gulp. Then he started again, though with a little more decorum, befitting the head of a noble family.

"Everything you have, has come from me and now you steal away as a thief in the night with my daughters and all of my family. If I had not been warned by your God to refrain from bringing you any harm, I would have ridden in here and wiped all of you off this mountain."

Although we would have been able to match him man for man and possibly even come out the winner, the surprise element would have been in his favour and much of our defence was out tending the flocks. However, my next surprise was from my father. His calm and respectful demeanour gone; it was his turn to demonstrate a pent-up anger that I knew had been brewing for twenty years. Also, buoyed by the assurance that Djoser had sent out messengers, while the women were taking care of the men under the awnings, and within a short time the full contingent of our armed forces would have arrived and surrounded the camp, Jacob literally let his frustrations free in the most eloquent, but deeply bitter choice of words and feelings.

"First of all, Uncle, you arrived here having ridden as fast as you can for weeks, totally convinced that I had stolen your family and your flocks and your gods, and without any notion of propriety befitting a man of your station, in front of all of my people and your own assembly of men, you have accused me of crimes that clearly you had imagined according to a logic that goes beyond any reasonable understanding."

Looking straight into Laban's eyes, Jacob, fuelled with memories he had thought buried, proceeded, "Now let me tell you a few facts that you may have clearly overlooked, and I will try and behave more as a respectful son-in-law than you have as a father-in-law, although given your current behaviour, I doubt I will find that to be much of a challenge."

Jacob was extremely angry. A very deep anger that welled up and hovered over everyone seated within that space. It was like a storm cloud that had been brooding, dark and threatening, for a long time, until, given this lightning strike of Laban's accusations, burst its full fury of thunder and rain, and all those years of slavery and exploitation tumbled out in a rage that even the red-faced uncle could not confront.

We have some very colourful expletives in the languages of our part of the world, borrowed and shared among many cultures. Given his years of torment, I could not blame my father for using a few of the most outrageous, but I have to admit they were absolutely called for and appropriate for the occasion. They totally expressed the issues that he was addressing. However, I won't share them.

Jacob continued, "I came to you as a nephew asking for help and also seeking a bride. I fell in love with your youngest daughter, and we sealed a bargain of seven years as a bride price. Instead, you exploited me for fourteen years and forced me to marry both of your daughters as if they were cattle ready to be purchased. That was disgusting. I have worked for you for twenty years and not once have I ever stolen from you. We had an agreement about the flocks. You would keep the unblemished ones and I would keep the speckled, spotted, and striped. But when you made this agreement, you took all the pure and healthy unblemished stock with you leaving me with only the very weakest and marked animals. As you are very aware, Adonai has been blessing me and He made sure that I could raise a large and healthy flock, while His sense of justice rebounded against you and your flocks became weak.

I worked fourteen years for your two daughters. Tell me, ask your neighbours, was that a fair bride price according to the rules that govern your lands? What about the gold and jewellery I gave you as a bride price, right at the beginning? Did you ever take that into consideration when you made a bargain with me for your daughters? Never have I stolen from you, not once. Even when wild animals ravaged your flocks, I was the one who made recompense. The fact is, you have become a wealthy man because of me, but you were too ashamed to let your shepherd nephew anywhere near your exclusive friends in Haran. Everyone knows that, and even your friends have seen through your deceit and your robbery from a close relative, not to mention the despicable sale of your daughters. I am very well informed and the fame and reputation you think you have in Haran is simply an empty shell. Behind your back, they all talk about your meanness, greed and beyond contemptible behaviour.

As to your gods, why would I ever consider stealing them as they are simply man-made idols of metals and wood and clay. They are no gods. It was not they who helped you become wealthy. They have utterly no value to me whatsoever. If you find anyone here in my camp who has stolen them, that person will immediately be put to death because of bringing such shame to my family and my people. Search as you will. Look everywhere to your heart's content and then be gone. And by the way, if you had any thought of violence against me or any of my people, you would find that your men are surrounded, and it would only take a nod from me before you would all be totally annihilated. Trust me, we have the ways and the means".

I think we all drew a very deep breath expressing both admiration and relief. Now, almost without moving, we awaited Laban's response. Halfway through my father's tirade, his head had dropped, and it was obvious, the words had struck a real chord. He looked cowed.

All he could say was, "Your words have penetrated deep within me, and I am feeling very hurt.

Hurt? He should have been grovelling!

Laban went on, "As I mentioned earlier, your God warned me not to do you any harm and so I have come to you to seek a peaceful reconciliation and an agreement that neither of us would do the other any harm in the years to come."

Peace and reconciliation, that was a far cry from the aggression with which he stormed into the camp.

"Let us make a pact and hold a feast and build a site of remembrance for all to bear witness to our agreement of peaceful coexistence," were his final words.

So, the fight had been knocked out of Uncle Laban. What ensued was a combination of a ceremony to mark a parting of the ways, a sacrifice on an altar raised by Jacob, that honoured both the God of Jacob as well as Laban's commitment and then a rather low-key sort of a feast to celebrate the end of any animosity and to ensure that nothing violent would occur between them in the future. Why Laban thought any of Jacob's family would want to travel such a long way north to wreak vengeance, I couldn't imagine. But it allowed him to somewhat save face. As to the gods, they were nowhere to be found. I later found out that it had been Rachel who had stolen them and when her father entered her tent, she had placed them in the bags of a saddle and had sat there protesting that it had been her time of the month so she could not stand. Clever lady. Actually, I found it quite ironic, that the gods of Laban were ostensibly being protected by a woman's menstrual cycle. Seemingly, quite a scene of absolute humiliation for Laban's gods to have to endure.

But in the end, the very next day, Jacob had demanded all idols be brought out, which was done discreetly, at night, all placed in one pile and by the morning, they had all been burnt and the ashes scattered on the stream beside our camp. That was the end of foreign gods among our extended family. Our people all gradually came to accepting Adonai as their God, not because they were forced to, but because it was clear that He was a God who was real and was playing such an important role in confirming His covenant through His multiple blessings to this family of Jacob and, in fact, to all who dwelt with him.

The pile of stones erected by Jacob, is still to be found at that site; I am told. The feast was simply a slightly expanded version of our normal evening meal with a few roasts, some stew, flat breads, and fruit. Then they were gone, and for the most part, forgotten. Meanwhile, a few days later, my father sent Ithai with a deputation to his brother Esau, asking for a meeting and offering his best wishes, hoping for peace after so many years had passed since his indiscretions.

Ithai returned after ten days with the good news that Esau seemed very amenable and would plan to travel north in the near future. Currently, he was busy establishing his camp in Seir which would require his attention for the next hundred days or so. This gave Jacob the opportunity to consolidate his own affairs and as one of the pressing elements was knowing exactly what he possessed, he sent Ithai, Djoser and myself out to make an inventory of the animals. Joseph begged to accompany us, and his father agreed as a special consideration to his having become a seven-year-old. So, the four of us left one mid-morning together with a couple of pack animals to carry our food and tents as we would be gone for several days. We all rode horses, Joseph mounted on a smaller, sturdy, and gentle pony, but he was very confident.

These few days alone, with just the four of us, must register as one of the happiest memories I have. It was a time where we all contributed to helping in any way we could. No servants, no one running around trying to please us, almost, I would imagine, like a campaign experience, without the violence. The weather turned out to be perfect, sunny days and cool refreshing evenings enjoyed around a blazing campfire. The scenery was impressive offering mountain landscapes splashed with the blossoms of late spring offering every possible variety or colour and aroma, and horizons boasting panoramic views stretching into the distance and beyond. The sunrises and sunsets were the most extravagant, decorating the sky with colours I had rarely seen; more than breath taking.

Every morning we would break camp just prior to the sun rising. A quick breaking of the fast, with flat breads and cheese washed down with fresh water from nearby creeks, or from wineskins we had filled with water from our own fresh Jabbok tributary. The size of Jacob's flocks and herds was such that several valleys were required to adequately feed them, so first of all we had to locate them and then we had to use the shepherds and herders to help count them. We usually shared lunch with these wonderful, friendly, and accommodating men. They were so uncomplicated, loved their jobs and treasured their lifestyle. They had also refined the art of living off the land. They could trap small animals such as hare, quail, and wildfowl. They understood the rivers and creeks as a resource for catfish, carp, and eels. The vegetation everywhere offered herbs, wild carrots, onions, and garlic as well as berries and nuts. Nature could be very kind if you understood it, and the shepherds had become experts. We thoroughly enjoyed participating in the bounty they had to offer.

By early evening of the first day, we had collected the information required, so after a final rural feast around a campfire, we moved on halfway to our next destination. Making full use of the slightly extended daylight offered by the approaching summer, we finally stopped and set up camp. We generally felt more relaxed being among our foursome for the night.

Only once did we have a brief encounter with the really wild. It was the morning of the next to last day. The landscape was, as usual, breathtaking. The early morning sun just bursting its light over the eastern mountains. After a short and very light breaking of our fast, we were all feeling quite confident of a peaceful and productive day. Ithai was leading, Joseph at the rear, when, for some reason or other his pony decided to stray into a break in the otherwise smooth hillside. It was almost like a cut away into a secret open cavern.

Unfortunately, the secret was not so secret because it had already been occupied, by a mother bear and her two almost fully grown cubs; a very formidable force especially when they were hungry. Joseph's pony reared up, spilling him onto the ground and then sped off, leaving him stranded. His shriek for help alerted us, and we raced back to observe a totally confronting scene of this little boy, grounded and helpless, with three large bears facing off within twenty cubits. It was a seriously precarious scenario. Jacob's favourite son threatened by three very large animals capable of considerable injury and driven by their code of survival. Ithai reacted almost instinctively, and whilst talking calmly to Joseph, who was clearly terrified, climbed off his horse, and edged slowly in the direction of the fallen boy. Meanwhile, he exhibited everything he could to avoid showing any aggression towards the animals, who seemed equally as surprised as we were.

His calm voice not showing any strain, although internally he must have been enormously worried, "Stay calm Joseph, keep absolutely still, I am coming for you. Don't scream or yell or make any noise or you'll frighten the animals, and they may attack. All will be well. Just stay calm and still. I'll be by your side in just a short time. I'm almost there. Don't move anything. Just stay still. Remain calm and don't move, I'm very close to you now. When I arrive, keep sitting and not moving. I'll talk softly to you and tell you what to do. Do not worry, all will be well."

It seemed like an eternity, a supremely dramatic scene, acted out in slow motion, as Ithai gradually approached Joseph. Poor boy, maybe his terror had acted in his favour as he did not budge a muscle. Moving slowly, cubit by cubit, Ithai eventually reached Joseph, then very slowly, and making sure not to make eye contact with any of the bears, he lifted him up and placed him behind immediately at his back. Then explaining what they were going to do, the two of them slowly walked backwards, still not looking at the animals, until they were close to the horses, when Ithai calmly lifted Joseph up behind the saddle, climbed up in front of him, and telling him to hang on, turned the horse around and coaxed it to walk away gently without any sudden movements.

We were a little further distant away, so could only watch as everything unfolded and, amazingly, at no time did the bears seem threatened. They simply stared curiously at these strange creatures that had entered their space. My heart was in my mouth. It was the most stressful experience of my life to that moment. I was petrified, but at the same time in absolute awe at how Ithai was handling the situation. At that moment, I firmly resolved to always trust him with my life were any similar situation to arise in my future. Djoser, meanwhile, had taken his bow from the side of his saddle where it was attached for easy access, and had an arrow poised and ready in the case of any emergency. Watching this amazing scene, I simply could not believe the bears did not attack. Later, Ithai explained, that they would only attack if they felt threatened, so moving slowly and not looking into their eyes, was the key to calming them down and assuring them that they were safe.

We rode on, poor Joseph, I could see, was shivering with the aftereffects of shock. He simply clung to Ithai with his head buried into his back. But he had been very brave, another feature of his nature which would serve him well in the future.

The sun was almost directly overhead by the time we had arrived overlooking the valley where we would conduct our final animal count. Ithai had decided to make it a rest day, so we set up camp on a small but flat ridge overlooking the valley below. By this time, Joseph had recovered sufficiently to ride his own horse which we had found grazing nonchalantly a few hundred cubits from where it had panicked. No one spoke of the recent event until a fire was lit and, since a cool breeze was blowing up at this altitude, hence the need for warmth and Joseph was wrapped in a blanket as he was still shivering slightly. We were all sitting comfortably around it, waiting for the fresh flat breads baking on our clay griddle, when Joseph burst out,

"Ithai, uncle, thank you. You were so brave, and you saved my life."

This was the first time I had ever heard Joseph refer to Ithai as uncle.

'No, my young friend," Ithai replied, "you were the brave one. Anyone else your age or even older would have screamed and run, and of course the bears would have chased after you and they are much faster than any human. You have really impressed me today, Joseph. I can see that in your future, you will always remain calm even in the midst of very stressful situations. That is the way to be, because with a calm head, you can think and always consider your options for survival."

And that said, we changed the subject and talked about the weather, the beautiful landscape and we began our midday meal.

The day passed peacefully, Joseph turned into the tent and slept, while we simply rested or talked about how special the past few days had been. Apart from that interlude of fear, shock, and amazing rescue, we had all been privileged with the most peaceful, productive, and profitable few days and a closely shared camaraderie we could have ever hoped for. The task, which we had imagined would be routine and rather mundane, had actually indulged our senses in a totally unexpected series of stunning natural spectacles, enjoying tastes of nature both rich and varied.

Once again, we rose early, and following another day of counting, we were fortunate to have finished early, so, not far from home, we enjoyed a leisurely return, and well before sunset, we were back in our camp. We were also blessed with the satisfaction that we could return with a report of a very healthy and significant tally of animals belonging to Jacob and his family.

That evening, my father had planned a special meal for our group and an opportunity to share our findings. Leah and Rachel had also been invited and this time, an awning had been set up outside Jacob's tent, a fire lit in front, and everything organised for a very pleasant opportunity for recounting our adventures.

First the food., which included a variety of different roasted meats, several stews, tasty vegetables sourced from nature, similar to those we had eaten during our journey, a variety of breads and finally fruit. My father had opened a wineskin and although none of our group drank excessively, it was delicious and helped to mellow the occasion.

Then My father commenced the discussion by saying,

"I hear we have a special adventure to hear about as a start to our evening's entertainment. Who is going to do the honours?"

Ithai quickly spoke up,

"Brother Tarku was there watching everything from a safe distance, and as he has a gift for sharing the dramatic, why doesn't he proceed?"

I was reluctant, as the two real heroes were Ithai and Joseph, but I nodded and began the narrative. By the time I had reached the point where Ithai was edging towards Joseph with three large bears staring at them, Rachel could hardly contain herself. She was listening wide eyed and clutching the cushion below her, small gasps every now and then, adding to the tension to an atmosphere already tightly drawn. Leah listened calmly and at one stage at a particular point when Ithai was drawing close to Joseph and the bears were there, staring at the approaching humans, she put her arm around her sister, offering comfort and identifying with the trauma a mother would be feeling for her child in such extreme circumstances. The story ended with relieved laughter and clapping and telling the two heroes how brave they were, all proclaimed with another cup of wine.

Then it was Ithai's turn to report on the animal inventory. Without any embellishments, he got straight into the numbers. He had carried with him several small tablets of moist clay wrapped in softened goatskin to retain the moisture. Each valley we entered that was occupied with My father's animals, he would take one tablet, identify the valley, mark the results of the tally, and leave it out in the open to dry and so ensure the marks remained clear and intact. He now took out the tablets and, identifying each valley as he read, these were the results.

Ithai began, "Valley one: Five hundred sheep, made up of fifty males, four hundred and twenty females with twenty lambs which are just beginning to arrive; three hundred goats, made up of twenty male goats, two hundred and fifty females and thirty kids.

Valley two: Nine hundred sheep, made up of eighty males, seven hundred and ten females, and one hundred and ten lambs; four hundred goats, made up of sixty males, three hundred females, and forty kids.

Valley three: Seven hundred sheep, made up of fifty males, five hundred and forty females, and one hundred and ten lambs; eight hundred goats, made up of sixty males, six hundred and eighty females, and one hundred and forty kids.

Valley four: Twelve hundred sheep, made up of one hundred males, one thousand females and one hundred lambs; six hundred goats, made up of seventy males, six hundred females and thirty kids.

Valley five. Eleven hundred cattle, made up of twenty bulls and a thousand cows and eighty calves; three hundred camels, ten male and the two hundred females and eighty calves; one hundred donkeys made up of ten males and the remainder females, no offspring yet this season but it seems there could be over seventy.

We relied on the numbers given by the shepherds and herders as well as carrying out our own counting. Although it was rather difficult to be totally accurate, hence the numbers being presented were rounded off. It should be added that as we were speaking more animals were giving birth, so day by day the numbers were increasing.

He handed the tablets over to my father and then sat back, finally being able to relax, a job well done. The evening ended with more stories and a lot of laughter. It was good to be back with the family.

Jacob had decided that he would take some of his camp members and all of his family across the Jabbok River for the meeting with his brother. He had sent several of his trusted men ahead to report back when they saw Esau approaching. That would give him time to prepare.

A few days later a messenger entered the camp bringing the news that Esau would be arriving in a seven days' time and that he would meet Jacob and his family on the south side of the Jabbok River. He would be accompanied by four hundred men. Now that was unexpected, so adding to his normal degree of concern, Jacob put together a bold plan of action.

The camp would remain as it was, even though a temporary set up. A forward party would cross the river and set up a smaller, even more temporary camp which would be reasonably comfortable for a few days. It needed to include accommodation for Esau, an area where his small army of men could camp, if he decided to stay, but it was also essential that a kitchen be prepared for entertaining this very large group of people over several days. The area had been explored and a suitable site selected, so Ithai crossed with a large group of servants and most of his warriors, to erect and establish the facility. Jacob made it clear that he expected something well planned, impressive, and comfortable, albeit small in appearance. Nefertari went with him to oversee the kitchen and eating arrangements. Mzia accompanied her as an assistant. Between the two, they had to prepare food sufficient, as in feasting, for almost six hundred people. These days anywhere Nefertari went, Mzia would follow, it was a lovely relationship between two bonded souls, and they were always privileged to be given their own private tent. It made good sense to keep both the head cook and the doctor happy.

Within five days everything was ready, and so the crossing began. Most of the animals remained in the valleys, but Jacob had selected several droves of animals and their minders as gifts for his brother.

Two days prior to the anticipated arrival, everyone crossed, all of the family, except Jacob. He remained behind but never really explained why. Later he told us that he had misplaced some small but important items and needed to look for them. However, that night, something miraculous happened. As he explained to me several days later after his meeting with Esau.

"I know it looked like I was sending everyone across the river as potential lambs for the slaughter, but that was not my purpose. I don't know why, but I just felt that was the right way to go about this meeting. I think it must have been inspired by Adonai, because that night as I lay trying to sleep, but tortured by so many what if's, suddenly a man appeared from nowhere. He challenged me, and as if I was in a dream, I accepted and there we were, the two of us, wrestling throughout the night. It went on and on and on, never ending and I was determined not to surrender. Thoughts kept racing through my mind as we tossed and rolled around on the grass outside the tent. Who is this, why is he wrestling with me, what if he is an angel? Finally, when it seemed, we had come to an impasse and neither of us was going to win, the man struck my hip which dislocated. Then attempting to break free, he made an extra effort to leave because, as he said it had become close to daybreak, but I would not let him go. Stubbornly, I refused and finally, realising that this must have been a heavenly being, I demanded that he bless me before he left. He asked my name. I told him, and he replied, and this was really strange".

"From now on you will be called Israel, because you have shown your
strength to both God and man and have prevailed."
Genesis 32: 29

"So now, it seems I have a new name, but more importantly, I have a new blessing from Adonai my God."

The following day, Jacob crossed over and joined us and, not having heard the story of the wrestling match, I was concerned at his having received some impediment on his right leg as he was limping. Soon after he had crossed a horseman came galloping into the camp, jumping off his horse, he went straight to the main tent where father had settled himself.

'They are coming Adoni, there are hundreds of them, and all are warriors and well-armed. Most of them ride camels but at least fifty are on fine Arabian horses. They are a very disciplined and impressive group of men."

I'm not sure whether this man reporting what he had seen, himself not a warrior, could tell the difference between a well-armed warrior and a horseman with a sword? But his report should have been enough to send Jacob into a mild panic. Any other leader of a group of nomadic shepherds would certainly have reacted in some extreme form of dismay. However, I should have anticipated his reaction. I had forgotten the Jacob of so many adventures. So, as in every previous occasion, Jacob remained calm, very observant, waiting, and watching. Later he told me.

"Of course, I was terrified at hearing that my brother was coming to meet me along with four hundred armed warriors. I had a sizeable force made up of professional soldiers and backed up by another forty or fifty people trained in a variety of skills including archery and slings and spears. But my over-riding fear was the prospect of any killing at all, either he defeated me and killed me, or I defeated him and killed him. I did not want any loss of life. I remember my mother telling me, that had always been her fear after we had manipulated my father's blessing. That a conflict between us would end up with one of us dead.

My message to my brother had to be one that spoke very clearly of my intentions. I was not coming back to Canaan to claim the birthright I stole from him, and it was furthest from my mind that I expected him to respect the blessing given to me by our father. The present reality was, that Esau was my brother, my twin, and I was seeking his forgiveness by instructing my people to address him as my lord, his younger brother's lord. I realised that along with his forgiveness, I needed to make recompense for my failures and lack of judgment. Over the years, I had come to understand that while blood is all important in any relationship, restitution was an equally important element in assuring complete absolution and pardon.

My sending gifts of my flocks and herds in advance of our meeting was not simply to bribe him to forgive me. It was also a statement that I was not returning to claim an inheritance. I was demonstrating that I was now wealthy and did not need to make any claims on my inheritance. I hoped that my gift demonstrated to Esau, whom I was led to believe now had a better understanding of animals, that the ratio of female to male animals would mean a rapid increase in his flocks and herds.

It was so important for me to demonstrate a public repentance, to show anyone who knew or cared, that I was truly sorry for all my past and that my return to Canaan was in my own right as a wealthy man with a wonderful family. My stolen blessing, though in itself of great value, was of no account now because I had, not only the blessing passed down from my grandfather Abraham, but also a new covenant of my own. Adonai has promised to bless me and through my seed raise up a nation that would honour Him and serve him, more numerous than the sands of the sea.

Yes, I admit my fear. So, over several days prior to my move across the Jabbok, I spent time on my knees, worshipping Adonai, and reminding Him of His covenant with my forebears and, more recently, myself, regarding the promised land of Canaan, and His promise to be with me in all that I did and all that I had accrued. Then His angel appeared to me and after a night of struggle, He renewed Adonai's promise. I believed, and my fears vanished. I was confident that everything would be as Adonai had promised. I am fully assured that Adonai heard my plea and all I had to do was to continue the implementation of His plan".

So that is how it played out. Jacob arranged three droves of a variety of animals. Each drove in order as he had planned, then he arrayed his family with the maids, Bilhah and Zilpah and their children first, then Leah and her children next, and finally Rachel and Joseph. He sent off each drove one by one with strict instructions to explain that they were from Jacob and were gifts for his brother Esau, his lord.

The first drove consisted of: *Two hundred female goats and twenty males.* Genesis 32

The second drove consisted of: *Two hundred female sheep and twenty males.* Genesis 32

The third drove consisted of*: Thirty milk-camels and their colts, forty cows and ten bulls. Twenty female donkeys and ten colts.* Genesis 32

Finally, accompanied by his family, he approached Esau and his four hundred warriors. As he drew near to his brother, Jacob bowed down low, spread out his arms in an act of obeisance and waited for the result - a sword, or a hug.

I was standing back but close, and just in front of Ithai and his warriors who were positioned in case of the need for some kind of organised retreat. This was another occasion for holding our breath. I could see Rachel tightly clutching Joseph's hand, while Joseph was looking up at his mother not fully understanding what was happening and why she appeared so anxious. Then, to our immense surprise and unexpected delight, Esau simply grabbed his brother in a huge bear hug and lifted him off the ground. From behind, I could hear several audible sighs of relief, and even some pent-up laughter. It couldn't have been more perfect. Arm in arm they walked into the newly established camp and sat down in front of Jacob's tent which had been set up with every possible show of comfort and luxury in honour of an esteemed guest. The years of animosity and discord and all kinds of imagined revenge seemed to have been quite easily washed away in that single and extraordinary hug. The peace pact and reconciliation now began.

"Forgive me for everything I have done brother. Please accept my gifts as a token of my repentance." Jacob, humbled, asked for forgiveness.

Esau's response was. "No, my brother. I do not need your gifts. I have sufficient in my own lands in Seir."

"Brother, I insist". Jacob continued, explaining, "I have everything in abundance. Please accept my gifts to remind you of my regret and remorse. I have selected from the best of my stock, and they will increase and give you a multiplicity of the very best flocks and herds."

So, Esau accepted everything offered to him and that night the feasting and celebrations continued in earnest. Everyone was celebrating, many of our people purely out of relief and others rejoicing at the peace and accord that this meeting had accomplished. Ithai found some of his compatriot Philistines who had joined in service under Esau, Djoser even found some Egyptian mercenaries, so the two camps combined as one in a massive display of solidarity. I was so proud of Nefertari and Mzia, they had prepared a feast like no other and it was obvious from the slightly controlled but semi raucous expressions of delight from the well wined and dined soldiers, that the feast had scored complete success.

In a more subdued environment, sitting in a smaller group just outside Jacob's tent with a fire to warm them and servants coming and going offering a constant stream of delights, Esau was over generous in his lauding the excellence of his younger brother's kitchen. Jacob introduced his children, one by one, starting with Reuben the eldest and finishing with Joseph the youngest. I noticed Esau's keen eye observing Joseph. He made a small but, what I considered, very perceptive remark expressing his opinion that in this young man you have a winner.

I was privileged to be part of the smaller group of family and even introduced as eldest ward and bard of excellence. So, given that initiation, I had never been called the family bard before, I was expected to perform, which I did, in fact performing several numbers all resulting in encouraging applause. Then it was down to business.

The family was excused leaving Jacob, Esau, two of his trusted leaders, Ithai and myself. Jacob, opened the conversation,

"So, brother, what of our father?"

"He is well," Esau replied. "He has recovered from his blindness and now is actively involved, together with our mother, and our esteemed friend Baruch, managing a very prosperous establishment. I retain a camp next to our fathers but have moved my main home south and east to Seir, where I have now developed a profitable business trading between Egypt to the south and Mesopotamia to the north. We travel along the King's Highway, of which I know you are familiar, and we prosper. Our grandfather, Abraham created a warm and hospitable relationship with the ruler of Rekem and they have become major partners. So, we are doing well. Why don't you accompany me to our father's house and then possibly to Seir where we can live amicably together and mutually prosper. Let us leave tomorrow, together as a family reunited."

Jacob responded, "Brother, I am more than delighted that we have reestablished our family ties as brothers and am overjoyed at your invitation to accompany you to Beersheba to see our father and from thence to your establishment in Seir. I would pray your indulgence to allow me some time as we have many animals that will need sorting and preparing for a long journey. So, please indulge your younger brother and, allow me to bring my family in a more leisurely time frame."

With a show of reluctance, Esau agreed, so with a warm display of affection, he departed to a camp set up not far away, by his own people, which in a rustic and nomadic way was almost the equal of what Jacob had to offer.

Esau had done very well over the past twenty years, possibly with help from his father but also with various alliances including the Hittites as well as the Moabites and the Ammonites. Although, I sensed a degree of caution from my father towards the integrity of his brother, as it turned out, Esau had clearly demonstrated, what seemed, a genuine affection for his returning twin. That evening, I was invited to stay with my father, he had a lot on his mind, and I sensed that he wanted to share some of his feelings safely with someone he completely trusted.

"It's good to have you here Tarku, my son," my father Jacob opened the conversation. "With all that has been happening, we have had little time to share, just the two of us. As you can imagine, I am extremely relieved and thankful to Adonai for the successful outcomes firstly with my uncle and then, most recently, with my brother. In my own strength and wisdom, I could never have expected anything like this would have come true. As my uncle said, Adonai warned him in a dream not to harm me or my family. And now I have established peace with my brother who had every right to cause me harm. I am feeling truly blessed. Come, lets enjoy a cup of wine to celebrate."

The next morning, by the time I had risen, Esau and his company of warriors were gone. We rested for two days and then pulled up our temporary camp and moved back to the other side of the Jabbok. We had crossed an enormous hurdle, and the relief was written very clearly across my father's face. He walked with a limp now but with a far more confident gait. We were back in Canaan, Adonai had blessed him, prospered him, protected him and was now with him promising a very confident future. As for me, I was simply holding my breath wondering and awaiting his next decision.

CHAPTER SEVEN

SUCCOTH

"Jacob went on to Succoth, where he built himself a house and put-up shelters
for his cattle. That is why the place is called Succoth (shelters)".
Genesis 33: 17.

Over the past many days, we had been crowded with adventures, one after the next, and as far as everyone in our camp family was concerned, Master Jacob had achieved victory on every occasion. Firstly, there was the arduous trek down from Haran, which was accomplished without undue trauma, although we were almost attacked by a band of brigands. Then, there was the encounter with a furious Laban, where Jacob triumphed by transforming a raging uncle into a petitioning relative seeking to ensure no harm came to his family. Finally, despite his fears of retribution from his brother for past betrayals, instead, to everyone's astonishment, he discovered a warm and forgiving sibling, proving to be another positive step towards settling peacefully in the promised land of Cannan. I should, perhaps, also mention another achievement; the wrestling match where he overcame a Divine opponent and received a final blessing, along with the new name of 'Israel'. However, now the most pressing decision seemed to be; where were we going to next, and what new obstacles would we face?

Fortunately, we didn't have long to wait. The very next day, Jacob gathered all of our leadership, which included Leah, Rachel, Ithai, Nefertari, Mzia, Nabu-Ahh, the senior herdsman in charge of the larger animals, the senior shepherd overseeing the flocks, and myself. A few days earlier, Jacob had sent out the two senior animal caretakers along with Ithai to search the area for the best possible location suitable for a comfortable, defendable campsite, as well as offering adequate pasture for the animals. The current location was too close to the King's Highway, without seclusion and privacy. Additionally, the scattered nature of our flocks and herds made them vulnerable to wild animals and marauding gangs. By evening, the men had returned with the good news that a close-to-perfect site had been identified. It would meet all our needs and was reasonably nearby. So, the plan was to remain in our present location for the near future, while the new location was established. Then the move would be implemented in stages, commencing with the animals. To ensure its suitability, my father Jacob, Ithai and I went to the location, and, happily, it appeared tailor made for everything Jacob had asked for.

Situated on a ledge overlooking the Jordan River and backed by steep cliffs, the new site offered a multitude of options for the animals without their being too spread throughout various remote valleys. It was less than half a day's journey away, although as the Hoopoe flies it would have been simply half a morning's ride, but the track was very narrow and meant for either walking or riding an animal. So, for carts it became a very time-consuming experience. The position overlooked the famed Jordan valley, which stretched from the Kinneret Sea to the north all the way down to the Dead Sea.

Our location was somewhat south so, from the site, looking down river, we could actually see the Jabbok River and its confluence with the Jordan. Our southern border would be the Jabbok, with another valley forming our northern boundary. The area was flat, and beyond the ridge in front, the ground sloped gently down to the river below. My father was delighted, and we returned to our campsite already discussing plans on how to configure all our people, programs, and future potential in this beautiful setting. This was to be our permanent settlement for the foreseeable future. Further investigation revealed that there was a small settlement just upstream which went by the name of Succoth. Interestingly, while returning to our camp in Mahanaim, my father confirmed the reason for this choice of location for our first real home in Cannan.

"In case you are wondering Tarku, yes, I did have a dream and the message from my God, Adonai clearly pointed to establishing ourselves at this place called Succoth".

The following days involved planning, moving, and establishing what we hoped would be our perfect residence. The arrangement was to be quite similar to our site plan in Haran. The first structures to be erected were the food and meeting tents, which would be located in the centre of our camp. On the southern side of these large structures, and protected from the winds of the northern mountains, a series of awnings were set up under which an assortment of kitchen facilities had been arranged. To the east of this area, close to the cliff face, there was a crop of pine trees, locally called berosh. In front of these trees, the tents of Jacob, in the centre, and his two wives were pitched, with Leah's tent on the right and Rachel's on the left. I suspect this change had come as a suggestion from Rachel.

Immediately beside Leah's tent, three additional tents were set up for her sons. As they were growing up, it was considered appropriate to give them more space rather than having them all sleep together. Dinah still shared her mother's tent. Beyond the boy's tent, a line of tents formed a semicircle curving around to meet another semi-circle commencing at Rachel's tent. Between the tents of the single men, on the right and the single women on the left, there were tents for married families, some with children. On the outer sides of the new establishment, both to the right and the left, there were several tents housing the warriors. The bathroom facilities for Jacob, his wives, and now the boys were located within the clump of pines, while the bathrooms for the rest of the camp were yet to be arranged, possibly beside a small stream flowing into the Jabbok.

In addition, corrals were built to house the horses, donkeys, and camels while the flocks and herds were spread out below the campsite and along the Jordan valley. Anticipating the possibility of wild animals even down here in Canaan, a series of folds, similar to the ones in our Haran campsite were erected. Not having any reason to hurry, the entire process of setting up our new settlement and then moving was stretched out over many days. First to move were the animals, followed by the bulk of our servants, making it easier to complete the final touches with many hands conveniently on site. Our band of warriors, now numbering close to sixty, moved in small batches, ensuring everyone and everything was protected at all times. Finally, we the family moved out, leaving only various structures to be dismantled and brought across. Scattered throughout the Jordan valley and the adjacent ridges descending down towards the river, occasional clusters of gnarled olive trees gave the location a very special, serene, and peaceful ambiance hinting of many years of peace and tranquillity ahead.

Jacob became more deeply involved in organising the daily routine and responsibilities of camp life with Leah by his side. They began by individually consulting the senior members in charge of each activity and discussing their specific responsibilities. For example, Nefertari, accompanied by three cooks, planned a timetable for meals and suggested sources for food supplies. People could be sent to nearby Mahanaim on the King's Highway, or even the smaller settlement of Succoth to purchase flour, spices, vegetables, and fruit. Hunters were tasked with bringing in a selection of wild game and, of course, there was an abundance of meat from our own resources. Ithai and Djoser were responsible for creating a schedule for guard duty and training Jacob's sons and some of the other young men in the uses and handling of various weapons. The senior shepherd and herdsman were to explore the surrounding area for grazing possibilities, keeping in mind the need for sustainability. Jacob had decided that the older boys from twelve years and up would spend time with the shepherds and herdsmen to learn the necessary skills for animal oversight and care including the handling of dogs.

Nabu-Ahh was entrusted with teaching the boys, and even Dinah started participating in the lessons. The discussions included subjects and the timing of the lessons. Not all the lessons were to take place inside the tents. There was much to be learned from exploring nature, including studying the constellations at night. To their astonishment, the boys were to be taught cooking and healing arts as part of their program. Finally, Mzia was consulted regarding the medical well-being of the camp family. She had been assigned two assistants whom she was instructing, and most mornings they could be seen searching for herbs and medicinal plants in the trees and along creek beds.

This first stage in our journey into Canaan was to be a very important time for preparing all of our people. In particular, Jacob considered this a significant opportunity for teaching his sons everything they would need to know in preparation for the day when they were given specific roles in managing and building all that Jacob had initiated and developed. Not content with his present achievements and wealth, Jacob anticipated considerable growth in every aspect of his business; his animal husbandry, his trading, and, whenever the appropriate occasion presented itself; crops, and fruit. Apart from their more or less formal academics, inside and outside the tent of meeting, the boys were also assigned to periods of living with the shepherds and herders and acquiring the skills and knowledge for surviving in the open away from the comforts of home, while responsibly caring for the animals. Jacob also spent time with them, mostly in the fields, demonstrating efficient methods for breeding healthy animals. Joseph, while still too young to be participate fully, still learnt almost as much simply spending time with his father discussing everything relating to the family business.

With the older boys fully occupied in their various learning ventures, I was able to focus more on Joseph and established a close and trusting relationship with him. Sometimes, we accompanied Mzia's assistants as they explored forests and riverbanks, while at other times we visited the shepherds tending their flocks by the river to learn their fishing techniques. The nights held a special charm, as all the boys would gather around the edges of the fire listening intently to fascinating stories from their apkallu as they explored the heavens. Stories of gods and demons, mighty celestial battles, heroes and adoring maidens, love lost and re-discovered. He had an unending collection acquired through his experiences with many different cultures.

One morning, while the boys were attending their formal classes, I found myself sitting under my favourite tree – an old oak that was quite rare in our area. It held a special place in my heart as it reminded me of happy times in Haran and it was also a place of solitude where I could ponder so many incidents that had led up to our present and greatly appreciated home. It was a private and uninterrupted time of reflecting on Jacob's God, Adonai. I was pursuing my thoughts and feelings about a growing conviction that He must be the one and only true God, architect, and ruler of all the heavens and indeed of all of His creation. I was becoming a believer.

At that moment, a young man named Naran approached me and politely asked if he could join me. I gladly welcomed him, recalling a first encounter during our journey from Haran. Naran wasn't officially part of our group, but his story intrigued me. I refrained from mentioning him to Jacob because I understood his eagerness to be part of our liberation from the oppressive rule of Laban. Naran had the potential to become a valuable asset to our cause.

Naran's father had been employed by my father's uncle as an expert in the art of winemaking, including tasting, procurement, and production. Despite dedicating ten years of his life to this position, his wages had never increased, and he felt unappreciated for his expertise, loyalty, and hard work. During one of the feasts celebrating Laban's annual sheep shearing, a visiting businessman offered him a job opportunity. This individual had attended the festival with the intention of purchasing wool, but he was unimpressed with the quality of the fibre. However, he had been captivated by the exceptional quality of the wines served at the event. During a conversation with Naran's father, sensing his discontentment with his current employer, the businessmen offered him a considerably elevated position with better pay and working conditions. Ultimately, Naran's father made the difficult decision to accept the offer - difficult, because he was worried about Naran's future. So, on hearing that Jacob was planning to leave, he encouraged his son to leave by somehow embedding himself into the exodus caravan. However, he cautioned Naran not to reveal his true identity to Jacob until they had reached Canaan. Naran's first task, upon arrival, would be to locate a vineyard and present Jacob Master with an offer of developing an exclusive vineyard with the most excellent wines.

"How can I assist you Naran?' I inquired.

Naran explained, "Well, as you are aware of my situation from our previous conversations, my father advised me to find a vineyard once we reached this land. So, I've been walking all over and among the hills and valleys nearby Succoth as well as further afield. Just yesterday, I stumbled upon an abandoned vineyard not too far from here. Situated on the side of a mountain. It would take about half a day's walk to get there. Although it is overgrown. Some of the vines still bear fruit, and upon sampling them, I discovered that the quality is excellent. I enquired about the owner in Succoth and learned that he had passed away, with none of his relatives being interested in continuing the business. Therefore, I believe the family would be willing to sell the vineyard at a very reasonable price".

'That's fantastic news, but how does that involve me?' I responded.

"Could you please arrange a meeting for me with Master Jacob?" replied Naran.

Knowing the reputation of Naran's father, I was certain Jacob would be eager to explore this potential new venture. So, I agreed, and instructed Naran to meet me at this same spot that evening after the meal. Following his departure, I searched for my father but was informed that he had gone down to the river to inspect some animals. Consequently, I had to wait until the midday meal to speak to him. I finally found him, having concluded his meal, and sitting under the awning outside his tent. So, I approached him. As anticipated, he showed quite considerable enthusiasm to talk to Naran and discuss his proposal. Extremely pleased with myself, I could hardly wait to tell Naran the good news. We duly met, and I escorted him to my father's tent, where I remained at his request.

Jacob commenced the discussion, "So, Naran, I have heard your story, and while I generally don't encourage people to join my caravan within an invitation, I am familiar with your father and his reputation. If you possess even half of his talent, I would be very interested in exploring this new venture. Quality wines are always in high demand. However, how can you ensure that this abandoned vineyard will yield the results you clam?"

"Thank you Master. Of course, I cannot match my father's level of expertise, but he has imparted a great deal of his knowledge to me. I used to work alongside him when he served your uncle, albeit without pay. It was part of my education according to my uncle. I'm not entirely certain, but I have tasted two different grape varieties at this abandoned site, I am quite confident that one of them is called bogazkere, very popular in and around Haran, and especially popular for making excellent red wines. The other is known as assyrtiko, and it has the potential to yield a highly flavoured white wine. These were the names my father used and would reference when discussing his products with wine merchants".

Jacob interrupted, "At this stage, the names and types of vines are not of utmost importance to me, but are you certain that you can revive an abandoned vineyard? After all, the vines may have grown wild. If you can salvage the plants, how long will it take before we can taste the results?"

Naran explained, "I will require some assistance, perhaps two people, and we should be able to clean, prune and prepare the entire area within thirty to forty days. It's not an extensive vineyard, estimating at probably between eight hundred to a thousand plants. From my observations, most of the vines are likely around fifteen to twenty years old, the soil is ideal, and there is an ample water supply for irrigation. The condition of the trellises is less than ideal, and that will be our primary focus for regenerating the plants. I anticipate that we will be able to harvest some fruit by this time next year. Additionally, since there is a considerable amount of unplanted land, we can obtain cuttings from neighbouring vineyards or the marketplace in Shechem to expand the vineyard, possible reaching a capacity five times its current size. I would estimate being able to provide you with close to one hundred to two hundred wineskins shortly after another year. I would also anticipate that number to increase significantly in the second and third years".

Looking very pleased, Jacob concluded, "Very well, Naran. I will give you two years to produce your first wine. If you succeed, you will have a job for as long as you desire. Meanwhile, please arrange to identify the owners and schedule a meeting for me to visit them. I will pursue the purchase as enthusiastically as you obviously look forward to creating excellent wines. If there is anything you require, simply inform Tarku and he will make the necessary arrangements."

So, it was settled. Within a month, Jacob had managed to purchase the property, allocated three young men to work alongside Naran and we had our first winemaking venture off the ground.

Like the flowing of the Jordan below us, time sped fast, with season following season. The boys grew taller and stronger and had become accomplished in both the wielding of weapons as well as the rearing of animals. Our camp population had not increased dramatically, with our people probably numbering close to three hundred including, of course my father's family. What did multiply was the size of our flocks and herds which had increased two-fold, so newly hired persons were mainly allocated to that purpose. Some were hired and some were purchased in nearby slave markets, but once they had joined our family, the quality of life offered was so much better than any they had previously experienced, so they could always be trusted to remain loyal and honest. There was plenty of grazing available in the nearby valleys branching off from the Jordan and all along the riverbanks was considered common land. A series of sheepfolds and goat pens had been erected along the sides of the hills close by the camp and more towards the Jabbok where the animals would be brought in each evening. Each fold or pen could hold around three hundred to four hundred animals and also had a small hut built at its entrance for the shepherds or herders with three or four dogs allocated to each fold. Camels, donkeys, and cattle were brought into paddocks fenced with, rocks, branches, and thorn bushes but the horses, some donkeys and several camels were kept in corrals near the camp and used for carrying loads to and from the markets.

Four years passed, and it seemed like only yesterday that we had set up camp in this beautiful site that has felt more like home than anywhere else we had lived. Several of the boys were now in their mid to late teens, almost grown men and demonstrating a lot of confidence. Joseph had grown into a very handsome and knowledgeable adolescent young man, very mature although he could be somewhat susceptible at times, perhaps a little too trusting.

Jacob was now a very wealthy man in anybody's estimation. He has accumulated very large flocks and herds and because of the quality of the animals, is highly sought after by meat merchants as well as those operating commercial trading caravans, from all over the region. The camels and donkeys have all been trained for strength and obedience, essential elements when out in the open and faced with a serious range of natural elements such as, sand or rainstorms, lightning strikes, rocky mountain paths and torrential river crossings.

A more recent development has been his entry into the wine market. Naran has proven himself beyond expectations with his selection of premier wines. Although rather limited in quantity, he has excelled in quality, so the demand is far higher than supply which, of course allows Jacob to price his product accordingly. The vineyard at Succoth now operates with close to two thousand producing vines and another three thousand still maturing. The availability of a plentiful supply of both natural fertiliser from the animals, and water, together with all the manpower Naran has asked for, has ensured astonishing growth and productivity. As soon as a donkey caravan of wineskins hits the Shechem market, every item is sold within the morning hours with no one questioning the cost. In fact, Naran has been asking to purchase additional land nearby to further expand the vineyard. I'm sure that will happen.

Jacob's success has gradually led him into trading. As I have mentioned, his animals are in high demand both for meat as well as pack animals, his wine is the best in the region, thanks to Naran. He has resumed the annual arrival of a caravan from Beersheba with trade goods from Rekem and beyond. He returns the convoy with items from the north.

The central marketplace for all these activities is Shechem, perhaps a half a day's ride from our campsite. Despite the almost twenty-five years that had passed since his previous journey through the city, Jacob has not forgotten the shame and anger he experienced. However, for the present, this city is convenient, and no one has shown any interest in this newly arrived prosperous family from Haran. Our products are of the highest quality, and we have given no one any reason to distrust us as all our dealings have been honest and reliable.

While Succoth has proven to be a very comfortable resting place where my father has been able to consolidate both his family and his fortunes, the reality of market supply and demand has dictated the need to be closer to a marketing outlet. And what better place than Shechem, a bustling town that almost qualifies as a city, with a population of around three to four thousand. This city-state of Hivites, is ruled by a king and his family, along with a small but elite class of nobility who indulge in a luxurious lifestyle far beyond the reach of the average citizen. These self-indulged autocrats live within the city walls, protected by an additional inner walled suburb, on a slightly raised elevation, and overlooking the central marketplace.

Although not particularly popular due to the heavy taxes imposed on every business activity, whatever its size or composition, this small but exceptionally wealthy group of rulers does offer protection, so they are tolerated. The walled off section where they live, has its own guards whose sole purpose is to ensure the exclusivity and security of the palace and royal residences. The city, walled and ancient, dating back many generations like most city-states in Canaan, governs a rural area where most of its population earns its living by working on the land. Within the city walls, possibly only half the residents are Hivites, with the remainder consisting of entrepreneurs from almost every Canaanite tribe in the region.

A large marketplace dominates the centre, surrounded by numerous shops adorned with a fascinating array of goods. The trade of animals, however, takes place outside the city walls where, in addition to all the facilities offered within the city, numerous semi-permanent buildings have been erected, offering lodging, food, and whatever happens to be the latest in entertainment. The traffic in humans, carts and pack animals entering and leaving the city gates is constant during the day. This human flow lessens considerably at nightfall when the first watch begins, and the gates are finally shut once the middle watch comes on duty.

Jacob decided that, while retaining his campsite at Succoth, it would be convenient to purchase some land just outside Shechem mainly for storage, corrals, pens, and accommodation for those delegated to carry out his business. New business ventures would be his sole, concern, but ongoing contracts and supply linkages could be delegated.

As a result, he purchased a sufficiently large plot of land to accommodate a full-scale camp in case he decided to relocate from Succoth. The land also included storage facilities and corrals for animals. Additionally, he built a house, or rather a large hall, where he could entertain business associates and guests providing accommodation in rooms adjacent to the main facility. Kitchens were added, offering the finest foods and wines for his business partners.

Once everything was ready in our new facility outside Shechem, Jacob called all his immediate family and senior personnel to join him. The journey, with the women travelling in carts and the men on camels and horses, took just over half a day. Further down the Jordan, not far from our campsite, was a ford that animals and carts could cross, as long as it wasn't during the season of the snow melt from the north, at which time, the waters would rise significantly and make the crossing treacherous.

Once the family and their retinue had arrived and rested, they were all summoned to a far corner of the facility, where my father had built an altar using carefully selected uncut stones. A small semicircle of wooden benches had been prepared for everyone to be seated. Jacob began the ceremony by explaining that this was to be a dedication, an observance to consecrate everything he possessed, both here and in Succoth, to Adonai, the only true God who had blessed him with such abundance in family and wealth. An animal had been prepared for the ceremony and as the sun set, assisted by two attendants, the sacrifice took place. The attendees stood and raised their hands in thanks and worship to El Shaddai. Admittedly, not everyone had yet transferred their devotion to Adonai, but most were becoming convinced of His reality mainly because of His blessings. It was an exclusive event, restricted to family members and the senior people who worked for them, without any invitations extended to the local community. During the following days, most of those who had journeyed from Succoth, took the opportunity to explore the city and browse through its shops. For protection, they were accompanied by Ithai and several soldiers, serving as a visible sign that this family group was under a well-armed watchful care.

While the boys explored the variety of weapons on sale, the women enjoyed browsing through the various displays of fabrics and showed particular interest at those establishments who employed handloom weavers on site, offering customers the opportunity to design their very own textiles. Most common were the pit looms where a small trench had been dug and the loom was set within its walls, mostly at ground level. This afforded a cooler temperature for yarns being used, mostly cottons. The weaver sat on a cushion at the edge of the pit, with her feet touching the ground inside. This form of weaving was especially popular as it permitted some very detailed and intricate design favoured by the people of Canaan. Having satisfied their curiosities, everyone drifted towards the food stalls where each one selected a delicacy of either chicken or fish or wild deer, wrapped in a small bowl of palm leaves. Then happily consuming it using our fingers, we turned for home. Following visits over several successive days, it was finally time to return to our campsite in Succoth.

Understanding the significance of security, our new facility, at Shechem, was enclosed by a modest barrier. Its primary purpose was to safeguard the animals while also ensuring the safety of the inhabitants within its boundaries. The base was constructed with rough-cut stones, that stood at a height of two cubits. The stones were complemented by an additional two cubits of solid hewn logs, giving the impression of impermanence despite its inherent strength. To further enhance security, a group of fifteen trained warriors resided within the establishment. They diligently carried out their duties as sentinels, visibly demonstrating their presence to any observers. However, their role was not to pose a threat but rather to serve as a deterrent. What set our warriors apart from typical mercenaries, who often prioritised financial gain, was their integration into our extended camp family. This fostered an unwavering commitment to the collective safety of our group.

Our full complement of professional soldiers consisted of approximately sixty members, I was never really sure of how many we had as Ithai handled the comings and goings of our security. We had an additional hundred men and women who had received some training, mostly in archery, with some opting more for close combat, but who primarily served in various roles at the campsite, with the animals, or in other aspects of Jacob's business. Given the size of the Succoth establishment, which encompassed multiple valleys where the animals would graze, maintaining reliable protection was an essential requirement. Guards were stationed around the campsite, and patrols were mobilised to cover the numerous locations where the animals were kept. While security along the King's Highway was generally ensured, there were always risks from rogue robber gangs or opportunistic raids by smaller Kingdoms targeting vulnerable caravans and businesses.

A year after the establishment in Shechem began, my father made the decision to bring some of the older boys to live at the newly purchased and built facility outside the city. This was part of their training in the various aspects of the family business. Erecting additional tents was all that was required to manage their arrival. Jacob wanted his sons to live separately from the business area, as he preferred their learning experiences to be gradual and controlled. Djoser accompanied Reuven, Simeon, Levi, and Judah. Our site, located in a valley not far from Shechem, had its own spring, ensuring an abundant supply of fresh water. The daily routine now changed for these older siblings, and their father encouraged them to explore the city centre, markets, and other facilities together, and as a group, acquainting themselves with everything that transpired within the city walls. The guards at the main gates grew accustomed to their presence so much so that they almost considered them to be local residents.

Then, just before the occasion of Dinah turning fifteen, exactly two years after the four eldest boys had moved to Shechem, she begged her father to allow her to leave the safety of their campsite in Succoth and visit the annual harvest festivals held in and around the city. This was a significant request. As my father had only one daughter, her security was of a paramount concern. Perhaps due to the attention she received from her older brothers or her status as the sole girl in the family, Dinah had matured into a strikingly beautiful young woman, appearing older than her innocent fifteen years. My fathers' concerns were understandable. The harvest festivities could become raucous, and rightfully, he worried. However, Dinah's consistent pleading seemed to have eventually outweighed Jacob's apprehension, and eventually her father relented. Strict rules were imposed on her whereabouts and companions.

Accompanied by her mother Leah, two maidservants, Ithai, three warriors and myself, we set off for Shechem. Dinah and her mother and the maidservants rode in a bullock-drawn cart, while the rest of us rode horses. By midafternoon, we arrived at our destination, and the women were promptly guided to two tents – one for Dinah and her mother, and the other for the maids. I sought out the boys, who were pleasantly surprised and delighted by my arrival. They expressed concerns about Dinah being present during the celebrations, knowing how rowdy people could become. They were eager to greet their sister, but I informed them that she was resting so they decided they would wait and postpone their reunion until after she joined them for the evening meal.

The atmosphere was joyous and infectious as the boys competed to share stories of their experiences since they last saw Dinah. As always, she relished the attention, allocating ample time to each older brother and maintaining a harmonious chatter among the five of them. Whilst she displayed sensibilities when it came to talking about the festivities, I could sense Dinah's struggling to contain her excitement at being near such a renowned city, especially during its vibrant harvest celebrations. One thing all the boys emphasized repeatedly was her need for caution.

Almost as in chorus they declared, "Dinah, dear sister, do not venture into the city or its vicinity without us or without guards. People become unpredictable during this time of the year."

SHECHEM

*"Then the sons of Jacob entered over the dead bodies of those who had been slaughtered
and plundered the city in reprisals for defiling their sister, they took the cattle
and donkeys, end everything else; ... everything they owned. Their children and
wives they took captive, and they looted whatever was in the houses".*
Genesis 34: 27-29.

The following morning, after breaking our fast, and the boys had been allocated the task of taking some of the animals out to graze in a nearby valley, Dinah requested permission from her father to venture into the nearby fields to gather flowers. She along with the maids, intended to fashion garlands upon their return to the facility. Initially hesitant, my father eventually acquiesced but insisted that Dinah remain within sight of the front gate. Dinah agreed and the three of them gleefully scampered off to collect flowers, revelling in the carefree spirit that this whole new adventure was offering. Unaware of their escapade, I would have joined them had I known. Thus, the subsequent events are recounted from the perspective of the maids.

"Our reason for going into the fields was simply to gather flowers to bring back to the master's hall, where we would make them into garlands. Each of us, basket in hand, ran into the fields like little children, laughing and crying out with the freedom we felt. And we had almost filled them with a wonderful collection of beautiful colours. Then, realising we must have wandered around the corner from the gate, we were just about to return to within sight of the entrance as our mistress had promised, when a group of horsemen approached along the nearby road. We really didn't even notice them, and we just continued laughing and frolicking lost in our happy collecting. But then the men dismounted and approached us.

Mistress Dinah asked them what they were looking for, maybe she thought they were looking for the city which was over the hill and couldn't be seen. The men smiled and nodded and without saying anything, kept approaching. Maybe they were upset because our mistress had questioned them and all three of us started to become a quite nervous.

Then, suddenly, the three men seized each of us, with their leader attacking Mistress Dinah. We were savagely thrown to the ground and, muffling our screams with their rough hands forced themselves upon us. In a very short time, although to us it seemed like ages, it was over. The two men who had attacked us, chased us away. Our screams must have been heard all over and across to our camp.

We could see some guards come running towards us. Just then the leader of the group, jumped up on his horse placing Dinah in front of him, and rode past us. The other two men followed, all laughing and joking about their adventure, and riding back towards the city. We just kept running until we had entered the gates and then we collapsed; we were out of our minds. It was the most terrible thing".

Months later, when Dinah was finally able to recount the tragic event, she shared her story with me. Allow me to narrate it in her own words.

"I was totally in shock. I had no idea of what this man was trying to do to me, and then the pain, oh the pain, it was something I had never felt before. I was terrified. Once on the horse, I screamed only to have my mouth quickly covered with a cloth, I can still remember the smell, it possessed a very sharp perfume and was extremely unpleasant. My whole being heaved with the horror of this man and what he had done. He had invaded the most intimate parts of my being to which only I ever had access. No one else had ever been allowed there and I was horrified, disgusted and very, very angry.

The next memory I have is waking up in a dark room, all alone on a bed. I was terrified, unable to fathom what had truly transpired. It was all so far beyond my understanding. I longed for my mother, and I couldn't bear to contemplate my father's reaction. Despite my fear, my reaction to this totally shameful act upon my person started to grow beyond my fear into a deep and hateful anger. Whatever this outrage was, it should never have happened. Who was this man, and how dare he commit such an abhorrent act against me? I was only just fifteen. Then, my mind began to wander, pondering what had really occurred. Whatever it was, it was utterly unacceptable. And then came the pain. Perhaps until that point, shock had dulled my senses, but once the pain became apparent – an intense, relentless pain – it refused to subside. Finally, every ounce of my resistance crumbled, and I wept. I wept and I wept, deep, wrenching sobs born of pain, loneliness, anger, despair, and fear. I felt so afraid.

At that moment, I heard a noise, and with tears streaming down my face, I looked up to see the door opening, revealing an older woman and a young maid approaching. They seemed friendly and eager to help. I remained half-sitting, half lying, until they indicated that they had brought clean clothes and water to wash. Although reluctant to move in any direction, I recognised that changing my clothes and splashing water on my face might provide some respite and fortitude to address this overwhelming feeling of distress. They gave me something to drink, I was very reluctant to accept anything to eat or drink and I wasn't sure what it was. For some reason they wouldn't speak, but they indicated that it would help me sleep, so I understood it was to calm me down and I thought maybe it would help the pain, which was still there but had become dull, deep, and throbbing. I was still distraught and increasingly furious, but these two women were not the cause of my turmoil, so I allowed then to complete their tasks, understanding they were acting on the instructions of whoever ruled this house."

Let me interrupt Dinah here, to explain about communications within the land of Canaan. Language did in fact, pose frequent challenges in this region. Dinah had grown up learning the Aramean language of Haran, as well as her father's language. The Hivites had their own language, and each of the various kingdoms in Canaan had their distinct tongues, all sharing similarities being Canaanite, but nevertheless different in vocabulary, aspects of grammar and certainly in daily applications. However, the necessity of communication between these groups, particularly for trade, resulted in a fragmented combination of several Canaanite languages, forming a hybrid or simplified language. It was crude and unsophisticated, but it served as a means for people to communicate. Dinah possessed a limited understanding of this amalgamated version and attempted to use it to convey, at the least, her anger and her outrage. Using all the strength she could muster to tone down her expressions so as not to scare away these two helpful women, she asked about her whereabouts, and what would become of her. I will let her continue the story.

"I managed to explain that my name was Dinah. The two women responded with half-smiles and some nodding, prompting me to continue. My father is a wealthy businessman who resides in a valley nearby. They appeared to comprehend. Realizing the importance of conveying that he would be searching for me, I added.

"My father will be looking for me. He is very powerful, and he will be exceedingly angry".

At that point, the older women abruptly left the room. After a brief interval, she returned accompanied by an elaborately dressed older man, likely the landlord or an important figure. His first question was".

"What is your name? Who are you, and where do you come from?' I was uncertain whether to feel angry, distressed, fearful or a combination of all these emotions. I was also unsure how my answers would be received. Despite everything I was feeling, I decided that a simple truthful response was what these people were seeking, as it seems they were also confused about my being here".

"My name is Dinah. My father owns a large business facility in the nearby valley. He is very wealthy, and he will be extremely angry when he learns of what has happened to me. His name is Jacob, but some call him Israel. The look of horror that swept across the man's face was enough to indicate that what had transpired was likely unplanned, and the perpetrator was unaware of my identity.

He immediately left the room, returning a short while later accompanied by several elegantly dressed women. They approached me with a semblance of friendliness and a desire to help. Gently lifting me up, they practically carried me out of the room, down a corridor, up some stairs, and into a much larger luxuriously furnished room with an opulent bed and exquisite drapes adorning the space. From glimpses I caught of the building as I passed through, it resembled a palace of sorts. Someone entered with a tray of fruit, while others brought various dishes of food and some wine. It was obvious that someone in charge was in a state of uncertainty regarding what to do with me. However, I took solace in the hope that my response might lead to an eventual release. I drank some water and, in an attempt to alleviate the persistent pain, I consumed some wine – recognizable as having been supplied by my father. Then I laid down and tried to rest, hoping that sleep would provide a temporary escape from the overwhelming circumstances engulfing me".

Meanwhile, back at Jacob's establishment, the two maids stumbled in, helped by the guards who had run out hearing their cries of distress. They were dishevelled and hysterical. They were clearly traumatised, both by their own experiences as well as the abduction of their mistress whom they were supposed to be protecting. They blurted out the details of what had happened before collapsing. Leah was one of the first on the scene, with my father Jacob and myself close behind so we were broadly aware of what had happened. Nearby women came to help the maids into the safety of a tent, where they apparently lay down and passed out.

My father stood there staring out towards the direction of the city. His face reflecting a mixture of deep and unrestrained anger, distress, and an almost violent desire for revenge. It was a sight I will never forget. If the evil culprit had been within reach, my father would have willingly impaled him, using any weapon at hand – a stake, a sword, a spear – anything. Having heard a little more about the catastrophe from one of the guards, I simply stood there next to Leah, shocked beyond words, waiting silently by my father. I could both see and feel the enormous conflict he was experiencing. On the one hand his almost uncontrollable fury at what had occurred to his beloved daughter, while on the other hand the catastrophic significance of what had just occurred and the very urgent need to consider what he should do next.

He gestured me to join him and instructed someone to fetch Ithai and Djoser. My father, now known for his remarkable ability to control his emotions at a time if extreme stress, quickly composed himself. This attribute, I noticed, had also been passed down to his son Joseph. The five of us gathered around a table in his business hall, forming a small but intense group. One could almost feel the shared intensity of emotions. My father's degree of control and focus became even more evident as he determined the next course of action. I had been astounded on multiple occasions by his ability to devise a plan that, in hindsight, proved to be the best decision possible. This was another one of those occasions.

"Now listen the four of you". My father began. 'The individual who defiled my daughter is no other than the son of the ruler of Shechem. His name is Hamor, and his son is named after the city, Shechem. I purchased this land from him, so they know who I am. They could amass at least two hundred guards, potentially a small army, to wipe us out. I'm uncertain about the abduction, but I'm not waiting to find out. We must act swiftly and decisively, preparing for any threats that they might present.

Ithai and Tarku, you will ride to Succoth without delay. Inform our family of the events and assure them that I will follow as soon as I ascertain Hamor's intentions. Once you reach our campsite, gather all the camels, donkeys, and carts, and bring them back here. Leah, I know you would want to remain to find out about your daughter, but I really need you at our campsite. Start packing our belongings and have everything ready for a quick departure if the need arises. Continue living in the tents with the bare essentials and, let me remind you, it is essential that you maintain an appearance of calm and control. We don't want anyone panicking. Ithai, explain the situation to the senior shepherd and herdsman and have them prepare to head south along the Jordan valley. They must await my signal before commencing the journey. Additionally, assemble twenty-five of your warriors and return with them here. Now go quickly and be back by early tomorrow morning". Jacob's instructions were simple, clear, and concise.

"Djoser, you will assist me in alerting all of our guards to maintain an increased vigilance around the clock. If we find ourselves surrounded and under attack, create a diversionary counterattack from the other side of our facility and while the main body is distracted, I will lead the main group of our soldiers and armed staff into the city, we will try and kill the remaining guards and set the palaces on fire. It's a risky plan, but for now it will suffice. Meanwhile load our carts and animals with as much as they can carry and send them across to our campsite. The carts should remain there but should not be unpacked".

So, this was the plan, and we set off to execute it. Ithai and I riding horses and Leah onboard a camel. From this point forward, I will let Jacob continue with the story, as I was away and across the Jordan at the time.

Jacob continues. "While Djoser set off to organise our troops, station lookouts, and collect our pack animals and carts, I focused on mobilising our remaining personnel to pack up our establishment, and at the same time mentally preparing myself for the task of informing my four sons, who were still out grazing the sheep and goats.

We were able to locate six carts along with the bullocks to pull them, twelve camels, and several donkeys. With the exception of the guards and twenty to thirty individuals who had received various forms of weapons training (some of them women who were among our best archers) everyone else was mobilized to begin packing up our belongings. We quickly realised that we would need more carts to accommodate everything that we would want to take with us. It made sense to leave behind our animals such as sheep and goats and also the wineskins that had arrived recently and had not been taken to the city markets. These could be easily sold as we could always find enthusiastic buyers. I also planned to leave behind the tents and other infrastructure that were of lesser value and replaceable.

I then assigned Djoser, accompanied by six of our servants who were weapon's trained, to lead the carts and pack animals to the other side of the Jordan. Most of our remaining personnel went with them. We were now left with our body of defenders consisting of fifteen professional warriors together with at least twenty others who could actively help defend our premises. Whilst pitted against hundreds of trained guards, it may have seemed paltry, but we were expecting reinforcements the following morning. Djoser was to return as soon as possible together with an additional six warriors. Then, I sat down at the gates to gather myself and prepare to explain the tragedy to the boys. I knew their reaction would be extremely violent.

By late afternoon, there was still no sign of any activity from the city when the boys arrived. As they entered the gates and saw me sitting there, they immediately sensed something was seriously wrong".

'Where is our sister?' Levi asked.

'What happened? Where is Dinah?' Simeon inquired.

"I led them into the building, had them sit down, and then began telling them the tragic story, or at least as much as I knew about it. As expected, the boys were furious and demanded that we attack the city and destroy it; immediately. They were inconsolable for quite some time. I allowed them to vent their anger and then suggested they compose themselves, sit down, and consider what would be in the best interest for all of us at this point in time. I reminded them that the ruler of Shechem had hundreds of trained soldiers at his disposal, while we had no more than fifteen. I advised them to sleep on the situation and come up with a plan by the following morning. And so, reluctantly they retired to their tents, and we all slept a nervous few hours waiting and wondering.

Early the next morning, as dawn was breaking, Tarku, Ithai, and our additional twenty-five soldiers entered the camp. They looked exhausted, but I was greatly relieved to see them. Everyone was on high alert. Ithai had organised the newly arrived soldiers into shifts, ensuring that while some slept, others stood guard. Revolving our manpower like this, positioning them in varying and visible locations created an illusion of a larger force than we actually had. I was about to hand over responsibility to Ithai, when I received a warning about a group of horsemen approaching from the city. I called for Tarku and Ithai and waited for them at the gate. Deliberately, I chose not to inform the boys. The group consisted of around twenty individuals, including a few of Shechem's nobles and fifteen heavily armed soldiers. It was clear that they were a delegation, intending on displaying their strength. As they dismounted outside the gates, I hoped they would notice our strategically positioned guards".

The leader of the deputation began, "We come on behalf of our noble leader, King Hamor, seeking an audience with you. We have your daughter under our care. His son deeply regrets his actions, but now discovers that he has fallen in love with your daughter and wishes to marry her. What is your response?"

Jacob was incensed, I could see that, and while he understood the need for diplomacy given whom he was up against, I agreed with him that an expression of his outrage could put this arrogant individual on the defensive. "How dare you approach me with such audacity! Who are you to hold my daughter against her will? I recognize some of you as customers and am appalled by your actions. Have you no shame? That boy's regret means nothing when he should now be facing the fullest consequences for bringing such dishonour upon his family".

There seemed no limit to this person's affrontery. He was possibly a senior nobleman in the King's court, and he continued, "As we mentioned, King Hamor deeply regrets the situation. However, it appears that his son has developed genuine feelings for your daughter and desires to unite our families through this marriage. The families of Shechem and Israel could coexist, with your son's marrying our daughters and vice versa. We could become one mutually extended and favourably disposed family".

Jacob maintained his stance, "I have only one daughter, and your ruler's son violated her. You well know the laws of our land as adopted from those of Babylon. This act is punishable by death. What do you have to say for yourselves? Let us witness the execution of the culprit and that will be the end of it. Where is my daughter, and why are you keeping her captive?"

With a complete lack of sensitivity towards what had happened, and an expression that clearly demonstrated his total indifference to the feelings of a father, he went on, "Rest assured that your daughter is safe and being well cared for. We understand that she has developed her own affection for the son of our ruler and is content within the palace".

Jacob almost shouted back, "Are you out of your minds? She has only just turned fifteen, and after enduring such violent treatment as if she were an object of no value, you claim she wishes to remain in the company of her assailant? You people are disgusting".

Now this obnoxious person, whatever rank he held, commenced an unsubtle threat, "Please consider esteemed lord Jacob. That we are a formidable city with a substantial military. We have the power to take whatever we desire. We urge you to contemplate reason".

Maintaining an aggressive appeal to the law, my father retorted, "What do you deem as reasonable? Your ruler's son has committed a grave offence against my daughter, deserving nothing less than a death sentence. And now you threaten me with your insignificant army of would-be soldiers? Do you even know who I am? Are you aware that I have influential and powerful relatives in the north as well as the south who could amass armies capable of obliterating you all?"

Jacob later confided to me, "I knew I was bluffing, although they were unaware. I needed to buy time".

Now it was Jacob's turn to demand, "Convey to your King that I will meet him face to face tomorrow, where I will deliver my response. We will meet at this very spot by mid-morning. If a single hair of my daughters' head is harmed in any way, rest assured that I will personally hold each of you accountable".

Without uttering another word, they mounted their horses and departed.

That evening as we sat in the hall, Jacob told me, "I'm uncertain of the outcome and whether my threat had any real impact on them. They live behind very solid walls, and it would take a large armed force a very long time to overcome such a daunting challenge".

True. But nonetheless, my father possessed the means to hire a substantial force, although it would take time, and the city would not yield easily, and the Hivites had friends in the region who would come to their aid, and maybe by then we could all be dead anyway. This had become a very complex situation.

I remained there, sitting quietly, while my father, without saying anything else, continued deep in thought, considering all the possibilities and opportunities. The boys had approached him earlier. They had again fumed at not being present when the delegation had arrived and after explaining to them that the situation needed patience and tact and a plan, and over reacting could prove fatal for all of us, Jacob asked them whether they had come up with a recommendation?

Simeon was the spokesperson, "After a lot of discussion and thinking, we have come up with a compromise. Our initial plan was to contact Grandfather Isaac as well as Uncle Esau and request for them to hire an army or two and then to completely destroy the city. We realised that would be a very expensive option and that it would take a long time to accomplish, however, having more recently heard of the proposal for a wedding, we now suggest sanctioning the wedding on one condition: all the members of the King's household, including his nobles and the guards, must adhere to the God of Israel, Adonai's law, which requires the circumcision of all the males in Abraham's entire constituency. So, we will only agree if all the males of the king's household including the nobles as well as the guards, were to agree to this ceremony".

I had been resting at the time, so my father later related this totally unexpected and somewhat extraordinary suggestion on the part of his sons. He continued, "My immediate reaction was a big, "What?" And after a stunned silence while I was trying to absorb both this audacious proposal as well as to understand why the boy's had given in so easily, I looked at each of my sons to see if they were really serious. Personally, I had no desire to, in any way, become aligned with the king's family, and I seriously doubted that my God, Adonai would approve. Nevertheless, perhaps this arrangement could work, and it might even have paved the way for our family to eventually rule over the entire land. It was an excessively naïve thought, of course, but, at that moment, my desperation to protect my family had possibly dulled my reason, so I reluctantly agreed".

To our astonishment, King Hamor arrived the next day at the precise time Jacob had demanded. He remained mounted on his horse, which reinforced my suspicion that he felt he held the upper negotiating advantage. He possessed my daughter and all the required military strength. However, without my realising it then, his weakness lay in his son's genuine desire to marry Dinah and being his only son and his heir, the king would do anything to keep him happy.

We were all there, including the boys, who, with great effort, had managed to keep their anger under control. "What have you decided Jacob?" the King asked with almost a sneer on his lips. He was so arrogant.

He was surrounded by a group of his nobles, who whispered among themselves, expecting my father to capitulate. He glanced around, acknowledging their approval. Then Jacob spoke.

"Your majesty, your offer of peace between our two peoples is indeed generous".

I noticed the appearance of veiled grins on several gloating faces.

"However, according to our laws, ordained by our God, true harmony can only be achieved if all the males of your family undergo circumcision. Anything less, and we are prepared to give our lives for our faith and our God".

Instantly, complete silence descended over everyone present. The whispers and sneers ceased abruptly. While circumcision was not unheard of among various Canaanite tribes, some viewed it as barbaric and excruciatingly painful. If it wasn't such a serious situation, it could almost have been humorous. There was a chorus of clearing the throat and embarrassed coughs before King Hamor, with a face that had suddenly become seriously flushed and almost uncontrollably outraged, forced his reply.

"Let me consult with my nobles, and I will provide you with an answer by this same time tomorrow".

It was a temporary reprieve. The remainder of the day and the ensuing dark night weighed heavily on all of us. Sleep seemed remote. I was sharing a tent with my father and noticed how he tossed and turned, clearly wondering about the possible outcomes. Even if they agreed to our terms, how would he reconcile this decision with his God, Adonai?

Finally, day broke, and at the appointed time, Hamor appeared, now accompanied by a group of visibly despondent nobles. He uttered only a few words.

"We accept your terms. After our season of festivals, in two days' time, the required procedures will be carried out. All male members of my family and nobility will undergo circumcision, as per your terms".

"And your guards?' Jacob interjected.

"What?" from the King.

"And your guards, many of whom are officers from your family". My father insisted. There was a heavy silence and then, seemingly resigned to the grim fact, the King concluded.

"Alright, we agree, and your people can be witnesses that everything is carried out according to your requirements."

"Thank you, your majesty, and in recognition of our accord, I will gift you two hundred of my best wineskins to help you through your ordeal". Jacob was clearly delighted although trying very hard not to show it.

Without any further comment, Hamor wheeled his horse around and they all sped off, heads bowed and significantly humbled. I am sure he made a very pointed observation to his son of the degree to which he and everyone around him have grovelled on his behalf. Shechem's reply, according to one of the maids of the palace, who had overheard the conversation, and told me quite some time later, was of one of pure delight. He had very little shame and seemed willing that everyone around him should acquiesce to his wants whatever the cost. Such confidence and arrogance. All he had to say was.

"Yes father, I am grateful, but after all, I am your only son and your rightful heir".

The next two days was a hive of activity. Even if Dinah agreed, and I am very sure she wouldn't, father had decided that we would leave this place. He had brought over a large quantity of wineskins, the marketable livestock and had purchased many carts, ostensibly for the purpose of moving our campsite from Succoth to Shechem. However, under the cloak of darkness, he had been transferring every possible asset back to Succoth. Meanwhile, selling off every sheep and goat that would fetch a good price so there had been a steady stream of family traffic backwards and forwards between Succoth and our site at Shechem.

Then, on the day of the final harvest festival, father shared with me, "I can't help but mourn the loss of my dearest Dinah. I am praying that she wouldn't agree to marry that monster, perhaps a last-minute refusal. His arrogance and lack of any sense of decency, such as asking for my forgiveness and blessing, forewarns me that my daughter would only be feted as long as this beast felt attracted to her, after which she would be destined to a horrible life of neglect and loneliness. Daily and agonisingly on my bed, I pray for Adonai's blessing and intervention".

About noon, a rider rode in from Succoth, urgently seeking to deliver a message to Jacob from his beloved, Rachel. She asked that he immediately come to her as she was in pain and wanted to share something very important. Not knowing what it could be but being very apprehensive, as she had always been delicate, Jacob dropped everything, called Ithai and me, giving us a list of instructions, and then in the company of another cart load of possessions, left after sunset. Ithai and several soldiers accompanied him.

Even as Jacob departed, the plot, totally unbeknown to me, thickened significantly. This is how the plan, also totally concealed from Jacob, unfolded. The motivation and idea for the scheme came from Simeon and Levi; both thoroughly consumed by anger and seeking revenge for what had occurred. The actual details of the plan were devised by the experienced and wise Ithai. I cannot help but comment on the fact that Rachel's call for my father's presence could have possibly been divinely inspired. Otherwise, the plan might have ended in complete failure.

According to the agreement, a select group from our Shechem establishment would travel to the palace and oversee the circumcision operations for everyone involved. Ithai ensured that this contingent included some of his warriors. Simultaneously, the promised wineskins would be delivered. However, after successfully accompanying Jacob to his beloved Rachel, Ithai would return and bring a potion to add to the wineskins. This potion, crafted by Mzia, would not only alleviate pain but also induce sleep in those who consumed it; a special gift from the sons so bitterly grieved by the cruel fate inflicted on their sister.

While the people of Shechem were not particularly fond of the ruling elite, who imposed taxes without offering much in return, it was crucial that no commotion or protest arose from that direction. Hence, another shipment of wineskins was brought over from Succoth, surreptitiously, and while Jacob was distracted by Rachel's condition, also infused with a potent sleeping powder. These wineskins were to be sold to establishments serving food, lodging and entertainment. The stage was set.

On the day of the operations, my father's appointed supervisors entered the section of the city walled off from the commoners, to ensure that every male, be he royalty, nobility, or guard, received proper circumcision. They were accompanied by cart loads of wineskins labelled as medicine for the ailing males. Concurrently, a large quantity of wineskins appeared in the marketplaces and quickly found buyers from the hospitality sector of the city, inside and outside the walls. Everything was in place. This marked the second day of the conspiracy, and as night fell the vengeance-soaked plan moved forwards to its critical phase of execution. Being exactly that – execution.

Once the operations had been completed, and darkness descended over the city, all of those supervising left, except for Levi, Simeon, and four of our disguised warriors who had helped overseeing the painful ceremony. Since all the Hivite soldiers had undergone the operation, the guards on duty at the changeover for the middle watch, were eager to depart and partake of the gifted medicine. The incoming guards then closed the gates and retired to their beds in the guardhouse, also with a wineskin for comfort. Now was the moment for all the planning to reap its intended reward. Throughout the city, peace and silence prevailed, as if the entire population had imbibed Jacob's wines.

The guards at the gates were quickly despatched, and the gates swung open. Led by Ithai, forty trained and experienced warriors surged into the city alongside Reuben and Judah fuelled by their thirst for revenge. Everyone involved was driven by a deep and consuming anger at what had happened to their beloved Dinah and their immediate focus was to exact the harshest possible punishment on every male of that evil family. Several archers were positioned in strategic locations in front of the inner gates as well as beside the main entrance in case of attempted escape or interference. As we were entering, Ithai turned to me and commented.

"I'm sorry Tarku, this is not your scene, but we do need every sword. Once we are confident that we have control, I would like you to return to this courtyard and supervise the loading. We can't have everything simply thrown into the nearest cart. If you can ensure that chests of fine garments, tapestries, bed covers, various household ornaments, and finally weapons are all placed in specific carts, so we know the contents of each one when we arrive back at our campsite. All the boxes of jewellery and silver coins should be placed on camels and donkeys. Since this will also be the location of the city's treasury, I expect we will find gold bars. They should be carefully loaded and particularly guarded. I'm sure you know what I mean. From the start, we need to ensure a carefully controlled management of what happens at the conclusion of this gruesome ordeal".

I'm about to face a horrendous slaughter and Ithai was already arranging the booty? But I knew what he meant.

There was minimal screaming, as many of the wives had also partaken of my father's generous liquid gift and they offered little resistance. The two guards at the inside walled gate, writhing in pain from the operation, met a swift demise. Room by room, sleeping body by sleeping body, every male within the complex and including the guard quarters, tasted the sword blade. That is, until they reached the palace chambers. Simeon and Levi had specifically requested the privilege of enacting this special act of revenge. Once the royal rooms had been identified, the two brothers were notified and very soon arrived, swords dripping red in their hands.

The first room they entered was the king's chamber, where his chosen wife for that night was cowering in a corner. Assuring her that her life was not in any danger, Simeon plunged his sword into the over indulged and bloated body of the tormented soul. Racing to the next room, where Shechem lay sleeping, Levi gazed upon the sleeping cause of all the tragedy that was taking place, closed his eyes, and with a sigh of relief, drove his sword down, deep.

Time to seek out Dinah. Then, not far away, hearing the sobs of a familiar voice, Levi entered a room, and there she was – his sister. He rushed over, embracing her tightly, lifting her off her feet, and with great joy, assured her that she was safe. Passing her onto one of the senior soldiers, Levi instructed him to take care of her and to escort her out to one of the carriages, and to stand guard until he arrived.

Once all the males had been dealt with, the instructions were to gather all the women and children in the courtyard, under the threat of death if they screamed. Then, the remaining personnel from our facility, who had been prepared and were waiting at the gate, were brought in. After securing all possible carts, carriages, and pack animals, under my supervision, they loaded everything of value, including hidden treasures like gold bars and silver coinage, their location extracted from the chamber maids who had lived a lifetime of abuse and so had no real loyalty for their masters. The entire operation took not much longer than the time to walk between Jacob's facility and the city. None of our contingent had been killed, although there were a few injured. Some of the palace guards who had not gone to sleep put up an attempt at resistance, but between the pain and the potion they had little chance. Leaving behind trails of blood throughout the complex, our warriors accompanied by the four sons of Jacob escorted all the women and children out through the main gates and onto the road towards Succoth.

This part was going to be challenging, considering there must have been at least two hundred women and almost another eighty children. While ten carts had been made available for the women and another six for the children, initially these were loaded with the wives and younger children of those men who had met their untimely death, given that they were mostly still suffering from both shock and possibly the doctored wine. Throughout the journey the elderly and frail remained in the carts while the younger ones took turns walking. The road surface was a mixture of dirt, gravel and grass and the gradient principally downhill, so that made it somewhat easier. Unsurprisingly, the servants and slaves, although not totally sure of their future, responded much more positively, particularly the latter. Their lives within the palace walls had not been easy, so for many of them this was a walk towards a new kind of freedom.

In total, the captured caravan must have totalled around sixty carts, thirty of them loaded with the wealth of the palaces, ten carts with some of our people and the last of what we wanted to take from our campsite. Sixteen carts catered for the captive women and children. While several carriages and all the pack animals brought up the rear. It was a slow-moving line, that would stop every now and then allowing our servants who had prepared waterskins to slake the thirst of those walking. Somehow, everyone managed to complete the trek and by late-afternoon the following day, we had arrived at the Jordan, another rest and then a short walk-up hill and we were in our camp.

I rode a horse up front with the boys, while a smaller carriage carrying Dinah and her maids followed behind us. Ithai brought up the rear, ensuring that everyone's needs were taken care of, especially the women who were not accustomed to walking. According to the two primary instigators, Levi, and Simeon, this was supposed to be a triumphant entry, I'm not sure whether anyone was really feeling triumphant, rather more like an after-battle exhaustion. I must admit, I had some doubts about my father's reaction. His family had just conquered a major Canaanite city. What was going to happen in response from the immediate region with the historical links local cities had with each other? It was not something we wanted to dwell on too much as it could have been disastrous.

With all the commotion from a caravan of this size, we fully expected our father to emerge from his tent in absolute disbelief. So, his reaction didn't surprise me at all. Here we were, forty plus warriors covered in blood, his four eldest sons also stained with the aftermath of the slaughter, thirty carts filled with every conceivable luxury item, two hundred exhausted women and another eighty or so children, some crying others hanging onto their mothers' skirts. All in shock. Meanwhile, as we approached the campsite, Ithai had ridden to the front. I suggested that Dinah lead the entire procession into the camp, followed by Jacob's sons who, I must admit couldn't help beaming over their victory. Ithai looked decidedly uncertain. As it happened, my suggestion for Dinah to lead was exactly what was needed to dilute father's possible explosive reaction.

And then, there he was, our father, stepping out of his tent. Fortunately, the first person to catch his attention was Dinah, carefully descending from the carriage. That was enough; everything that followed was simply a very happy story to be told.

Our father rushed to his daughter, enveloping her in his arms and seeming to weep on her shoulder. Leah was right behind him, touching her, stroking her hair. Then turning to Ithai, my father, in a voice expressing his complete incredulity, asked.

"What is this? What have you done? What were you thinking?"

Ithai simply replied, "Master, forgive me, but we had no choice. Once the Hivites had recovered from their circumcision, they would have sought revenge and would have done exactly the same, if not worse, to us. Hamor was pure evil as was his son. All they wanted was to satisfy the greedy lust of Shechem. They would never have accepted us, shepherd nomads, as their family. After obtaining his bride, Hamor would have seen no reason to spare us from his shame and public disgrace. We would have all become victims, both in Shechem and also here in Succoth. At least we saved their women and children. I accept full responsibility my lord."

My father stood there, thinking, trying to absorb everything he saw before him, filling his mind with questions, doubts and so many new fears. Then he answered.

"Yes, of course, you're right, Ithai, my grief over the loss of my daughter clouded my senses. I should have anticipated a violent reaction from the Hivites and even had we left, they would have pursued us, that is clear to me now. What have we remaining in Shechem?"

"Nothing of any real value Master, other than the altar, the kitchens, some of the larger pieces of furniture and some soft hangings on the walls". Ithai replied. "I made sure everything of value was brought with us, and in addition we have the wealth of Shechem's nobility. We brought everything we could find; we have over thirty cart loads of bounty, and several of their finer carriages. We have been repaid for Dinah's disgrace".

But father could see the other side of our revenge, "No, Ithai, in that you are wrong. Nothing can bring back the shame and horror of what happened to Dinah, and now it seems the price has become the destruction of hundreds of lives, that is a very costly retribution. One atrocity has led to another, growing in volume and outrage. However, as you have said, we have also saved hundreds of our own lives, which is our first responsibility. I need to think. Please arrange everything that is necessary. Particularly look after these women and children. Sort them out into family groups. Separate the royals and nobles and the servants and slaves. But treat all of them equally. I will talk further in a little while, after I have collected my thoughts".

Kindly but firmly, all the captured women and children were guided into the meeting tents and instructed to sit down. Families were sorted and grouped together. Several additional tents were set up to offer some privacy and a place to sleep for the various groups that had been separated. Nefertari organised her cooks to put together some stews which they distributed along with flat breads. Then, ushering each group, nobility, servant, or slave, into the newly erected tents, everyone was encouraged to rest until well into the evening after which they would be told about their future. Finally, a gentle warning was given that if anyone attempted to escape, they would be subsequently tied and gagged and isolated, a very uncomfortable result they really should not wish for. Each of the tents were then guarded by several the soldiers who had remained behind in the camp while those who had been involved in the Shechem attack, were afforded time to refresh themselves, change their clothes, eat some food, and take some rest.

The weather was relatively mild and warm and within a short time almost everyone was asleep. I really felt for them. They had nothing to do with the shocking attack on Dinah. But they had to endure the unbelievable pain of watching their menfolk put to the sword; innocent or guilty. Every one of those men paid with the price of their lives because an arrogant young man, their future king, abused an innocent girl. What could it have been like, for these women and children to watch the slaughter of their husbands and fathers, without a word, and now to realise that their feted lifestyle, which used to be their expected daily norm, was very likely forever ended? Each had become just another captive among several hundred with a future that could bode slavery or even worse. That was sadly the reality of how events like this played out in our part of the world.

The four boys joined their brothers, still high with the excitement of this their life's most exciting adventure, sharing story after story of their escapade. I marvelled that these young men, having been involved in the most terrible slaughter, could so calmly continue with life as if it had all been just another day's experience. I suspect that reality would eventually set in and the dreams and mental images that would plague them within the near future would be something I would have to help them deal with.

Ithai, Djoser and myself, all indulged ourselves in washing off the effects of the last night's events. None of us were particularly hungry as we couldn't be as glib as the young men after experiencing what Ithai had rightly pointed out, was completely bloody and ruthless, but had to be done. To answer a question about my role, yes, I did participate, actively, though very reluctantly. Not that I disputed Ithai's decision for what had to be done. Nor did I see any alternative because once the king's son had committed such a terrible act, as my father pointed out, worthy of the death sentence, he had cast the dice of his and his family's fate.

But it was probably the most distasteful and hideous act in which I have ever, although reluctantly, taken part. Looking back to that event so many years ago, I have to say, what we did was so typical of the violence tragically common in our land of Canaan. It was harsh, it was brutal, and it was often so unfair. But for now, enough, I lay back shut my eyes and tried to forget for just a short time, while I sought some relief, hoping for sleep. One thing though I was sure of, was my complete confidence that Jacob would know exactly what to do. His was an amazing ability; one he would most likely attribute as a divine gift from Adonai. I tend to agree. But for now, sleep.

'Tarku, master is calling for us." It was Djoser. I roused myself, poured some water over my head from a basin just outside the tent and headed straight for my father's dwelling. A thousand thoughts swept through my brain. It was all well and good for Jacob to realise, as a result of all the spoils of the recent bloodbath, that he had become an incredibly wealthy man, but the challenge was to ensure that he was able to keep that wealth. Would there be a price on his head? Would armies around the region be after him and the treasure he stole? There was so much intermarriage between the royal families of city states that reinforced alliances, how was all this to play out? Within days, most of the cities of northern Canaan would be aware of what had happened.

I entered my father's tent and found Leah, Ithai, Djoser and, to my surprise, Joseph, already seated and waiting. I apologised for my delay and promptly sat down.

Jacob started immediately, "I'm sure you have all been wondering, what next? Well, a little while ago, I had an interesting visit from my youngest son who came to me with a proposal that I think you all should hear".

Could Joseph really have a proposal worthy of his father's consideration in this moment of crisis?

Jacob, then indicating to Joseph, encouraged him to explain. "Joseph, my son, please share with the others what you suggested to me earlier".

Joseph, looked up, half smiling, some would have considered precocious, but I knew it was simply a well-founded confidence. "Well, I was very surprised when you all came into the camp with so many people. They all looked so tired. Some of them could hardly walk. I felt so sad for the children. They were hanging onto their mother's skirts, and they looked so frightened. So many of them were the same age as me. And where were their fathers? I felt really sorry for them. So, once they had eaten, I wandered around and sat down with some of them and talked to them and told them how bad I felt for them. Then some of then told me their stories. What has happened is so terrible. It was totally unacceptable what they did to my sister, but she is still alive, and all of their fathers are dead. No, I am not saying you did the wrong thing because I just don't understand what happened. But I was thinking, if I was my father, what would I do now?

I do know this, that many of the ladies who are from rich families didn't start their lives in Shechem but came from the royal families of large cities in our north. I also know that many of the maids come from villages all around Shechem. I think that it would be a mistake for my father to keep all of these people because they do not belong with us. I think that we should find out where everyone came from and offer them the chance to return to their home cities and villages. We could give them some of the money we have or some of the jewels the ladies had, and that would make them happy and when they arrived in their cities or villages, they would say good things about us. That's all. That's what I wanted to say".

This from a boy not yet fifteen. I was quite astounded as was everyone in that tent.

Now Jacob took Joseph's suggestion and put it into action, "Leah, I would like you to take a few of our female staff with you, trusted and sensitive, like Nefertari and Mzia and interview all the women. Sort them out into family groups and identify the wives and concubines of Hamor, plus the various noble families. We need to know who the servants were and who were slaves. Treat everyone equally with kindness but we can only devise a plan once we understand everyone's identity.

Tarku, can you unload all the carts containing clothing? They should be in chests. Place them on the ground in an orderly fashion so they can be easily accessed. Also identify all the chests of jewels and bring them to me. Then unload all that has been collected in silver coinage and gold bars and place them in my tent. If you run out of room in my tent, store the remainder in the tents of Ithai and Leah. We need to count what we have.

Ithai, can you check on your soldiers, make sure any wounded have been taken care of. Check the carts with weapons so you know what we have gained. Rest your soldiers and those who were not involved in Shechem, have them all return to duty and surround the camp, as well as setting lookouts at the Jordan including the Kings Highway so we are alerted in case we have unwelcome visitors.

Djoser, advise the senior shepherd and herdsman to commence the movement of our flocks and herds down the Jordan river valley. If they arrive at the crossing adjacent to the city of Jericho, they should halt there and wait for us. Ensure that everyone relating to our animal husbandry accompany them and make sure those who have had weapons training are fully armed. I would estimate at least fifty to sixty men should be involved. Identify a dozen of our warriors to accompany them. That should afford sufficient security. However, let me know whether they will be sufficiently looked after in terms of security.

I am hoping that within two days we should be ready and prepared to break camp, and head south. Our journey will be along the King's Highway as we will have many carts that would not be suitable for the way through the Jordan Valley. Thank you everyone, let's get busy. We'll meet again tomorrow at daybreak".

That evening, as I lay, exhausted, emotionally as well as physically, something I'm sure we all were sharing, I pondered over the last few days; the bad news commencing with the defilement and abduction of Dinah and ending with a terrible massacre and capture. Then there was the good news. As we were leaving my father's tent, Jacob put his hand on my shoulder, drew me aside and whispered, and for the first time in a long while I saw a brief smile on his face,

'Rachel is going to have a baby'.

CHAPTER NINE

BENJAMIN

"God said to Jacob, 'Get up and go to Bethel and live there, and make there an
altar to God, who appeared to you when you fled Esau your brother".
Genesis 35: 1

The sun was gently rising over the Eastern mountains, my sleep had been both deep from exhaustion and troubled by the previous day's event, when I heard a soft call.

"Tarku, we have been called," it was Ithai.

Within a very short time, we were all once again gathered in Jacob's tent. He commenced with.

"Blessings on you all this morning, we have a lot to do and a very short time to do it in, so let's begin. Leah, can you tell me what you have discovered regarding the women and children we have in our keeping? This is a challenge we have to resolve as our first priority."

Leah began, "Yes, ba'ali, my husband. Let me commence with the most senior. The king had three wives. His senior wife is the younger sister of the king of Hazor, she had one son, Shechem, who was the cause of everything that has happened. The other two are much younger and are the daughters of noble families in Megiddo. Between them they have seven children. They also have around fifteen ladies in waiting all from the north, some with children of their own and some single. The king also had several concubines, the most significant are two sisters whose father was the legitimate heir to the throne in Shechem but he was ousted in a palace coup. He and his sons were banished and now live in Ashtaroth, while the two daughters were taken hostage as security against any further attempt to regain the throne by their father or brothers. They were then forced into becoming the king's mistresses. These also have several ladies in waiting. The remainder of the women who were married to the Shechem's nobles are from various northern Kingdoms, some as far away as Damascus. Most were marriages of convenience and alliances. In all, counting the wives, the ladies in waiting and their personal maids and slaves, there would be around one hundred and thirty women and more than sixty-five children. Without exception, they were hoping that they would be released to return safely to their relatives even if it required a ransom. The remainder of the women were mostly household servants, and a few were wives of the more senior officers of the guards.

My father sat quietly, thinking, and then commented.

"Of this number, how many of them are slaves and how many are servants?' He asked.

Leah continued, "They were rather reluctant to volunteer that information, however, one of the maids pointed out a group huddled together and very fearful for their future. There would have been around forty-five made up of very mixed origins. Apparently, many of the servants were local and only remained in the palaces during the day, so residential servants only numbered about a fifteen to twenty, the rest were slaves. So, in all there are about sixty women of noble birth including ladies in waiting; forty-five personal slaves; and fifteen personal maids who were residential.

A second group that had separated themselves from the elite of the palace, were the concubines of various nobles. These numbered almost forty and the majority came from a village or community within the city state's borders, so they are all Hivites. These were all young and several had at least one child with them. The remainder of the women, who had also separated themselves from the nobility, were servants or slaves working in various chores throughout the various palaces.

Once more, complete silence pervaded our group, as my father considered all the details before him. Finally, appearing to have made up his mind, he responded, smiling kindly and clearly impressed.

"Thank you, isha, my wife, this is what we will do, and you will need help in carrying out this task. Separate the noble women and any of the ladies in waiting who are from the north. Take them to some of the chests which I would ask Tarku to arrange in front of my tent and permit them to select garments suitable for themselves to travel in. Then permit them to identify their jewellery boxes and they can take one of their favourites, only one, and return to the group. Make sure they are held accountable to each other and that what they select is truly theirs. Permit the senior wife of Hamor to select three items. We will also give her an amount of silver and gold for her return to Hazor, so she does not arrive penniless. Any servants willing to accompany their mistresses north may also select some traveling clothes. Each servant will also be given a small purse of silver coins but do this discretely without their mistresses' knowledge otherwise they won't be keeping the purse for long.

As to the concubines and servants who remain, any of them wishing to return to their villages will be given a purse to allow them a resource with which to commence a new life. The others will be welcome to join our camp family. However, that will only occur once the caravan leaves for the north.

The slaves, all of them, will remain behind and in time we will determine what to do with them. Treat them kindly and allocate their number appropriately between the various tasks in our camp, including Nefertari, Mzia and yourself. Then prepare all those heading north for the journey along with food and water for the way.

Now, looking at Ithai, Jacob continued. "Ithai, I would like you to prepare three of the carriages, one for the senior wife and some of her ladies in waiting, a second for the sisters of the royals in Ashtaroth and some of their maids, the third for the most senior wives. The rest of the women and all the children will be loaded into carts with fifteen per cart. In the senior wife's carriage place a bag of silver coin, amounting to three thousand shekels and two gold ingots. In the carriage for the two sisters, place another two thousand shekels, plus two gold ingots, and in the third carriage place two thousand silver shekels. Each of the servants accompanying their mistresses are to be given a small bag of silver coins enough that they can hide them in their clothing. Our Matriarch Leah can help you with all of this. I would like all these women to have left our campsite by tomorrow mid-morning. We need time to prepare ourselves for our journey south and to put as much distance between us and the northern cities as possible. I am hoping that by sending their women back safely, along with an incentive of shekels, that this will be sufficient for the alienated royals to focus on reclaiming their throne rather than pursing us".

Then it was Djoser's turn. "Djoser, I would like you to select five reliable soldiers to accompany you as guards for this journey north. Also take with you several camels for the drivers to ride on their return. We will talk further about a strategy for your role in this plan and where and how to leave the carriages and carts once you reach Ashtaroth. Be prepared to leave with your men by midmorning tomorrow".

Then turning to Leah, Jacob inquired. "By the way, I have been meaning to ask you Leah my wife, how is Dinah? Although this sounded as an afterthought, I know it definitely wasn't.

Leah's response was short and rather sharp. "Dinah is suffering considerably. We have not told of her of the aftermath of her abduction because that would only increase her distress. What has happened is a tragedy encompassing both our family as well as that of the ruler of Shechem. I am convinced that it will also go down as one of the less memorable tales of this land, a tragedy of monumental proportions. My husband, I hold you totally accountable, although I do understand that the plot was beyond your control. Dinah is now in the hands of Zilpah, and we will spend all the time necessary to ease her back to normality. But thank you for asking."

Jacob bowed his head momentarily, not used to such strong words from his senior wife in public, and then continued. "Now go everyone. There is a lot to be done. It is important that we are not seen to be packing up our camp before the women leave for the north. Of course, some of that has already been completed. Despite all that has happened, please focus your minds on your tasks and ensure everything you are responsible for is ready for when we depart. It is essential that the women from Shechem do not become aware of our plans. Tarku, would you please remain behind for a short while." Jacob concluded his instructions, nodding and smiling as people departed.

I wondered whether my father had sat up all night putting this plan together. The last thing we needed was a group of elite women in our midst that would encourage rescue from the various city states from which they had originated. Sending them off via Ashtaroth would mean a rescue for the two sisters held as ransom and should provide some level of incentive for that family to focus on reclaiming their throne. The gold and silver accompanying the carriages would help in re-establishing the women in their home cities. How it was used or distributed was in their hands and as they had all been living in the palaces as one extended family, I'm sure there would be some level of equity and accord. Timing seemed to be of extreme importance. I hoped that Djoser, and his soldiers would be sufficient to look after that many women and children, but then again there were the drivers who would also have been weapons trained. I'm sure my father would work out a realistic plan for delivering everyone safely while allowing Djoser and his men to escape any possible repercussions. Ashtaroth was at least two days journey, three if Djoser initiated further delays.

"Right then Tarku, about the gold and silver", was father's first comment as the others left.

I did not have time for an accurate count, but there were six camel loads of gold bars, taken from the King's treasury, and twenty-five donkey loads of silver shekels. So, I estimated around twenty talents of gold and thirty talents of silver. But that is a very rough estimate based on talking to our wiseman, Nabu-Ahh. Apart from the ingots and the coinage, there are several carts in which are an assortment of items made from gold and silver like candelabra, plates, dishes, and goblets, not to mention the jewellery. These have also been unloaded and I have stored them in a separate tent as the volume was so great. I have arranged for guards to be placed in front of each of the tents as extra precaution".

Jacob commented, 'That's a lot of gold and silver. On the morning of our departure south, I would like you to organise for the gold and silver to be loaded onto the backs of the camels. Assign a trustworthy herdsman to lead each camel and talk to Ithai to allocate a soldier to ride alongside each of the animals. That wealth will help us reestablish ourselves once we arrive at our final destination in Canaan. Thank you Tarku, I know this has been particularly stressful for you. Your prime responsibility was to look after Joseph and then help with the other boys and here you are, a warrior, a minder, an accountant, my loyal assistant, our family bard, and my eldest son. Thank you. The next few days will determine our success or failure, but I am confident that Adonai will continue to bless us, protect us, and guide us to where he has planned for us to settle."

I left, wondering what else was going through his mind? So much to think about, so much to plan, so much still to organise. As I exited his tent, I turned and asked. "How is Rachel?"

He looked up and smiling said, "She is doing well, but needs the rest. She is quite far along in her pregnancy. She didn't want to tell me until she was sure that she would keep the baby, so we have to look after her as the child could arrive at any time. She will have to ride in one of the carriages we brought from Shechem, and her sister can ride with her. I am so glad you added the carriages to the treasures we collected. They are much more comfortable and pulled by horses, offer a much gentler ride."

Indeed, I thought, if my father and the rest of our family managed to leave this place safely and put a few days between us and any potential pursuit, we should be able to cross the Jordan and reach the land of the Perizzites, who have a long-standing conflict with the Hivites and others further north. In fact, Jacob would depart from our Succoth sanctuary as a very wealthy man. However, while he might find happiness in having his only daughter back, it had come at a very high price to his self-esteem and his reputation. I am confident that Jacob would have never contemplated such a massacre, regardless of the justification. He has always upheld the sanctity of every human life.

Yes, I remember my father telling me about the curse he had laid against the king and his family those many years ago, but, as he further explained, this was invoked against them for a punishment to be meted out by his God, Adonai. The thought of administering a revenge of the magnitude that had recently taken place and, in particular, led by his own sons, would have been abhorrent to my father. I should also add that more than twenty-five years had passed since he swore that curse and now Jacob worshipped a just and merciful God, and he firmly believed that it was Adonai who would ultimately administer justice.

However, as I pondered over recent events, any solution other than what had taken place was beyond my imagination. Ithai was absolutely correct when he stated that, once the wedding had been achieved, Jacob and his kin and, indeed, the lives of every member of our camp family would have been forfeit, facing, most likely, cruel, and merciless deaths. This was a time when I really felt for my father, for sadly, in addition to all he had to deal with, he was confronted by a hostile Leah who holds him solely responsible for all that has occurred. I decided then and there that leadership of this nature was definitely not of my calling and I would do everything to avoid its temptations.

Meanwhile, Jacob has something far more pressing to consider: his beloved Rachel is very close to delivering their second child, and she will require a great deal of care. Other than leaving our campsite safely, nothing could be more important right now. We had never before planned or managed a caravan of this magnitude. As Jacob would say, 'we can only do our best and the rest is totally in the hands of my God, Adonai'.

The following morning, all those destined to travel north were gathered together. The carriages and carts were ready, food for the journey had been loaded onto the backs of several donkeys, so after everyone had satisfied the breaking of their fast, they were boarded in their respective vehicles and, guarded by our trusty Djoser, they departed.

Immediately they were out of sight, a feverish energy was released and everyone, having been programmed as to their specific responsibility, sprang into action. Tents were lowered and loaded. Many of the carts previously brought over from Shechem had been emptied and repacked more efficiently and in a more orderly fashion, so we knew where to locate anything we might need during our journey. Several carts were allocated for kitchen equipment, but much of the remaining items, unless they were too large, were packed onto the backs of animals of which we had an abundance.

Most of the concubines and maids who had been brought across from Shechem had enthusiastically accepted the offer of freedom and a purse of coins. In a change of plans, they had all left the previous evening. Some, however, expecting a less than enthusiastic welcome following the demise of the royal family and the end of the benevolence they had enjoyed from their relative's employment, decided to remain with Jacob's camp family.

Jacob's timetable had focused us on commencing our journey by noon. So, the cooks had prepared food packs for everyone as our objective was to arrive beside the eastern side of the Jordan across from Jericho by nightfall or soon after, however long it took. We were not stopping, except for one brief respite to stretch our legs and rest and water the animals. The plan was to cross the Jordan at first light and establish a temporary campsite where everyone could relax and recover.

Carts were available for everyone who could not ride. It was a tight squeeze, but the motivation and drive to leave this place, beautiful and much loved as it was, mobilised everyone and when all were on board, and every load was ready, a little after noon, we left with an enormous feeling of relief. All the boys, including Joseph, rode horses. Our security had been enhanced by another forty men who had proven their ability with weapons, not in the same league as our soldiers, but still an effective defence when called for. These, along with our corps of warrior's rode, in their case, mostly on camels. We also had, in addition, a group of thirty women who had become accomplished in the use of the bow and were always available if called upon.

With Jacob leading, our journey began on a small track leading from Succoth to Mahanaim, and eventually, veering southeast, it merged with the more substantial King's Highway. The initial leg of the exodus proved to be time-consuming, however, as we progressed, the route became smoother and faster. Centuries of travel along the highway linking Mesopotamia in the north to Egypt in the south had identified the most efficient terrain in terms of ease and gradient.

The convoy consisted of carriages carrying our beloved Matriarchs, Leah and Rachel, several senior and respected camp personnel such as Nefertari, Mzia and Nabu-Ahh, along with some of the older men and women. The carts followed, they seemed to go on forever and someone mentioned they had counted over one hundred. I thought that sounded somewhat exaggerated, but I do know there were many carts. Then came the animals carrying both personnel and possessions, in all making the entire procession a long and cumbersome affair.

Throughout the journey, Ithai rode up and down the column ensuring everything was safe and efficient. Any break downs or holdups could not be afforded given the urgency of our migration. No one looked back, and for the first portion of the journey, everyone remained very subdued and quiet.

Through the winding mountainous terrain, the convoy pushed ahead, determined to reach our destination, the Jordan River, and the ancient city of Jericho on the other side, as quickly as possible. The awe-inspiring natural beauty of the country provided a contrasting backdrop to the urgency of our mission, making the whole experience both formidable and captivating.

As planned, we stopped once, people thankfully alighted and stretched their legs. The herdsman and drivers watered the animals, although they remained attached to their carts and loads. Some of the warriors, who had been assigned to a rear guard were despatched further back to keep watch in case we had been followed. Then it was back onto the road with the next stop, the Jordan.

It was almost dark by the time we reached the famed river. Sometime earlier we had branched off the King's Highway, turning west and finally arriving at the flat plain running along each side of the Jordan. Standing on a slightly elevated position, we could see the vague outline of that ancient city, in the far distance. Everyone was exhausted, physically as well as emotionally, so we all simply lowered ourselves to the ground and rested while the herders led the animals to the water. Only the bullocks and horses were released from their carriages and carts. The camels retained their loads but didn't seem to mind once they had quenched their thirst. Guards were posted around the caravan, a tent was erected for Leah and Rachel, but the rest of us were expected to find a comfortable spot and make that our bed for the night. Even our leader, Jacob had refused the convenience of a tent, choosing, instead, to join the rest of us under the stars. Meanwhile, several fires had been lit and our company gathered around, opening the provisions we had received earlier that morning. Cooking for such a large group on the move was out of the question. By the middle of the first night watch, most had fallen asleep.

The morning sun rose warm and welcoming, by which time, everyone was awake and up. Fruit, cheese, and bread, baked previously and carried on the backs of several of the camels, was distributed, washed down by water from the Jabbok River transported in old wineskins. Everyone's mood had lifted considerably, in complete contrast to the day before. People were laughing and sharing stories of our journey, and children were running around enjoying the sand and soil beaches of the riverbanks.

Now, it was time to cross, but before this happened, Jacob had to ascertain whether he would receive a friendly reception from the royal family of Jericho. This grand and revered city had a history thousands of years old stretching back before any other tribe in the region. One of the slaves that we had rescued from Shechem, was an aged scholar, by the name of Hanno, meaning gracious or favoured, who had been cruelly sold into slavery by a disgruntled noble of Jericho, simply because he had been teaching his children the principle of equality between genders and that girls should have the same rights as boys when it comes to an inheritance. He had been purchased by the royal family of Shechem and had been tutor to Shechem the son of Hamor, king of that city. I had met him a couple of times when I visited Shechem in the days before the recent savage act of revenge.

I was surprised to see him among those who had been brought over to our camp in Succoth. His story is riveting. Finding him sitting there on the banks of the Jordan looking across at what had once been his home, I sat down beside him, and patting his shoulder, I asked,

"Hamor, old friend, how did you survive what happened back there at Shechem?"

His answer was intriguing. "Thank you for asking Tarku, I do want to share my story as that always helps relieve the huge amount of tension that builds up after such a violent experience. In fact, it was the women of the king's private quarters, with whom I had established a special relationship because of the many stories I would share. Not having access to much entertainment, the queens found them fascinating and would regularly call for me. Apart from their embroidery, weaving and the occasional call to the king's bedchamber, life, for them, could be rather monotonous. Being older, I was never considered a threat. At the time of the attack by your people on the royal residences in Shechem, I had been in the middle of a tale of palace intrigue, so, the women dressed me up in their drapes and shawls and smuggled me out into the carts awaiting our transportation across to your campsite in Succoth".

Intrigued as to why Hanno didn't accompany the women north, I asked him, "Why did you remain with Master Jacob's caravan since you were so popular with the women?'

Hanno replied, "The women of the royal palace had their own private quarters simply referred to as 'the Chambers of the Royal Women' or more commonly 'the Chambers'. I was considered simply as a distraction and of no more value than an entertainment. I had no future with the royal women once they had returned to their home cities; I would most likely have become a servant or slave of a very low order due to my age. So, I opted to accompany Master Jacob's family".

Always interested in history and the varied and colourful cultures of my land of Canaan, I have subsequently spent many fascinating evenings with Hanno. Given the opportunity of freedom, he opted to remain with Jacob's family, finding a like-minded friend in Nabu-Ahh, a brother teacher. As we sat on the banks of the Jordan River, I asked Hanno about the city of his birth.

"It's like this," Tarku, he began, "Our city of Jericho is perhaps the oldest in the whole region and has been occupied by numerous people groups, the most recent by an estranged branch of the royal family of Jebus. So, the ruling family are Jebusites, although the remainder of our population is a mixture of possibly every Canaanite tribe in the region. When the current royal family descended on us with their small but powerful army, they were faced by almost impregnable high walls. Then, miraculously, we are not sure whom, some people actually opened the city gates to them. As the previous royal incumbents had been very greedy and oppressive and all we wanted was security and justice, they were accepted as our new rulers. Thus far, it seems to be working out very well.

Our city began thousands of years ago, and the present structure is built on the foundations of several previous establishments, the most significant being one with solid stone walls fifteen cubits high and six cubits deep and having a tower twenty-five cubits high and twenty cubits wide at the base. Our present city covers a much larger area than those days, but the infrastructure of the defence is not nearly as strong. Nevertheless, Jericho is still a powerful fortress and would require a very significant force and a long siege to defeat. Although, I must say, these days most city states are more concerned with trade rather than conquest".

Now, Jacob had to determine whether Jericho would remain friendly and allow us to cross without hindrance. His solution was money, for as he had often commented, 'money talks an open road into the most defensible fortress'. So early on this first morning following our escape from Succoth, he crossed the Jordan at the site usually accessed by caravans of our size together with Ithai, several armed guards and myself. Djoser remained behind to ensure the caravan was adequately protected.

We approached the gates, large and impressive and overlooked by a platform on which were several sentries. The gates were open, but on seeing our approach, several guards around the entrance blocked our passage, demanding to know our reason for entering the city. Jacob, refusing to dismount from his horse, implying that he was many stations above the level of the guards, replied that he had come to pay his respects to the ruler of this great city. He mentioned his name and his relationship to Abraham whose name was renowned throughout this region after he had rescued Canaanite Kingdoms from the oppression of their Mesopotamian overlords.

Abruptly, and with considerably greater deference, he was welcomed to enter and led into an inner courtyard where several senior officials, having been notified, had arrived to greet him. We all dismounted and followed our hosts into a rather sumptuous palace, resplendently supported by marble columns, and surrounded by walls adorned with beautiful frescoes. Once inside, we were offered seats in the middle of a large, we assumed, throne room and very politely requested to wait. So far, everything seemed positive.

In no time at all, a group of very well dressed, most likely counsellors and nobles, entered the room led by a younger, but very confident individual, who, firstly bowing to us, then seated himself on a raised platform, his throne. He addressed Jacob with.

"We bid you welcome, Lord Jacob of the family of Abraham. Your lineage is well known and highly respected among my people. How can I help you?"

Jacob replied, "Noble King, I simply wish to cross the Jordan so I can re-establish contact with my father Isaac of Beersheba. Additionally, in respect for your honourable self, your family, and your impressive city, I have brought a gift which I hope will cement a long and prosperous relationship between us."

Jacob had brought a chest full of silver shekels topped with a dazzling display of gold jewellery. A sight I would think no one in their right mind, however noble, would have refused. The chest was opened before the King.

I was watching intently and couldn't help but witness small gasps of amazement and delight from some of his officials. In essence, Jacob was more or less saying; 'between my father and his wealth and the potential of my having the buying power to recruit a large army, we could replace you at our leisure.

There was a silence, and I was impressed that the king understood the protocol apportioning an appropriate time first to reflect upon, and then to consider this offer; not too quick to appear greedy, and not too long to foster doubt.

"Noble Jacob. I know of your father Isaac, long may he continue to live, and of his wealth and power. I can see that you have inherited his abilities that have also contributed to your considerable establishment. I bid you welcome. With gratitude and thanks, I accept your gifts and would request you to likewise accept our invitation to reside with us and let us celebrate a new bond of friendship."

Taking a moment to pause, Jacob replied, "Your majesty, I have been away from my father and family for many years and my earnest desire is to meet him again as soon as possible. I ask simply that we may cross, and after remaining here for a few days, continue to a long-awaited reunion with my beloved parent. I will be delighted to accept an invitation to your honoured house to cement a long-standing pact of friendship sometime in the future. But, for now, I beg your indulgence to allow me to reside with my wives, and children in our tented establishment."

With a treasure chest such as he would not have seen for some time, how could the king not agree? So, he bowed and with a flourish of his robes, left the room. Of course, without visibly showing it, my father was delighted. Behind him, and not far from the Jordan, was the powerful city of Heshbon, of the Amorites and they were far less predictable than the Jebusites. So, leaving without much further ceremony, we returned to our camp across the Jordan and made plans to cross the following day. It was a fascinating opportunity for me to witness the reality of my father's strategy; that money does indeed move mountains. Although I was also very sure that Jacob's God had a lot to do with everything that seemed to be going his way.

The next morning, we crossed. Jacob decided that this was a good opportunity to rest and reorganise. So, once across, all the animals were unpacked, the carts had already been well arranged according to their contents, so they remained as they were. Tents were erected for everyone, the silver, gold, and chests of jewellery were brought into those belonging to Jacob, Leah and Ithai. Awnings were set up for the kitchens. The weather was very pleasant so everyone would be able to enjoy life in the open plain and next to Canaan's principal river. We had still not heard from our shepherds and herdsman who were journeying slowly down the Jordan River valley, so father requested Ithai to send some of his warriors to find out where they were.

Around midafternoon, emissaries came from the king inviting Jacob and his entourage to attend a feast of welcome. I know, from comments he had made, that my father had other things on his mind, but cementing an understanding of peace and cooperation was always something that could rebound to future benefits. The Jordan was a popular crossing and having an ally guarding it, could never be considered a bad thing. So, Jacob attended, along with Ithai myself, and half a dozen of our best warriors. It never hurt to remind local rulers that although without walls and bastions, our family had the wherewithal to mount all kinds of aggression if called for. The feast was a pleasant relief after so many days of tension, and apart from a short ceremony of accord between the King and my father, it was simply another feast. The music, the dancers, and the food were all very acceptable, but I know our celebrations have always been that much better.

Jacob now decided his next important move was to identify a place where he could settle. All of this area was friendly. However, he was particularly keen on Hebron as there were fertile valleys all around watered by numerous springs and small streams. But first he had to return to the site of his first encounter with Adonai, just outside Luz, or as he re-named it, Bethel, House of God. Allowing a few days rest to recuperate from the demanding journey down from Succoth, he commenced to make plans for our next venture up into the Central Highlands. Djoser had returned from accompanying the women to Ashtaroth. There had been no complications. As planned, he had left the carriages and carts outside the city gates after they had been closed at the second night watch instructing the women to make themselves known and had then ridden off with his contingent of warriors and the drivers of the carts and carriages, arriving safely at the Jordan. Then all they had to do was cross.

Meanwhile, the senior shepherd and herdsman also arrived in the camp to report that they were nearby scattered alongside the Jordan and up into some of the valleys. They had crossed further up at a commonly used ford where the water was shallow and less turbulent. As it was now nearing the middle of summer, the water level was lower, and crossings were more easily navigable. So, now everyone had arrived, it was time for our pilgrimage west and up into the mountains.

Leaving Ithai behind to watch over the temporary encampment in the Jericho valley, our small convoy set off up the rather steep climb into the Central Highlands towards the ancient cities of AI, Gibeon, Jebus and Bethel. My father Jacob, riding his horse, his two wives, Leah, and Rachel, their two maids Zilpah and Bilhah in a carriage, several servants, male and female in a bullock drawn cart, and myself along with Joseph also riding our horses. Having successfully ridden down from Succoth, nothing was going to convince Joseph to get into a cart or onto a camel. Six additional camels were loaded with everything we would need to make a camp each one being led by a herdsman. My father had also brought along Djoser together with several of his warriors so as to discourage any wandering bandit groups who frequented the remote parts of these rugged mountains looking for easy prey coming up from Jericho. Jacob's family had been carrying out business with most of the major centres in these highlands so there was little risk of confrontation from city patrols, nevertheless, a show of strength was always an effective deterrent.

This was to be a family pilgrimage as my father wanted to introduce his wives and his favourite son to the site where he first met his God, Adonai, and received the covenant previously given to his father Isaac and grandfather Abraham. This was to be a sacred journey which, during the evening before, he explained had been ordained by Adonai.

"I have asked you to join me for a short explanation regarding our visit to Luz. Or, in fact, just outside the city. This is the site where I first encountered my God, Adonai. Not so long ago, I was visited in another of my dreams where I was instructed to return to this location and make an offering of thanksgiving to Adonai in recognition for his covenant and the many blessings that He has bestowed upon me and my family. I want you all to be part of this very special occasion. I'm not planning to spend too long here as I would then like to visit Hebron and determine whether that is the most suitable location for our next family home. Hopefully, our forever home in Canaan".

I had wondered how Jacob managed to leave his other ten sons without their objections. However, as he explained, "I called the boys in and told them I was going on a pilgrimage with their mother and her sister, following which I would take Rachel to Efrata for the approaching birth. I needed some responsible family members back with the camp to ensure everything was functioning as it should. I placed Reuben and Judah in charge as I considered them the most responsible. Levi and Simeon didn't mind as they were still euphoric about their role in the events at Shechem. I also added that, if they all cooperated with Ithai and that were I to receive a positive report once I had returned, I would have a special reward awaiting them. So, all was accepted, and they happily agreed".

After a rather gruelling passage up the mountain passes, we arrived at the very spot where Jacob had received the vision of a stairway to Heaven filled with Divine beings passing up and down. I could sense his excitement, as he climbed down from his horse and strode eagerly towards the pillar he had erected those many years earlier. He stood silently, head bowed and then looking upwards I noticed his lips moving in silent prayer.

I was particularly concerned for Rachel, so I went to the carriage and helped her out, supporting her as we walked to a group of trees where she could rest while the tents were being erected. Without any need for instructions, everyone became busily involved in the task for which they had been brought. By the time the sun had commenced its descent beyond the distant sea to the west, everything was ready. The cooks had erected an awning under which several pots were bubbling away. A large tent had been allocated for Leah, Rachel and their two senior maids, the latter of whom were now actually looked upon by most of our people as Jacob's junior wives. An awning had been added outside where Leah and Rachel were reclining on comfortable rugs and cushions, enjoying the evening breeze. Zilpah and Bilhah were inside preparing the accommodation for the night. My father, Joseph, and I were to sleep in the same tent next to the ladies. At some distance several additional tents would house the remainder of our small caravan. Just then the herders returned with the animals which they had taken to a nearby stream for water and grazing. It was a beautiful and peaceful setting, almost perfectly located for the family's celebration of thanksgiving.

The evening meal over, the ladies retired to their tent for an early night. Rachel looked relaxed and I knew she would be in good hands. While the cooks were cleaning away the leftovers, my father, Joseph, and I sat around a fire, Djoser was also seated oppositive, not speaking very much, simply enjoying everything that the evening was offering, with the night sounds of owls and an occasional howl from a wolf commencing its hunt, the stars appearing, and now and then a grunt from the camels tethered nearby. Then our father started up a conversation about the next day.

"Tomorrow we will build an altar, right alongside where I erected the pillar those many years ago. Djoser can go to nearby farms and purchase our sacrifice and by evening we will be ready for our ceremony. I don't want to stay here longer than another two days as I can see Rachel is in need of some serious help. She is putting on a brave face, but I know she is feeling quite uncomfortable. I would have left her back in the camp except I know these people in Efrata and they have the best mid-wives who have delivered all their children successfully. Maybe you remember them Tarku, because some of their people would accompany my father's caravans up to Haran each year."

'I smiled and nodded saying, "Once I meet them, I will know if I recognise anyone."

Jacob concluded the evening with, "All right everyone, let's get to bed, it's been a long day and tomorrow will be special, but also a very busy day. Djoser, you should post some guards around the camp to look out both for animal as well as human intruders. Keep the fire going." And with that we retired, looking forward to a peaceful sleep.

Dawn broke next morning, and everyone was up and already busy with delegated duties. Djoser reported that the only incursion during the night, was a small pack of wolves looking for food but were quickly chased away. After a quick breaking of our fast, Jacob gathered his servants and a few of the warriors, and organised them into building the altar and preparing the sacrifice. Early evening was the designated time when everyone would come together to observe a simple but sincere ceremony, finally culminating with a celebratory feast enjoyed by all around a huge campfire. While the summer days could become quite hot, up here among the Central Highlands, prevailing winds from the west, coming from the Mediterranean, would cool the temperatures quite considerably, so a fire was welcome, not only for some warmth but also because of the celebratory features of fire, sparkling embers rising into the night sky as well as the camaraderie of family and friendship.

And it all went to plan. The evening was always a propitious time for observing a ceremony of reverence and thanksgiving to a deity in this land of Canaan. However, this was no ordinary deity, but to all the family gathered, they were here present to give thanks to the one true and only God, Adonai. The sun was setting, and for our leader Jacob, this symbolised the end of an era of significant change involving first of all, his flight from a past life and the threats of his brother, to a new beginning in Haran, and now, following our second traumatic escape, and this time from Succoth, an entry into a new life of celebrating the promises of his God, Adonai. Now, so different from his first journey north, having a large and significant family, enormous prosperity, with a renewed covenant, we could all look forward to a blessed future in what we all hoped to be our new and final home. However, right here, was his Bethel, the House of his God, and it was in this most significant place, that he would, first of all, before anything else, worship, adore, and thank Adonai for all His promises and His blessings. This was a covenant between God and man, with a reciprocal commitment between man and God; to follow, worship and obey.

A whole new chapter was unfolding; ordained, blessed, and prospered by Adonai, something that Jacob explained, repeated, and emphasised to everyone gathered. Each station of the ceremony progressed in quiet but reverent order. First the assembling of the family, then the prayer of offering as everyone bowed before the altar in humble thanksgiving of the Divine will, and finally the sacrifice. After years of resistance, the family had finally accepted that Jacob's God was the Almighty, more than for any other reason than how He had blessed every step of Jacob's life, and consequently the life of the family. The other, non-family members of the gathering joined in, bowing because of their respect for their master and, to some degree, of his God who had truly prospered everything in which he had ventured.

The highlight of the evening had to be the sacrifice, two lambs and a heifer followed by freshly baked bread laced with the best olive oil, a wine offering and finally a carefully selected combination of herbs and incense. This was all so new for Jacob, and he was making it all up as he went, but he assured me that all along he experienced a very real prompting of what to do next. The part that was my favourite, and of which I frequently recall with very deep emotions, was when he called Joseph up to the altar and with his left arm around him, raised his right hand in an act of reverence, praise, and commitment, as if he was dedicating his favourite son to the divine purposes of his God. It was a supremely beautiful ceremony, heartfelt and sincere. I truly believe, as I watched the proceedings, and I am sure it wasn't a quirk of the evening light, but I observed a real aura surrounding and enveloping everything and everyone within our family circle; a special glow, divine or not, it was real. That evening as we were preparing to sleep, Joseph, looking earnestly at me, said.

"Dearest brother, I still cannot understand or explain everything I felt when my father brought me to the altar and putting his arm around me, prayed and blessed the sacrifice. All I know was my real conviction that he was committing me to his God and bringing me into the life-changing covenant that he and my grandparents had received. I will never forget that experience of awe and reverence that we both shared as he held me. It was as if he was introducing me to Adonai, in order to secure His divine blessing for whatever lay ahead in my future. I know, I am still very young, and am nowhere near having the connection my father has with his God, but I am starting to feel an understanding of a divine entity, and a confidence that He, a Supreme Being, is overseeing and guiding my life. It's all so new, all so fearful but yet exciting".

Now I must share how we enjoyed the remainder of that special evening. Wrapped by the enchanting mood of our surroundings, the cooks surpassed themselves with a brilliant feast, consisting of an array of delectable dishes. Roasted lamb on the spit, stews of beef, hare and wild fowl, vegetables of every possible selection both wild and cultivated, all enhanced with delectable wines that we had brought with us. It was magnificent. Then there was the setting; all we had to do was look up. Nothing short of breath-taking - an idyllic scene under a starlit sky, surrounded by vibrant living nature and the whispers of a gentle breeze. Behind and beyond were the dark silhouettes of the mountains offering their shadows of protection and blessing. With hearts overflowing with joy and gratitude, we united in thanksgiving for a divinely ordained and blessed day. As the evening unfolded, a contagious euphoria enveloped our gathering, uniting us all, an extreme mixture of tribes and nationalities, in a shared sense of spiritual fulfilment and gratitude. It was a profound connection with the divine, where both faith and festivity intertwined, leaving an everlasting imprint on our souls. We sat there, relishing the tastes, basked in the magic of the evening, and finally appreciating the beauty of the silence. I really don't think anyone wanted this to end.

Then breaking in on our reveries, came Jacob's voice, "My sincere apologies to everyone, but tomorrow, we are leaving. So, let's pack up what we can, and I would like us to leave shortly after daybreak. All of you know what needs to be done. Good night to you all and my sincere thanks to everyone who contributed to what has been a truly memorable evening". And very soon, we were all in our tents catching up on a well-earned sleep and preparing for the next day.

Morning broke, a stunning sunrise over the mountains to the east highlighting the tops of the cedars, oaks and even our olive groves. Much earlier, the birds had begun their welcome chorus. The servants had risen early and already a fire welcomed the slightly chilly dawn. While we breakfasted, the tents were dismantled, and all the animals packed and ready for our imminent departure. By mid-morning, we were on our way.

Our journey was not long and within the midafternoon we were riding into ancient Efrata, a small but very conveniently positioned town just south of the great walled city of Jebus (sometimes known as Salem and later Jerusalem) and providing an excellent stopping off site between Father Isaac's camp city at Beersheba and the numerous markets in the north of Canaan. While helping Rachel out of the carriage I noticed she was in a very significant degree of distress. Our hosts were out and welcoming, so I passed her into their care, albeit, but with great concern as she did not look well at all. The birthing of Joseph had been carefully planned and with a significant amount of support. But here, I was not sure, it would not be a normal delivery. Jacob had earlier sent Djoser ahead to warn the hosts of our arrival, so by the time we had reached our destination, everything was as ready as could be expected given the short notice. From here, let me hand over to Leah who was present throughout the ordeal.

"We took my sister straight into an upstairs room along with Bilhah and Zilpah. Midwives and healers were already there waiting. The weight of anticipation and anxiety hung heavily in the room as the midwives and healer began administering herbal medications and preparing Rachel for the birth.

Already in the throes of labour, my sister was clutching her abdomen, enduring the relentless contractions that gripped her body with each spasm. The pain was consuming, waves of agony washing over her as she braced for the arrival of her child. Sweat glistened on her brow, and her breathing became louder and more strained.

We three women surrounding Rachel could only offer words of encouragement and soothing gestures, but as parents ourselves, we knew that this path of motherhood was a path Rachel had to walk alone. The echoes of her cries filled the room, an outcry of pain and perseverance that tore through our hearts. Meanwhile, the midwives and healer were providing skilled hands in supporting and guiding Rachel through her travail.

As we watched, we could see Rachel drawing from deep within her a determination and fortitude that was transcending the bounds of her physical pain, with what seemed a realization that there would be an end, producing a much loved and longed-for child. With a final surge of effort, and a chorus of cries, her baby was born, another son, and a formidable testament to the strength of her love and commitment.

But while we breathed a sigh of relief, with growing fear and alarm, we began to realise it wasn't over. Very gradually but assuredly, Rachel's life force showed signs that she was about to face an even greater challenge. As her newborn son began to draw his first breaths, her own breaths became more and more shallow, and her strength waned with each passing moment. With a sense of horror, we realised despite the efforts of the midwives and healer, and the love and prayers of those surrounding her, that Rachel's journey was about to come to a heart wrenching end.

 The baby, now wrapped in soft linens, was taken outside to show Jacob, and then gently cradling his son, he entered, along with Joseph and Tarku, their faces drawn tight with worry and dread. Now Tarku, you were there, you add what you experienced in Rachel's final fatal scene, I am still far too upset to re-live those terrible and more than agonising moments."

I stood at the foot of the bed, tears streaming down my face, on either side kneeling and clutching Rachel's hands were Jacob and her son Joseph, both weeping quietly but profusely. I looked towards Rachel, her hair soaked and her face glistening with tears and sweat, I have never seen her looking more beautiful. Through all her pain, she was smiling as she glanced from side to side, once at her husband and then to her son, and with such a gaze of tenderness and intimacy, she said.

"My beloved husband, I have given you another son of our love. Look after him for me. I know he will give you great joy. My dearest son Joseph, I am confident that God has great plans for you. Be wise, be kind and always trust in Adonai for His mercy and His grace."

'Then, still smiling at her beloved family, embracing each of them into her loving gaze as if to take their memory with her, she was gone. Gone from our lives. But with such a presence of beauty and peace on her face I couldn't help but let out a sigh of relief as her pain was over, a passing both tragic but also triumphant. We all remained there, Jacob and Joseph still kneeling, the rest of us standing, for a long moment, trying to take it all in. A beautiful baby born from his beloved, but in giving Jacob another son, she paid the ultimate price, surrendering her own life in exchange.

Jacob was inconsolable, absolutely shattered. The joy of new life in his arms now contrasted with the deepest sorrow of a treasured loved one lost, gone forever. Taking the baby from Bilhah who had been holding him while Jacob knelt beside Rachel, Jacob cradled him for a short moment, his lips moving in a prayer, and then handing him back, head bowed, tears streaming down his face, he walked out of the room. Rachel had been his soulmate, the one who had captured his heart from the moment he had laid eyes on her. Their love had endured trials and tribulations, and they had shared dreams of a future filled with joy and happiness. Now, those dreams lay broken, and Jacob was left to grapple with the profound emptiness that her absence had now created. We did not see him for the rest of the evening and well into the following day. Where he went and what he did we will never know, only that his grief was so complete and so all-consuming that he could never share that side of the passion and all-consuming sorrow that he felt for his beloved; no longer sharing his life. One thing I was absolutely sure of was that he would continue to mourn his loss for many, many years after that fateful evening.

In a simple but moving ceremony, Rachel was buried just outside Luz. Jacob had a large rock called a standing stone, erected on her grave. Those that mourned her passing at her graveside were all of our camp family who had accompanied her on this her final journey as well as quite a large number of local residents, who had known the family through their trade ventures and had wanted to show their respect for the daughter-in-law of Isaac.

Eventually, after a period of respectful silence our gathering gradually moved away. I remained behind in case I could be of any comfort to my father and then I too left, with the intent of finding Joseph who had disappeared soon after Rachel's interment. Jacob remained beside the grave, well into the night, bidding his final farewells to his beloved. Later in the evening, I went to look for him, worrying that he might do himself some harm, and there I saw him kneeling, hands outstretched, appealing, and calling,

"Rachel, my heart, where are you?"

I melted back into the night. This was not a time for my interference. My father had to deal with his grief in his own way.

I eventually found Joseph sitting on a rock and looking west towards the setting sun. I placed my arm around him and in recognition, he touched my hand, then with a strained voice, he said.

"I don't know what to feel Tarku. I don't have the words to express how broken I feel, how empty my heart, how lonely my spirit. I have just lost my mother and I will never see her again. I simply don't know how to keep living without her".

Then turning towards me, he placed his arms around me and with deep heart wrenching sobs cried on my shoulder. Tears were pouring down my cheeks. I just held him tight trying to share both his love and his loss.

In the days and years that followed, as Rachel's two boys grew and thrived, her spirit would live on in their laughter, their dreams, and their legacy. And while the pain of her passing felt by all of us, but especially by Jacob, would never fade, the enduring memory of her bravery during that exceedingly brutal and painful birth would forever be a testament to the strength of a human spirit and the sacrifices made in the name of love and new life. Indeed, both her boys, but especially Joseph demonstrated throughout their lives, every element of personality and strength of character that was Rachel.

CHAPTER TEN

HEBRON AND HOME

*"I am El Shadai. Be fruitful and multiply. A nation, indeed, a group of nations, will
come from you; kings will be descended from you. Moreover, the land which I gave to
Abraham and Isaac I will give to you, and I will give to your descendants after you".*
Genesis 35: 11-12

As much as I loved my adopted father, Jacob, at this point my heart went out to Joseph. The mother who had doted on him for all of his eleven years was now no more and although his father had expressed, without any hesitation, his love for his mother and for his son, his absolute favourite, Jacob was always so busy, to whom was Joseph to turn to? It had to be me.

The very next day after Rachel's burial, Jacob called several of us to his tent and gave us his instructions for our next move. This was the pragmatic Jacob, tortured and in turmoil within, but outwardly in control, demonstrating a strength that so attracted confidence and loyalty. We were to proceed to Hebron which he intended to be our new home. His explanation, although he didn't really have to make one, but that was his nature, was to make sure we understood his plans and his reasons. These included: that the local population of Hittites were friends going back to the time of his grandfather, Abraham; the area was excellent for pasturing our flocks and herds; but possibly the most important factor was the tomb of his grandfather and grandmother at Machpelah, as well as his beloved mother, Rebekah, near the Oaks of Mamre just outside Hebron. We were to remain in our present temporary camp for another day while he scouted ahead with Djoser, looking for a favourable site in and around the valleys of Hebron. Meanwhile we were to start packing ready for our departure the following day.

Jacob returned that evening and as we sat together in his tent, Joseph and myself, we listened as he described the location of our next forever home.

"I think I've found the most excellent situation for our new campsite," he commenced.

Despite the despair that must have been eating away at him like an open wound, a constant nagging at his heart reminding him that such an important part of his life was gone, I was quite surprised by his relatively optimistic description. If I didn't know any better, I could even have sensed a small degree of excitement.

Jacob continued, "Upon arriving at the city, I decided it most important to pay my respects to the rulers of Hebron. On arriving at the city gates, I requested, through the officer in charge, for an audience with the family of Het, rulers of the city and its surrounding region. On learning my name as the grandson of Father Abraham, a very old friend of the Sons of Het, the king immediately invited me into the palace.

I was warmly welcomed, and after some polite discussions regarding something of my history, I explained that, since this illustrious family had been such good friends of Father Abraham, I was aspiring to settle my family and establishment in a suitable location outside the city walls as I had large flocks and herds needing pasture. Interestingly, the story goes that the 'Sons of Het' referred to my grandfather as 'a prince of God among us'. So, where would they suggest, and could I be assured of their blessing? They discussed my request among themselves, during which time a young man approached me and introduced himself as the grandson of Efron, from whom my grandfather purchased a tomb called Machpelah. He also offered any assistance I would need in the future. Then the ruler, also called Het, responded with".

"Honoured guest, and grandson of the most revered Abraham, friend of Hebron, we would recommend the valley of Hebron, which some also call the valley of Abraham, located just north of our city. With open hearts and many blessings, we welcome you and your family into our city and region. The location we recommend has good pasture, although you may also need to explore a wider region depending on the size of your flocks and herds, but it has a good water supply and would be perfect for a campsite of the extent required by your company".

Jacob continued, "After being offered some refreshments and further details as to the perfect location within the valley, not too far from the ancestral cave where my grandparents are buried, I apologised for taking my leave, although they offered me accommodation, and I promised to return once we had established our camp premises. Then I visited the valley of Hebron, and on receiving further directions from people living there, I was able to identify the exact spot designated and as promised, it will be perfect."

It was a sombre company of people who left our Efrat campsite. Jacob rode ahead with Djoser but remained silent simply staring ahead. I rode alongside Joseph, glancing at him now and again, as he too was completely quiet, perhaps trying to come to terms with his horrendous loss. He knew I was there for him, but even at such a young age, he was also aware that he had to deal with a new future, one now without a mother. Leah, Bilhah, and Zilpah rode in the carriage carrying the newborn, whose name, pronounced by Rachel just before she died, was Benjamin. By early afternoon, Jacob had guided us to the section of the valley he had visited the day before. It was in every way as good as he had described.

The region around Hebron is characterised by its hilly and rugged terrain. The site selected was on one of the hillsides running north south, overlooking the valley and, following an assessment of the location, Jacob began planning for a terraced arrangement of our camp. As he explained.

"Commencing at the top of the ridge, semi circling down, this level will consist of a row of tents for our warriors. On the next level below will be my tent and awning, on the right-hand side will be Leah's tent, and a tent for each of Bilha and Zilpha. Bilhah will become the surrogate mother for Benjamin, for now at least until he is old enough to join me in my tent. Several tents for the boys who by now have almost reached the full status of manhood, will follow. Until they are married, there will be two boys to a tent. On the left side of my tent will be a tent for Tarku and Joseph and beside that, Ithai's establishment. I understand that Ithai will be returning to Gerar to find a wife soon, so he is to be given a reasonably sized dwelling for himself and his anticipated family. The next level down will be a row of tents for families. Then the next level will be for the singles: on the left for women, then a gap and the several food and meeting tents, and on the right for men. Then, finally down the bottom and nearest the spring fed stream will be the accommodation for married couples and families plus several sheltered constructions for bathing; the women's below their accommodation and the men's below theirs. So, family, this is my overall plan, but of course we may need to make additional adjustments as we put it all together. I will be leaving tomorrow to arrange to bring up the remainder of our camp family, but in the meantime, you could commence setting up our campsite as I have explained".

The hilly elevation provided a panoramic view of the valley below where our family could look down upon settlements and dotted fields of various grains and orchards. It also afforded the capture and enjoyment of sunrises, sunset and any cool breezes wafting through. The valley offered water at the bottom with a small but reliable spring fed stream. There was ample land available for growing crops and the base of the valley was clearly fertile. For the immediate future, there would be sufficient pasture for the animals, but it was obvious that the shepherds and herders would have to look further afield for the future.

The location was perfect as shelter from any extreme elements and a proximity to the city was convenient for a number of reasons including protection, social interactions, a range of services, and trade. Probably the most important reality, was the protection that came with the assurances from the Sons of Het in the city. Given their patronage, Jacob could grow and expand his establishment without threat or competition.

We had never before had to consider such a large population within our family. Aside from some of the newly acquired women, which included concubines, servants and slaves, whose villages had been nearby the city of Shechem, but who had preferred to commit their future with us hoping for a decent lifestyle and fair treatment, Jacob even had a scheme, still to be put into practice, whereby slaves would accrue a system of savings, according to the years they spent with us and once they had turned sixty-five, they could access these and, if they wished, they could settle down somewhere nearby as free men and women.

But first we had to bring our camp family up from Jericho. Leaving Djoser behind with most of the warriors to guard the family, Jacob left us to return to the Jordan. Arriving in the river valley, everything appeared normal, except for an overwhelming and totally unexpected sense of doom, immediately noticed by Jacob. I will pass this over to him to explain what happened next.

"As I rode into the camp, I sensed a very real tension. I stopped outside my tent and within a very short time, Ithai arrived to bring me news of a serious threat across the other side of the Jordan. Apparently, while the rightful heirs of Shechem had successfully regained their throne. The King of Hazor, although receiving his sister, the senior wife of the former King of Shechem, together with the gifts of silver and gold, had decided that the treasure accumulated by Jacob was vulnerable and without a great deal of protection, so he had gathered an army and descended south to take possession. He was still on the other side of the Jordan as, for some unknown reason, it had started to flood. So, crossing for the time being was not possible.

I, accompanied by Ithai, visited the King of Jericho to assess what he was going to do about the situation. He declared neutrality. His army was not large, and he had trade links with all the city states of the north. We had very little time as we had no idea how long the Jordan would continue to prevent the crossing. I was desperate. So, I sent Ithai down to Esau asking for his intervention. At the same time, I sent another of my senior warriors with a message to my father Isaac to see what help he could offer. Then I prayed.

Ithai returned immediately he had presented my plea for help to Esau, as he realised, I would need help trying to prevent the Hazor army from crossing, but he did come with a promise of assistance. The next several days proved to be some of the most stressful I have ever experienced. Ithai had placed our archers under protected barriers but on full alert in case the Hazor army attempted to cross, although, in its present state, it would have been suicidal as the river was very wide and quite fierce. Each morning I would wake up early and go outside to see the condition of the flow of water. Every morning I gave thanks to Adonai for His ongoing protection, and every evening I would pray that He would keep the river torrent flowing.

Then one afternoon to my great astonishment and delight, a small army of mercenaries rode into the camp, coming up the Jordan valley. It was a miracle. My father had recruited and sent fifteen-hundred men-at-arms; some from his friend the King of Gerar and the remainder hired from various cities, but all professionals and loyal. In addition, Esau had sent a message to Jacob, saying that he would take five hundred of his soldiers up along the east side of the Jordan and ready himself for when the main body of armed men crossed over. At which time, he would attack the Hazorites from the rear. Then came the second miracle, that evening we noticed the water level commencing to lower and the torrent slowing down.

During the night, our guards monitored the situation and once it became clear that by morning, we would be able to cross, everyone prepared themselves. Just as the sun began to climb over the mountains in the east, we signalled Esau's lookouts. Immediately, his men attacked, so as to distract the Hazor troops from the river and then, covered by a constant stream of arrows from our archers, we crossed. The conflict was bloody but short. With Esau's men attacking from the east and our own, close to, seventeen hundred mustered men confronting them head on, we had outnumbered and out manoeuvred the army of Hazor.

Within a very short time, we had control, and the King of Hazor at my feet. It was an amazing victory. Instead of stealing our well-earned treasure, we stripped the king of everything of value he possessed, along with the horses and weapons of his small army and sent them all home on foot. That was revenge enough as in every city and region he travelled through, he would have to endure the shame of defeat, returning home with nothing. The greatest loss being his honour and reputation. It was brilliant.

Next on my agenda was Jerricho. Without delay, very soon after we had despatched the Hazorites, and together with Esau, his captain in charge, the leader of my father's contingent, and Ithai, we approached the city gates and demanded entrance. The king actually came out to address us. Why did he not protect us and why did we have to endure the stress of being threatened by kings of the north? What could he say? We had only recently completed a mutual agreement of protection. He had renegued and left us almost vulnerable. But now, as we had the numbers, and we could have added his city to our accomplishments, we were in a very strong position to demand an accountability. Of course, he could have shut his gates and defied us entry, in which case a siege would have been long and expensive. However, declaring us and our friends throughout the south of Canaan as enemies would have cost him dearly in terms of trade, which in turn could have cost him the allegiance of his people, so admitting his fault, whatever the consequences, was his next best option.

City states in Canaan, were not in the habit of maintaining standing armies and usually limited their authority to a few hundred guards. However, as we were to be almost neighbours, and given the wisdom of diplomacy, we agreed on a long-term solution. He was to agree in a publicly announced proclamation, along with his nobles and priests, that he would for the future remain an ally to Jacob and his family. As recompense for his cowardly neutrality, he was to pay four thousand shekels of silver to Jacob, four thousand shekels of silver to Esau and another four thousand shekels to my father's hired warriors. That would remind him of the influence and power of the family of Abraham in the region.

Interestingly enough, around one third of the survivors of that short but very intense battle, requested Esau's captain together with the leader of the Gerar contingent if they could join them as mercenaries. These were single young men who did not look forward to returning to Hazor in shame and possibly facing punishment, unfair as it may have been, to bear the blame for the failure of their King. They were accepted by both Esau as well as the Gerar militia, again to the increased shame of their king.

That night was one of momentous celebration. Once the victory had been declared our cooks got to work, realising they were to cater for thousands, dozens of pots started bubbling away. Nefertari, helped by Mzia were in their elements. They were going to make us proud. Our servants prepared the grounds, with a raised platform, as usual facing east, covered by an ornate awning and laid out lavishly with carpets and cushions, for Esau and the other troop captains, all greatly honoured guests. In a series of U shapes, one behind another, in front of the raised platform and on both sides, additional U shapes had been formed all facing where the honoured leaders were to be seated. In the middle of the initial U was an enormous fire. In the centre of each additional U was another smaller fire. The organisation that had gone into this celebration was more than impressive and, on the evening, it was a sight to behold.

Thousands of victorious warriors pumped up with winning a short but vicious battle; the food, as usual, was testament to Nefatari's magic and it simply kept coming. The wines were the best that the Succoth vineyards had produced. By the end of the evening, everyone was more than replete, filled with the most delicious array of meats, roasted, stewed, and basted on a spit, vegetables of a magnificent array, and fruits, sweet and juicy. Everything washed down with the very best of wines. After a heavy day of battle and another heavy night of feasting, all were ready for a very well-earned sleep.

Many tents had been erected, but for most of these hardened campaigners, they preferred sleeping under the stars. Guards were posted – just in case the Hazorites considered sneaking back, but without weapons that would have been a fatal decision. Nevertheless, we always had to ensure worst possible scenarios, including an attack from the recently humiliated King of Jericho. Fortunately, nothing happened and the next day, everyone, beaming with smiles that recognised not only their mercenary fee but also more bounty shekels in addition, departed. Esau and his contingent stayed an additional day, and I appreciated the opportunity to spend time with him, discussing our father's business."

"How is father and his establishment?" I asked Esau.

Understanding my concern and the many years away from my father, Esau offered the following, which I found especially comforting.

"Father is well, I believe you knew that our mother passed away two years ago and was buried in the Cave of Machpelah where our grandparents are laid. She was a wonderful woman and I know you had felt her loss then and the loss of your beautiful wife more recently. I grieve with you brother. I have a new life now, having married the daughter of our cousin Ishmael, and I can reflect on my past as I am sure you have with yours. I can see now why our mother acted the way she did on many occasions and while I still believe you were her favourite; she was also motivated by the preservation of our father's welfare and all he had built up. I miss her too, very much."

Esau continued, "In fact, father is looking forward to meeting you once you have arrived on the other side of the mountains. I believe you will be settling in Hebron, in the same valley where our ancestors are buried. That is a very wise decision, Jacob. The Hittites are old friends of the family and Hebron is a very convenient city for protection, for trade and the land is excellent for your flocks as well as crops."

Jacob replied, "Thank you brother Esau, firstly for your very timely arrival in our fight against the Hazorites. I trust your men are satisfied both with the bounty from the King of Hazor's camp as well as from the recompense exacted from the King of Jericho. Yes, I will be settling my camp just outside Hebron. The Son's of Het have granted me open access to the Hebron Valley, and I look forward to continuing to do business with them and, in fact, throughout the region."

He continued, "I am planning to visit our father and given his age, I am planning to bring him and his company to live with us in Hebron. I am sure he will leave a good proportion of his business in Beersheba to you as you are closer in Seir, and I understand that you also keep a residence in father's camp. I have more than an abundance to look after all of my people's needs and plan to grow my business even more over the years. I have twelve sons and a daughter, and they will all eventually create their own households. If there is anything you need at any time, please remember that I will be only delighted to assist."

What a wonderful story of blessing and of course Jacob gave all honour and glory to his God Adonai. Father continued telling me his story regarding the frenetic demolishing of their camp site, packing everything up and heading south to Hebron. The flocks and herds were sent on ahead, allowing them to take their time climbing up the highlands and then down towards Hebron. Oh, I forgot to mention, every one of the boys had been desperate to join in the battle, but their father had them cloistered away, under guard. He was not going to lose any more of his family. Three days later, our camp family arrived in the Hebron valley.

As to their promised reward, Jacob congratulated them on their cooperation in helping Ithai during his absence as well as their maturity when confronted by the Hazorites. As a reward, he promised each one of them a new and special horse, the best available in the local markets, once he had established his new campsite at Hebron as well as a bag of silver shekels which they could spend in Hebron at their leisure. They were, without exception, all very well pleased.

The following few days were rather disruptive as our tent city began to grow, but by the end of another thirty additional days, most of the structures had been raised, including the corrals, and pens for those animals that needed to be kept close to our camp, either for riding or for transporting goods. One afternoon, many days later, following the midday meal, father asked me to come and sit with him along with Joseph and there he outlined his plans for the future.

"It's always good to spend time with you Tarku and my son Joseph". He began.

"What do you think of our new home, my son?" This was to Joseph.

"Its wonderful father,'" Joseph replied. And I enjoyed watching a satisfied smile cross Jacob's face. We had a tent erected beside Jacob's tent, exclusively for Joseph and me.

Joseph continued. "I have my own tent with brother Tarku now, and that allows me time to think and even to write. I have obtained, through the help of Apkallu, parchment brought up from Egypt and whenever anything of importance occurs, I write it down".

Jacob was both impressed and curious, "what kind of things are important enough to write them down Joseph?"

"Well, father," Joseph continued, "I wrote down your recent war with the King of Hazor, that was important. I wanted to write about what happened in Shechem, but no one has really been willing to give me any details. I think most people don't want to remember that time. But then there are my dreams. I still have strange dreams and I am never really sure what they mean, so I am recording them. Not all of them, just the ones that seem to be special. Some evenings, I share them with Tarku, but he is as unsure of their meanings as well. I am also learning the language of the Egyptians and Djoser and Nefertari are helping me. Their civilization is so old and so blessed with great thinkers. One day I would love to go there to learn".

Jacob responded, "Well my son, as to going down to Egypt, that is not high on my agenda for your education. Your great grandfather Abraham went there, and, under strange circumstances, the Pharaoh loaded him up with gifts and sent him back to Canaan. I'm not sure we are very welcome in the land, as Egyptians look on foreigners as unclean, especially we people from Canaan. With relationship to your dreams, as you know I have had some extraordinary dreams myself, and some amazing encounters with Divine Beings, so if you ever want to share something with me, you are very welcome. After my experiences with Adonai, nothing will seem astonishing or unbelievable to me ever again.

Now let me share the reason why I asked you both to come here," Jacob went on. "I am planning for this to be our permanent home if Adonai grants us this time of peace and prosperity. I have done enough of running from one place to another and I firmly believe my God has brought me here. We have large flocks and herds. We have more than sufficient manpower to look after them, even if they will need to be taken to places further afield. We have professional warriors to guard everything we possess, and we are situated beneath the city walls of powerful friends to protect us. For now, I would encourage you, Joseph, to continue your learning from your teacher and to be guided by Tarku. He is a Hittite, and they are a civilization so much larger and stronger in their nation to our north, and they have a lot to offer a curious young man like you".

"Yes father," Joseph responded, "but the Egyptians have had thousands of years to study their lands, the winds, the ocean currents, the seasons, and mostly the stars. Tarku's people are mainly warriors. Of course, soldiers have a part to play particularly for protection and, sometimes for conquest, but my interest is in the knowledge that Egypt has acquired and even written down covering so many more aspects of life; about the land, society and how it can best function. They understand about managing everything from growing crops and transporting them, even about their safe storage. They can predict the weather. They understand the sky and especially the stars. Not only have they managed to rule an enormous area of land, but they have even mastered the seas. There is no end to their knowledge".

Jacob had to interrupt his son's enthusiasm, "Yes, Joseph, I agree, the Egyptians are an old and very knowledgeable civilization, but don't forget that every nation is ruled by a small group of powerful people, mainly men, who seek wealth and authority and often care little about the poor whom they are ruling. You may not know it, but I have heard that the Egyptians have recently been overrun by a people from the north, who themselves were overthrown and expelled by the Hittites. So now the rulers of Egypt are no longer the traditional owners of the land. To fully understand and appreciate the history and contribution of a people like the Egyptians, you must also take into consideration, their politics.

However, my son, I applaud your curiosity and would totally encourage you to continue to pursue every aspect of knowledge that you are interested in, including the Egyptians. And learning their language is not a bad thing. Now let me continue with the purpose of this meeting. Tomorrow, I am planning to travel down to Beersheba to meet my father. It will be an emotional time as we have been separated by a long distance and many, many, years. I would like you both to accompany me".

Joseph almost jumped off his cushion, "Oh, father, that is so exciting. I have always imagined my grandfather's tent city and everything that went on there and his journeys to Rekem, and my beautiful grandmother Rebekah."

Jacob again had to interrupt his very excitable teenager. "Settle down Joseph, I'm afraid I have to tell you, your grandmother Rebekah is no more. She passed away a couple of years ago and is buried not far from here. This I can tell you, yes, she was very beautiful and if it wasn't for her, I wouldn't be here, and you probably wouldn't have been born. We owe her everything. So, once we return, we will make a pilgrimage to her tomb and the tombs of my grandparents and make a special sacrifice in their names. But for now, you two need to get ready. I have a lot more I want to tell you both about my plans, but I can see Joseph is too animated to listen to anything more from me. Tarku, would you please ask Ithai to come to my tent immediately. He will accompany us."

The next morning, we left early. Leah was designated as in charge of the camp with a lot of capable and supportive senior members who would do anything she asked them to. Our company consisted of my father Jacob, Joseph, Ithai, half a dozen warriors and four of our best archers, and myself. It was not a long distance, simply a day's easy riding, although the landscape was very barren, and we saw not a soul. Joseph was ecstatic to be back on his beloved pony and had to be restrained constantly by his father from riding ahead. There was a reason to have brought a small but professional escort. This was open desert and home to a wide range of occupants who made their living from transgressing the law of the land, and living off vulnerable groups of travellers, whatever their ethnicity or cultural heritage. Ithai sent scouts ahead and behind so as not to be caught unawares. Although he had left Beersheba almost thirty years previously, Jacob was familiar with the territory. We were almost at our destination, when suddenly, appearing over the top of a rocky ridge was a troop of warriors, well-armed and numbering around twenty.

Ithai called in his outpost, and we all retreated to a rocky and raised outcrop behind us and waited. Within a short time, the group rode up to within calling distance and its leader announced his name and where he was from and demanded to know who we were and where we were headed.

Ithai let out a very audible sigh of relief and rode out to meet the group. This was a contingent from Gerar and he was an old friend of their leader. Within a very short time, he beckoned us to follow him and soon all of us were headed towards Father Isaac's camp. The Gerar commander explained that there had been several attacks and robberies in this area recently, and they were on the lookout for those responsible. Once they were located there would be no mercy. Ensuring the security of both travellers and traders was essential for a thriving local economy where everyone felt safe.

Within a very short time, we had arrived on a small rise overlooking the camp where Jacob had grown up. It was impressive. Although Jacob's father and grandfather had been more or less itinerant and had wandered the length and breadth of the land of Cannan, what we saw below us seemed a very permanent and very established settlement.

Within a very short space of time, we were approaching the camp, and there was Father Isaac, standing alone, flanked by Baruch, clearly excited, impatient, full of the anticipation of meeting his son after so many years. I couldn't hold back the tears as I watched Jacob leap of his horse and race towards his father, falling to the ground and placing his head on Father Isaac's feet. I glanced back at Joseph and even he was surreptitiously wiping away tears. It was a very emotional homecoming. We were greeted by Baruch, still watching over his master's life and property, and having handed over the reins to retainers, we were led to where we would be staying. This was a very significant time for father and son and realising this, we left them to consolidate all those years of separation.

The camp was used to visitors and being close family, we were offered the best available in terms of food and lodging. They even provided bathroom facilities with warm water and young ladies to help in the bathing. However, I was not interested in the young ladies and Joseph was too young, so we both accepted all the luxury, without the maidens, and very shortly afterwards, appeared freshly clothed and ready for whatever feast was on the menu. And it was also luxurious.

However, just as we were preparing to join in the feasting and festivities, Jacob sent a message asking both Joseph and myself to join him in Father Isaac's tent. With a feeling of awe and some trepidation, we entered, and seeing Father Isaac seated on a raised platform in a sea of exquisite cushions, I bowed very low to the ground, with Joseph following suite, hoping that this was the appropriate greeting to a legend among the family; the second Patriarch of Adonai's covenant. I noticed Joseph staring with his mouth half open, absolutely mesmerised at being in the presence of such greatness. Jacob came over, lifted us to our feet and directed us to seating nearby.

"Joseph my son," he began, "you can stop staring now and allow me to introduce you to my father. Come over here."

Timidly and a little reluctantly, Joseph rose up and followed his father until he was standing right in front of his grandfather Isaac, looking down at this old, revered and very stately man. As he approached, he bowed his head.

Placing his hand on his father's shoulder, Jacob said, "Joseph, this is your grandfather, you may kneel down in front of him so he can look you in the eye."

Joseph knelt, and for the first time in both their lives, their eyes met. It was a very special moment. That shared look – Joseph in awe – Father Isaac with love. I was transfixed.

Then Isaac spoke. "My dearest son Joseph, I am so filled with joy and peace at meeting you. You have grown up to be a very striking figure, which makes me proud to having gained such an impressive grandson. Let me give you a blessing. Place your hands on my thighs and I will pass on to you the same blessing that our God Adonai has covenanted with me and my father Abraham, blessed be his name".

Unsure about this request, Joseph looked around at his father, who nodded and a little cautiously, Joseph placed both his hands on his grandfather's thighs and once more bowed as Father Isaac placed his hands on his head. Then came the blessing. It was a very emotional moment, and tears started running down my face.

Isaac, looking upwards as if to heaven, intoned,

"May our God, Adonai, bless you and make you fruitful until you become a community of peoples. May He give you and your descendants the blessing given to Abraham that He would be with you in all circumstances and bless everything you do. May Adonai bless you with wisdom from above, courage to face every circumstance, and victory over every challenge. May you become a leader for your family and bring great blessings to everyone with whom your life comes into contact. And may Adonai preserve you no matter what danger befalls you."

'He sat back as if exhausted from the flow of emotion, and from the energy channelled to Joseph through him from his God. Looking straight into Joseph's eyes, he continued.

"Joseph, my son, I can see that you will become a blessing to your family, and everyone associated with your family. In fact, I have the assurance that Adinai will bless you and make you a blessing for a great many people. Trust Him, speak to Him and wait on His directions".

Joseph was a little overcome with all this attention and for a while remained silent, taking everything in, but eventually he managed to reply simply but firmly.

"Thank you, grandfather. I am so overjoyed and honoured to be here in your presence. I have heard so many stories of your life and all your achievements. I am humbled by, and truly grateful for your blessing, and will indeed strive to remain true to my God Adonai no matter what comes my way."

Without any further exchange, he dismissed us. "Now go the two of you, let me spend a little time more with my son. I have not forgotten you Tarku and am impressed by all you have done in watching over my grandson. Remain loyal to him no matter what eventuates. I have a feeling that he is destined for greatness but will always need you beside him. Enjoy the entertainment outside; we shall speak further tomorrow."

And enjoy we did. Father Isaac had anticipated his son's arrival, and so had planned an exceptional event of celebrations, entertainment, and the very best of foods from all over the region. We had never seen such a variety and every dish tasted better than the previous one. Although I would hesitate to say it, but truly this even surpassed Nefertari's best efforts.

Joseph and Ithai and myself were housed in a smaller but beautifully decorated tent. I was told it had belonged to his grandmother Rebekah. It had been a long day and so the two of us had decided to make it an early night, while Ithai continued celebrating with his old friends. Just before falling asleep, Joseph asked.

"Brother Tarku, what did my grandfather mean when he gave me his blessing and then said he expected me to make all kinds of contributions to my family and to a lot more people. It really left me very confused. I am not used to all this fuss with blessings and Adonai's covenant".

'There was not much I could add in terms of enlightening him, so all I could respond with was. "Don't worry about it, Joseph, if you trust in your God, Adonai, He will reveal everything in due time."

The next morning, shortly after we had broken our fast, Jacob called for us again and we entered his father's tent for the second time. We sat down and immediately, Father Isaac began.

"I have decided to leave Beersheba and join my son Jacob in Hebron, so now it is a time to distribute my wealth".

We were all shocked. Father Abraham had commenced this site so many years ago. It had become a tent city in a very complete and substantial sense. It accommodated hundreds, perhaps thousands, of people and supported many more thousands of flocks and herds, as well as producing a wide range of crops. How would all this be divided between the two sons?

Father Isaac continued, "To my eldest son Esau, I apportion two thirds of everything and to Jacob, my youngest the remaining one third. I am fully aware of the birthright and blessing due to my eldest, which, though stolen, is rightfully Jacobs'. Yet, following recent discussions with my son, we have agreed that the portion due to an elder son will go to his brother Esau. Over the following several days, I will arrange to have Jacob's portion packed up and sent to Hebron, leaving behind Esau's inheritance, which will remain here as he also has an established residence within this settlement. Jacob has made a few requests and as a result my master of crops will travel with me to Hebron together with those members of my family who were dear to my Rebekah and who have been with me since the time of my father Abraham. Now, all of this will take place immediately. I have messaged Esau, and he will be arriving in the next few days after which I will leave together with Jacob and the newly acquired members of his inheritance".

Given that the camp population would possibly have been well over one thousand persons, this would mean several hundred people to add to Jacob's family. Fortunately, the Hebron Valley was large, and we had been apportioned a significant amount of land by the Sons of Het. Almost half of those accompanying Father Isaac were old and had ceased working and while their contribution would not be physical, their knowledge of breeding and cropping would be immensely valuable. I was hoping that some of the cooks that had produced such an amazing feast the previous night would also be part of our entourage. I was sure that Nefertari would appreciate their presence and make appropriate use of their wonderful skills. The Philistine warriors were also to remain with Jacob as Esau had sufficient armed men for his needs.

Esau duly arrived two days later, and the three of them. Father Isaac, Esau, and Jacob spent considerable time working out how everything would be distributed. I was pleased to learn that Father Isaac's trade with Rekem was to come to Jacob as he had once been directly involved, and in any event, Esau had already established his own links with Rekem. More rapidly than I had expected, everything was agreed, written down and sealed, and within a further three days Jacob's portion was packed up and by mid-morning of that day, we all departed.

We were more than two hundred and fifty souls, made up of twenty-five families ranging from grandparents down to babies, fifty warriors most of whom Isaac had hired as additional security, over sixty-five single men to look after the animals, eight experts in planning and growing various crops, and the rest an assortment of skills to assist in support activities like the kitchen and cleaning; and those wonderful cooks were included. Father Isaac rode in a carriage accompanied by a healer and another young man to provide support. The warriors all rode horses. The older men and women rode in carts, the herdsmen and shepherds walked alongside their animals, and the remainder walked or rode in carts according to their capabilities and responsibilities. Jacob had sent messengers ahead to alert Leah of our arrival. She was to arrange temporary accommodation until the whole Hebron camp scenario had been re-configured.

By late afternoon, we had arrived, and everyone having been instructed as to their duties on arrival, commenced settling in, erecting a new settlement besides ours but slightly further south. A meal had been prepared by our cooks so once the accommodation had been arranged for everyone, we all gathered together for an evening meal, and a time to meet and make new friends.

The sun was setting and still the two families continued sharing and exchanging, well into the night. Joseph had eaten and then retired early. I found him sitting up in his bed several hours later, simply staring out of our tent, lost in thought, and reliving those few days that for him had become incredibly significant. His final words to me before sleeping were.

"Brother Tarku, I am still trying to understand what my grandfather said about my future. Maybe it is to do with my dreams, but I never shared any of that with him. So maybe he is trying to tell me something passed on through Adonai and that something is still to be revealed to me so I can make sense of it."

He didn't wait for a reply, because his emotional and physical exhaustion simply sent him to sleep.

"Good night brother Tarku, I am so glad you are with me, otherwise I would be very lost and confused." Were his last words before falling into a well-earned asleep.

As I lay there awaiting sleep, pondering, like Joseph, about the blessing he had received from his grandfather, Isaac, I also wondered about his future. What had Adonai planned for this gifted and very special young man. Would he, in fact, share in the covenant blessings of his ancestors? Was he destined to become a blessing to all around him? One thing of which I had absolutely no doubt was this; that under the benediction of his God, Adonai, Joseph couldn't be in better hands.

POSTSCRIPT

Looking back with a sense of wonder on all that had transpired in the recent past, I could never have envisioned the subsequent cascade of events that would propel both Joseph and me out of the safety of our home in Canaan and into the famed kingdom Egypt. He had once expressed a longed-for desire to visit this ancient land because of its history and all its accomplishments - but not under these horrendous and cruel circumstances.

We faced slavery, imprisonment, deep despair and then, miraculously, Joseph ascended to become the most powerful figure in the land, second only to Pharaoh. Endowed with the responsibility of saving not only Egypt but the entire known world from starvation, our journey unfolded in ways unimaginable.

I trust you will relish the thrilling narrative revealed in the sequel to this now completed chapter in his life, titled 'The Story of Joseph".

ETHNIC WORDS, PLACES AND REFERENCES USED IN THE NARRATIVE

WORD	LOCATION, REFERENCE OR MEANING
Adonai	Meaning 'My God', the term used by Jacob for his God
Adonenu	My lord
Akhet-Hapi	The inundation, or flooding that occurred yearly in Egypt, between June and September, caused by heavy summer rains in the Highlands far to the South.
Anatolia	Present day Turkey
Ashtaroth	An Amorite city in Gilead in the North and East of the Jordan River
Beersheba	Also called Beersheba in the South of Canaan, where Abraham set up his campsite, and continued by Isaac
Babylon	Bavel, a possibly the largest city in Northern Mesopotamia
Beit Chazom	Place, or house, of prophecy
Beit mishte	House of feasting, or banquet hall
Bethel	Originally Luz a city of the Perizzites in Cannan. Jacob called it Bethel (Beit-El) meaning 'House of God'
Berosh	Cypress pine
Bethlehem	Bethlehem, meaning 'House of Bread'
Caphtor	The island of Cyprus
Caucase	Also known as the Caucasus region around the Black Sea area
Cubit	An ancient measurement from the elbow to the tip of the fingers, approximately eighteen inches.
Damascus	A large and significant city in Mesopotamia
Dead Sea	Or, Sea of Arabah in the South of Canaan into which the Jordan River flows
Efrat	Bethlehem
Gerar	A Philistine city ruled by King Abimelech
Gomorrah	A Canaanite city near the Dead Sea
Hapi	The Nile River, called Hapi by ancient Egyptians, because that was the name of the river's god.
Harappa	The Indus Valley Civilization in Northwest India
Haran	A large walled city where Abraham settled when he left Ur and where Laban lived with his two daughters Leah and Rachel
Hebron	A Canaanite city ruled by the Hittites and where Jacob eventually set up his home camp after returning from Haran
Heqa	An ornamental crook, representing a shepherd's staff symbol of power that shepherded the people of Egypt.
Hot Sunu	Egyptian (hwt swnt) loosely interpreted as 'House of Planning'
Hyksos	Probably pronounced 'Heq-khasut', meaning foreigners. Coming from Anatolia, they conquered Egypt and ruled there for over 150 years.
Ibis	A popular Egyptian bird considered sacred

Ineb-Hedj	An alternative name for the city of Memphis
Jebus	Also known as Salem and eventually Jerusalem. Mount Moriah was just outside the original city walls.
Kalasiris	Egyptian tunic, and when finely embroidered, worn by women of wealth
Kemet	Meaning Egypt
Kinneret	The Sea of Gailee
Jebus	Salem and later, Jerusalem
Jericho	An ancient walled city in the Jordan valley situated beside the Jordan River
Jordan River	Also, Yarden, major river running North to South the length of Canaan
Mahanaim	Machanayim, in Canaan on the Jabbok River, West of the Jordan where Jacob camped temporarily, and Laban and Jacob established a peace pact.
Mari	An Ammonite city in Northern Mesopotamia
Mira	A Luwian city on the Southern Coast of Anatolia
Mishbar	The nickname given to Joseph's cream sandstone palace by the Nile.
Nasi	Meaning leader, or prince
Nekhakha	A flail, consisting of a handle with three beaded strands attached to it, an Egyptian symbol of power and authority to enforce order
Nemes	Egyptian fine linen headdress worn by nobles and senior dignitaries
Penuel	Also, Peniel, where Jacob wrestled with a divine being and claimed that he had seen 'the Face of God'. Here he was first renamed Israel
Rekem	A city in the Negev South of Beersheba where Abraham, Isaac and Jacob traded.
Retjenu	An Egyptian term referring to people of the northeast of Egypt, most likely Canaan, from which people came and settled in the Nile Delta
Sea of Galilee	Or Lake Kinneret in the north of Canaan
Shechem	A large walled city in Northern Canaan where Jacob established a trading post and where the King's son defiled Jacob's daughter Dinah
Schenti	Or shendyt, an Egyptian kilt or skirt
Sodom	Also, Sedom, a city near the Dead Sea in Southern Canaan that was destroyed by fire
Succoth	A site beside the Jordan river where Jacob established his first permanent campsite having arrived in Canaan from Haran
Ta-meri	Meaning 'our beloved land' - Egypt
Tzazu	A fever in ancient times possibly caused by a parasitic infection
Urkesh	A Hurrian city in Northern Mesopotamia
Xia	The first of China's dynasty's existing around the Yellow River Valley
Wadj-Wer	Meaning the Great Green which was the Mediterranean Sea.

CHARACTERS IN THE STORY OF JACOB

NAME	BIBLICAL NAME	MEANING	IDENTITY
Abraham	Avraham	Father or many nations	First of the Patriarchs and father to Isaac and grandfather to Jacob
Abimelech	Avimelech	My Father King	King of the Philistine city of Gerar
Adonai	Adonai	My Lord, Master	Jacob name for God
Al-Masih	Al-Masih	Messiah	Arabic word meaning Messiah
Ammiel	Ammiel	God is with my people	Crop master who accompanied Father Isaac to Jacob's campsite in Hebron
Apkallu	Apkallu	Our Wise One	Teacher of Jacob's sons. Original home - Babylon
Benjamin	Binyamin	Son of my right hand	Youngest son of Jacob and Rachel
Chedorlaomer	K'dorla'omer	Servant of Lagamer	King of Elam whom Abraham defeated. Lagamer - his god.
Djoser	Djoser	Having divine authority	Egyptian warrior and second in command to Jacob's soldiers
El Elyon	El Elyon	God Most High	Jacob's reference to the One and Only true God of his family and Israel
El Shadai	El Shadai	God, Almighty, All-sufficient	Jacob's reference to his one and Only true God
Ephron	Ephron the Hitti	Stag or deer	This is the man who sold Abraham the Cave of Machpelah
Hagar	Hagar	Sojourner	Egyptian, maid to Sarah
Hamor	Hamor	Ass, suggesting strength	Hivite King of Shechem
Hanno	Hanno	Origin of this name would be Phonecian	Babylonian teacher and storyteller and friend of Nabu-Ahh
Het	Also, Heth	A name associated with the Hittites	Sons of Het, likely the royal family of the city of Hebron – The House of Het
Isaac	Yitzhak	He laughs	Second Patriarch, son of Abraham and father to Jacob ab Esau
Ishmael	Ishmael	God has heard	Abraham's son through Sarah's maid, Hagar
Ithai	El-Ithai	God with me	Philistine warrior, given to Isaac by King Abimelech, also called Nasi, or leader by Tarku

Jacob	Y'aakov	Supplanter	Third Patriarch, son of Isaac often referred to by Tarku as Avi or Avi Jacob
Joseph Joseph ben Jacob	Yosef	May God increase. Joseph, son of Jacob	First and favourite son of Jacob and Rachel. Grand Vizier of Egypt, second only to the Pharaoh
Judah	Y'hudah	One who is praised	Son of Jacob and Leah
Lavan	Laban	White one	Cousin to Isaac
Leah	Leah	Weary one	First wife to Jacob and mother to eight sons
Levi	Levi	Joined or attached	Son of Jacob and Leah
Malachi	Malachi	Messenger	Crop Master for Jacob
Mashiach	Mashiach	Messiah	Hebrew word for Messiah, Anointed One, Saviour
Mzia	Mzia	Sunlight	From a village in the region of Kartli of the Caucasus. A healer.
Nabu-Ahh	Nabu-Ahh	Our Proclaimer	From Mesopotamia and Teacher to Jacob's sons
Naran	Naran	Popular Babylonian boy's name	Naran's father was the grape master or vintner for Laban an Naran set up Jaco's vineyard in Succoth.
Nefertari	Nefertari	Beautiful women	Egyptian and chief cook
Pelethite	Pelethite	Unclear	A warrior group of the Philistine people
Rachel	Rahel	Ewe, gentle and nurturing	Second wife and favourite of Jacob
Ragil	Ragil	Enquirer or curious one	Joseph's nickname when he was a boy
Rebecca	Rivkah	To bind	Isaac's beloved wife
Sarah	Sarai	Princess, noble woman	Abraham's wife, previously called Sarai, meaning mockery
Shechem	Shekhem	Shoulder or ridge	Son of king Hamor of Shechem, who defiled Dinah Jacob's daughter
Simeon	Shimon	One who hears	Son of Jacob and Leah
Tarku	Also, Tarhu	God of Storms	Hittite and narrator of the story of Joseph
Yeshua	Yeshua	Saviour	Hebrew term meaning Saviour

MAP OF CANAAN

Mediterranean Sea

Sidon

Mt Hermon

Tyre

Dan

Upper Galilee

Hazor

Bay of Haifa

Sea Galilee

Ashtaroth

R Kishon

R Yarmuk

Mt Carmel ▶

Meggido

Jezreel

Edrei
Ramoth-gilead

Mt Gilboa ▲

Beth-shan

Dothan
Tirzah

Pella
Jabesh-gilead

Zaphon

Samaria

Mt Ebal ▲

Succoth

Mt Gerizim ▲

Shechem

R Jabbok

Zarethan

Bethel

Ai

Mizpah

Jericho

R Jordan

Gezer

Gibeon

Gibeah

Heshbon

Gath

Jerusalem

Ashdod

Bethlehem

King's

Ashkelon

Lachish

Hebron

Dibon

Dead
Sea
(Salt
Sea)

En-gedi

Highway

Eglon

R Amon

Gerar

Beersheba

R Zered

Way of the Land of the Philistines

Wadi el Arish

Way to Shur

Arabah

20mi   0

Brook of Egypt

50km   0

The Land of Canaan

Kadesh Barnea

Way of Mt. Seir

© Bible History Online

MAP OF THE MEDITERRANEAN

The World of Jacob and Joseph and their Journeys

- Jorneys of Jacob
- Jorneys of Joseph

© Bible History Online

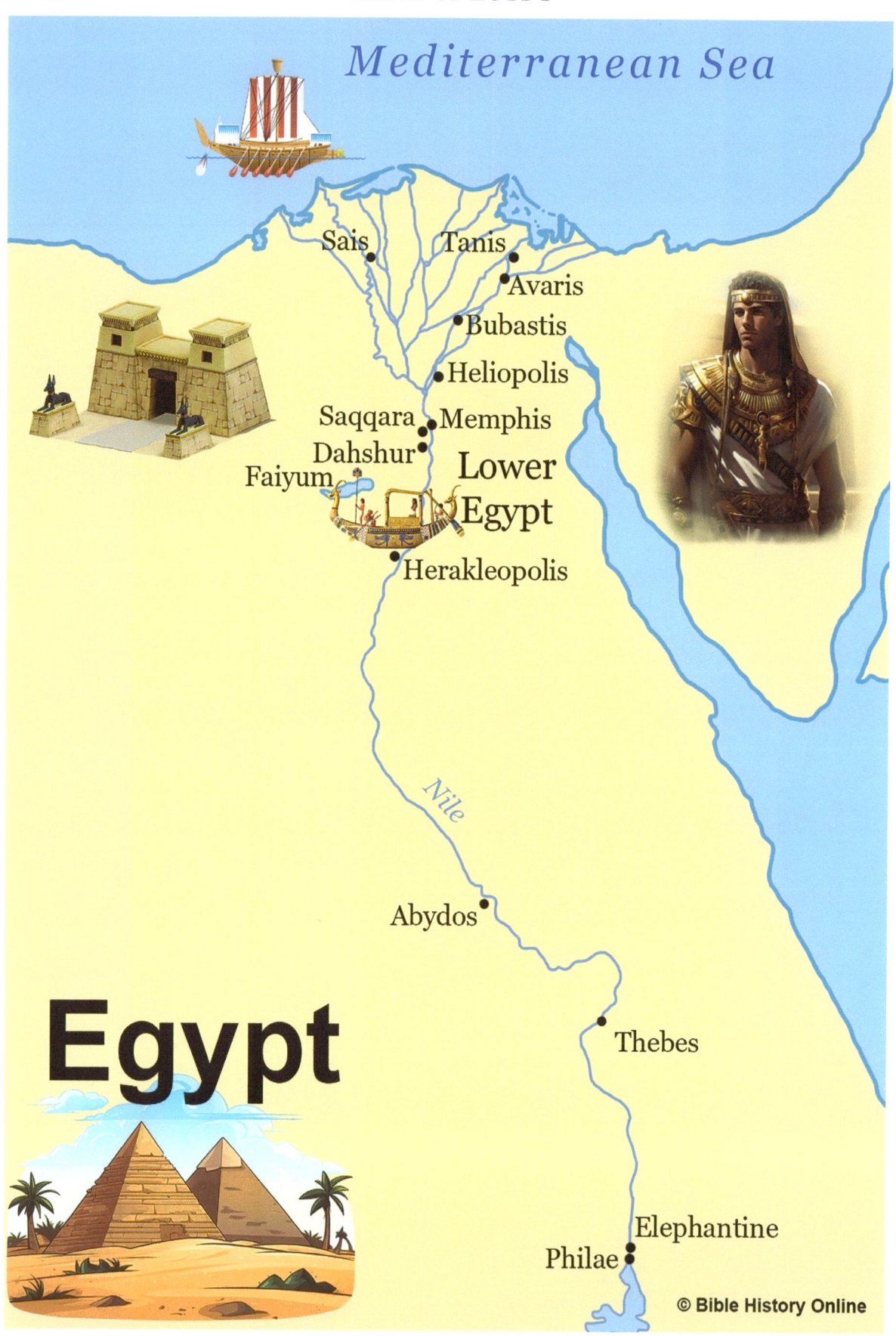

Mediterranean Sea

Sais

Tanis

Avaris

Bubastis

Heliopolis

Saqqara · Memphis

Dahshur

Faiyum

Lower Egypt

Herakleopolis

Nile

Abydos

Egypt

Thebes

Elephantine

Philae

© Bible History Online